Brother Orondi,

SOVEREIGN EVOLUTION

Manifest Destiny
from
"Civil Rights" to "Sovereign Rights"

EZRAH AHARONE

_11-22-10_

AuthorHouse™
1663 Liberty Drive, Suite 200
Bloomington, IN 47403
www.authorhouse.com
Phone: 1-800-839-8640

First published by AuthorHouse 12/24/2008

ISBN: 978-1-4389-3858-5 (sc)

Printed in the United States of America
Bloomington, Indiana

This book is printed on acid-free paper.

authorHOUSE®

Dedicated to my parents and all my living and transcended family members, including those in Africa who I never knew and never will know, with special recognition to all African ancestors who came from sovereign kingdoms and cultures in Africa, and aspired to regain their sovereign freedom throughout their captivity in America

Special Thanks To:
Prince Prophet Jervey L. Thomas, Sharon, Benaiah, Sereema, Queen
Mother Bariki, and the late great Rev. Dr. Charles Kenyatta

SOVEREIGN EVOLUTION

Volume 2: of the "STONE SERIES"

"…And these **STONES** shall be for a memorial forever"

"…The **STONE** was cut out of the mountain without hands …"

"And the **STONE** that smote the image became a great mountain …"

"And he took his staff in his hand, and chose five smooth **STONES** …"

"The **STONE** which the builders refused is become the head of the corner"

Table of Contents

Photos, Illustrations, and Documents

Introduction

Equality, in political terms, differs from equality in mathematical terms where the computed values of two sums prove to be identical. Political Time also differs from Linear Time, which is calculated by the stroke of clocks. Today's world exists in a political dispensation of time that's light years away from the 1960s mode of politics in which our freedom is rooted.

We therefore, as African Americans (who I refer to as Africans in America), could benefit from a 21st-century inquiry into our 1960s conceptuality of freedom and equality. Perhaps we would find that freedom can ascend to a height of "Sovereign Equality." This work therefore offers a 21st-century approach to freedom and equality, using sovereign principles as its interpretive lens to analyze and evolutionize our current Political and Ideological Self-Identity.

Though its content centers on Africans in America, *Sovereign Evolution* has wider political implications that equally relate to the future progression of Africa and Africans in general. In this regard, *Sovereign Evolution* is both the title of this work, as well as a transformative political concept to advance sovereign ideals, interests, and institutions.

Sovereignty is an inborn political desire for self-government that is as natural as the change of seasons. Since the dawn of humanity, people have engaged what I call "The Human Quest for Sovereign Powers." To establish a foundation of legitimacy for Africans in America to join this valiant quest, I use the words and philosophies of European notables like Aristotle, Plato, Thomas Jefferson, Thomas Paine, Ralph Waldo Emerson, Albert Einstein and Alexis de Tocqueville, as well as notables of African descent like Harriet Tubman, Marcus Garvey, W. E. B. DuBois, Martin Luther King, Malcolm X, and Kwame Nkrumah.

This book however does not promote a sovereign movement of political independence for Africans in America. It rather shapes the sociopolitical substance of our historical experience into a sovereign consciousness. It encapsulates the issues and political language necessary for sovereign and intergenerational dialogue. I also advocate for sovereign curricula to be infused into Africana Studies at Black universities, so students can academically learn to "self-apply" the concept of sovereignty and develop worldviews based on sovereign-minded frames of reference.

Another key factor that distinguishes this work from typical political works of Africans in America, is that it does not regard "Civil Rights" as the standard or goal by which our freedom should be measured or aspired. I rather circumscribe "Sovereign Rights" in a universal and historical context that effectively confers us with just as much integrity and authority as any other people on earth to espouse and employ sovereign standards for ourselves.

Having civil rights, as I assert, is mere "par for the course" of human dignity and decency between every government and society. A government therefore deserves no more "credit" for treating its citizens civilly, than a man deserves "credit" for not beating his wife . . . simply because men should not beat women in the first place.

Just as importantly, the granting of civil rights and voting rights should not be viewed as a marker of a government's legitimation, since a genuinely moral government would never make its citizenry "fight for civil rights" in the first place. However, a stark political reality of this world that I elaborate upon is that – "Un-Sovereign People Pay Un-Sovereign Consequences." Although we live in a sovereign nation, the sovereignty of America belongs to Euro-Americans who have abused their sovereign powers as a political weapon of control.

Katrina and Jena became modern touchstone episodes of protest, involving record numbers of young demonstrators who were instilled with the notion that we may need a renewed Civil Rights Movement. However, it is an indefensible affront for any government to have a people engaged in a protracted struggle for hundreds of years to be treated civilly. Let me tell you something – If after centuries, a people still find themselves fighting to gain or protect their civil rights, then they are in a wrong political relationship; because it does not take centuries to determine the true character and intent of any government.

To this end, I perform keen critiques into "Governments, the Governed, and the Ungovernable." Just as both Thomas Jefferson and Marcus Garvey affirmed, I too conclude that: "A government's authority is legitimized by the *consent* and *will* of a people to be governed." Accordingly, there is nothing permanent or infallible about the US government that supercedes our "Sovereign Rights to Exist." Furthermore, contrary to conventional protocols of today's political world, we have never had official representation to sign any binding bilateral agreement on our behalf with the US government regarding "consent."

Presumably, the Emancipation Proclamation and various Civil Rights Acts speak on our behalf. But these documents, like slave-related documents, are unilateral mandates – not agreements. Although Euro-Americans have "forgiven themselves," slavery is a universal crime against humanity wherein the offenders have no moral or political legitimacy to exercise authority over the aggrieved . . . George Washington therefore had no more legitimate authority to enslave us, than Abraham Lincoln *seemingly* had to Americanize us.

Though this has been a non-issue to date, whenever a people begin to peer at their historical and political circumstances through sovereign lenses, certain issues automatically enlarge in scope and significance. Matters that once were unimportant can suddenly gain primacy and urgency.

From emancipation to segregation to integration, we have undergone evolving States of Freedom, where each level was accompanied by elevated awareness and standards that in turn rendered the former level unacceptable. To demonstrate, consider our enslaved ancestors who were overjoyed to be "emancipated." They considered themselves "free," even though they had no real rights to speak of. We however, would deem such a state as unacceptable today. To take our evolution a step further, I examine our current state of "Civil Rights, Integration, and Citizenship" to determine its acceptability compared to the Euro-American state of "Sovereignty, Independence, and Statehood."

Sovereignty, as I exclaim, is the next state in our centuries-old political evolution to regain true freedom. I use the term "regain" because facts herein will show that Africa comprised sovereign cultures, kingdoms, and civilizations long before the arrival of Europeans. With this being true, I extend the political ramifications of slavery into an unresolved current issue, by showing that the institution of slavery not only deprived us of freedom in the past; its reverberations have disinherited us of sovereignty at present.

The enormity of this reality however, has been supplanted by the psychological enormity of "American Exceptionalism," which is the notion that America "is a unique nation, blessed by God to play a special (religious/political/economic/military) role in the world." The irony of our embrace of Exceptionalism is that we are among the greatest fatalities of its callous contradictions. . . . We have fought and died in military combat on foreign soils to secure and defend the freedoms *of* this democracy, while we've simultaneously fought and died in the streets of America to secure and defend our freedoms *from* this democracy.

Our need for a *Sovereign Evolution* is not diminished by the 4 or 8 years of Barack Obama's presidency, given that America as a nation is approaching 2½ centuries in the making. In many ways his rise is more of a victory for this establishment than for us, unless we can excavate beneath the surface of all the "Placebo Politics and Progress" that appeal to our political emotions, but otherwise leave our ailments largely uncured. Within these pages I identify Political Placebos and delve into the deeper, unveiled sovereign meanings and messages conveyed through all the emotional excitement that Obama has generated in America and throughout the world.

First of all, it is a mistake to credit his presidency to "racial progress" as the establishment would have us believe for its own self-aggrandized benefit. Spinmasters and the media attribute his rise to "opportunities of equality" that now exist. Conversely though, it is due to America's "political limitations" that, out of nearly 40 million Black people, only one of us has reached Obama's stature after nearly 400 years.

The reason there are no more "Obamas" is because the "Manifest Destiny" of Euro-Americans did not only apply to their westward expansion of territory, it likewise applies to their sovereign and ideological dominion over government and society. Black president or no Black president, we need our own political "Manifest Destiny," because their version of "Manifest Destiny" ensures that America will always politically remain majority-owned, fully controlled, and absolutely governed by "Anglo-European" principles, practices, and policies.

But now that the "Obama Genie" is out of the bottle, we should not fail to see the dormant but massive capacity of our own sovereign potentiality. If given a fair chance, we excel in everything from sports to politics. Jackie Robinson was the first to baseball what Obama is to the presidency. However, the deeper sovereign meaning and message that we should not miss, is that we are a great people because of our intrinsic greatness – Not because "America" per se makes us great. That would be like believing that "America" makes the Grand Canyon great. We are great because greatness is encoded in our genes.

On his own merit, Obama politically out-dueled and stood head-and-shoulders in intellect above all other candidates. Using words and phrases of their own political language and ideology, he exposed the intellectual clumsiness of the best and brightest that Euro-Americans had to offer, Bill Clinton among them. His political prowess and magnetism has set a new pinnacle in this country for what a real president should look like, sound like, and be like. It's fairly certain that America will soon be viewed as B.B. and A.B., or "Before Barack" and "After Barack." But I hasten to caution that America has systemic and establishmentarian ways that exceed the controls of any president.

Since many Blacks read and believe the Bible, I communicate a few allegories here and there to draw parallels, as I'll do here to characterize the messianic atmosphere surrounding Obama. The Biblical Joseph (Genesis 41) was a former slave who surprisingly became a wise and electrifying young ruler over all of Egypt, yet his people still had to ultimately be liberated by Moses because of all the otherwise existing evils and immoralities that gripped Egypt, like America, to its core.

To avoid anyone becoming racially confused, let me specify that sovereignty has nothing to do with segregation. Segregation is an unjust, immature policy-creation of Euro-Americans, designed to protect their ill-gotten gains from our enslavement. Sovereignty however, is not only honorable and noble, it embodies the highest level of political accountability and responsibility that a people can undertake.

This work therefore is far from an attack on Euro-Americans or an attack against "bringing everyone together" as per Obama's mantra. Its essence and purpose transcend Euro-Americans; it reaches high into the realm of our historical and ancestral obligation to be a sovereign people, with our own political and ideological self-identity. Sovereignty in this sense is a necessary and inevitable extension of the non-monolithic nature of who we are as a people.

In a related context, Euro-Americans share common bloodlines with the British, yet they see themselves through two different political mirrors and have two distinct sovereign identities that the world now accepts. Anyone who understands and respects their sovereign rights as a people should therefore equally understand and respect our sovereign rights as a people to do the same.

Clearly, not all Africans in America have sovereign aspirations. Conversely, neither do all appreciate Americanization. But there is no reason for those who desire Americanization to feel a challenge to their values, since the lessons of history verify that a *Sovereign Evolution* can be beneficial to us all. In this regard, I point to examples and established precedents to demonstrate how the best interests of those who desire Americanization can not only coalesce, but flourish alongside a *Sovereign Evolution*. What we must strategically realize as a people is that, based on our historical circumstances – We have rightful political claims to both Americanization and sovereignty.

Nothing is therefore wrong with our yearnings for sovereign freedom, and nothing is wrong with all Africans in America offering moral support of the ideal. Since a Black president supposedly indicates that America is a less racist society, now is the perfect time to give this establishment the ultimate test of "equality," by knowing its position on our "sovereign equality."

The worldstage is certainly big enough for us to share a sovereign place among the family of nearly 200 nations. I have utmost confidence that the world would be a better place if we contributed our politically unfiltered sovereign voice and vision. Though this may seem improbable, imagine for a moment the power and elation that our sovereignty would bring, as part of a global continuity and extension of our White House victory, which likewise seemed improbable at best.

In the final analysis of contemporary politics, there are two kinds of people: Those who are sovereign, and those who are un-sovereign. Although we are among the latter, we definitely do not lack the collective intellect or wherewithal to become a strong and influential sovereign people. However, there is no handbook, and Americanization is not designed to "justly undo, what it has unjustly done." So we therefore, must possess the commensurate political will and audacity of courage to effectuate a *Manifest Destiny from "Civil Rights" to "Sovereign Rights."*

"You Do Not Raise Your Children With Borrowed Food."
Igbo (African) Proverb

"A man does what he must – in spite of personal consequences, in spite of obstacles and dangers and pressures – and that is the basis of all human morality."
President John F. Kennedy

"History is the record of an encounter between character and circumstances."
Donald Creighton, Canadian Historian

1
The Human Quest for Sovereign Powers

Recognizing Our Sovereign Heritage

In today's complex and unpredictable political world, there's one absolute – Sovereignty is the ultimate prototype of freedom and the highest expression of political authority. Freedom comes in varied forms, including integration, but there is no existing political ideal or application of freedom that transcends sovereignty. An entirely new political instrument would have to be originated and exercised to supercede its authority. Undoubtedly, the holders of sovereignty sit atop the "Pinnacle of Freedom."

Although the term "sovereignty" doesn't date back to the ages, people throughout the ages have fought and died to acquire and preserve what the world now knows and defines as sovereignty. Some nations have used this power for peace and genuine good. Conquerors, crusaders, and colonialists have spared little in their wake to seize sovereignty by way of violence and brute force, oftentimes preserving it through use of fear-based psychology.

Since the dawn of modern capitalism, the sovereignty of nations (particularly European nations) has been largely driven by ravished forces of greed for natural resources amongst governments. This same greed forms a measurable portion of the underpinnings and short fuses that have ignited the political/religious turmoil now festering around the globe. In a certain sense, the contiguous and ongoing string of political/military conflicts that occur throughout the history of man, along with every just and legitimate freedom struggle for self-government, can be summarily termed: "The Human Quest for Sovereign Powers."

Indigenous and politically repressed people worldwide, from all continents and time zones, are pressing forward with this same quest at this very moment. Issues related to "Sovereign Rights" are now raising a new variety of unanswered questions that require modern responses which are bound to alter the political landscape of today's world. In early 2008, I wrote a paper, *"Rights and Reasons for the Sovereignty of Africans in the United States,"* for an international conference on sovereignty in Melbourne, Australia that was convened to address some of these transformative questions, such as:

Which human groups should be recognized as possessed of sovereignty and who should be excluded? How do sovereign states accommodate the presence and competing claims of other sovereign states without compromising their own autonomy? Is there a higher power to which sovereigns can turn to have their disputes resolved or is sovereignty's only ultimate sanction violence? Are sovereigns subject to their own law or do they stand outside it? Can different sovereignties overlap and coexist or is sovereignty monolithic and exclusive?[1]

To better understand this primal pursuit let's examine the etymology of "Sovereignty," which according to Webster's, dates back to

Old French (*soverain*) in the 1500s.[2] It comprises 3 component parts: *Sov*, the prefix; *Reign*, the root; and *Ty*, the suffix. Note that the word "Reign" is situated at its heart. *Sov* is derived from Latin and refers to being "super or superlative." *Reign* refers to "possessing or exercising power to rule, or to be predominant or prevalent." *Ty* refers to "the quality, the condition, or the degree of."

By definition, "Sovereign" in the political sense means to be "superlative in quality; of the most exalted kind; supreme in nature; having undisputed ascendancy; possessed of supreme power; unlimited in extent; absolute; autonomous and independent."[3] To hold "Sovereignty" means to possess a state or condition of: "Supreme power especially over a body politic: freedom from external control and influence."[4] When a people are truly sovereign, they possess political and governmental powers that are "supreme, unlimited in extent, absolute, and independent from external controls."[5]

For a more academic understanding, the Stanford Encyclopedia of Philosophy states:

> Sovereignty, though its meanings have varied across history, also has a core meaning, supreme authority within a territory. It is a modern notion of political authority. Historical variants can be understood along three dimensions -- the holder of sovereignty, the absoluteness of sovereignty, and the internal and external dimensions of sovereignty. The state is the political institution in which sovereignty is embodied. An assemblage of states [like the United States] forms a sovereign state system.
>
> The history of sovereignty can be understood through two broad movements, manifested in both practical institutions and political thought. ... Contemporaneously, sovereignty became prominent in political thought through the writings of Machiavelli, Luther, Bodin, and Hobbes. The second movement is the circumscription of the sovereign state, which began in practice after World War II ...[6]

By being a "modern notion of political authority," you therefore won't find the word "sovereignty" historically associated or commonly used in references to describe the kingdoms, empires, and civilizations of Africa prior to 1619. But make no mistake about it, what the modern world characterizes as sovereignty today, was fully known and actualized in Africa long before our ancestors ever arrived as captive laborers in the Western hemisphere.

Mention is commonly made however that we as Africans are descendants of kings and queens. T-shirts and posters depicting this regal lineage are popularly sold by venders all around the country. Revered and late scholar John Henrik Clarke even advised Budweiser on its "Black Awareness Campaign" to produce the *Great Kings of Africa* poster series, which profiled some prominent figures who "reigned" in Africa's past.[7]

Granted, some of us descended from kings and queens, but how does or should this knowledge impact and translate into modern times and terms? What are the present-day coefficients of this past reality? I pose this inquest since we have capitulated to the political ways and ideals of Euro-Americans who come from completely different historical lineages. After being a people with our own sovereign nations and cultures (in Africa), we seem to have adjusted quite well to a diminished stature where our sovereignty is not even a subject of open discourse.

This inquest should also awaken us to some overlooked realizations about ourselves, which should in turn cause drastic shifts in what we think about sovereignty and shifts in what we politically desire to achieve during this 21st century. One such realization, which is also central to the body of this work, is that – Slavery did not just *temporarily* "deprive us of freedom" ... Even more damagingly and more importantly, slavery has thus far *permanently* "dispossessed us of sovereignty."

In the final analysis after all of our theorizing, protesting, voting and civil rights legislation, the one fact that remains fixed and unchanged from our past enslavement is that we have been *disinherited* of our "Sovereign Rights to Exist" as a free and independent self-governing people.

The real-life enslavement of Prince Abdulrahman Ibrahim Ibn Sori, known as Abdul Rahman, is a testament of our sovereign heritage that supports this point. His story is a narrative that unveils our blood-tie to kings and queens in ways that should motivate us academically to retrace our sovereign footprints of the past, and mandate us politically to reconstitute them in the future.

Photo 1. Abdul Rahman

According to the PBS documentary *Prince Among Slaves*, Rahman was a prince in the current country of Guinea, West Africa where he grew up in a politically structured and intellectual nation that had a written constitution.[8] As the son of a king he was educated in Timbuktu in Mali. He married, had one son, and was the military commander of 2,000 men until his capture and enslavement in 1788 at age 26.

Prince Rahman was then shipped to Mississippi where he immediately saw that the development and quality of life were far less than he was accustomed. There, he married and fathered 9 children into slavery, all while spending 40 grueling years as the chattel property of a poor, uncouth, illiterate farmer who was nowhere near his intellectual or cultural sophistication.[9] Using his knowledge and leadership skills, Prince

Rahman became indispensable as he transformed a small unprofitable farm into a thriving cotton and tobacco plantation that showered wealth upon the owner.

Circumstances eventually allowed him to write a letter to his family in Africa in 1826. Somehow the letter arrived in Morocco into the hands of the Sultan, who then diplomatically interceded with a formal request to President John Adams to free Prince Rahman. After being subsequently freed with little resources, he was forced to leave his wife and children behind as he departed to return to Africa. Unfortunately, he died in Liberia before reaching Guinea. However, the descendants of his American-born children still live in America.[10]

Historically, Prince Abdul Rahman represents far more than just a lone individual who happened to become an enslaved prince. He, like untold others, represents paramount truths and realities of our sovereign heritage that have been redacted deliberately from the pages of US history ... Truths and realities which attest that Africa not only comprised sovereign constructs, but that some enslaved Africans were also rulers and potentates themselves. This explains why the Sultan showed respect by responding to the sovereign substance of Prince Rahman's letter.

Another great documentary, titled *From Palace to Plantation to Glory*, provides further evidence of early African sovereignty. It focuses on the vast number of sovereign "city-states" that were located throughout the current territory of Nigeria, prior to our enslavement. These city-states had formally structured governments and societies that comprised kings, princes/princesses, chiefs and government ministers, who were also captured and shipped into slavery to the Americas. The Teacher's Guide to the documentary, written by Dr. Bayo Lawal at the University of Lagos, Nigeria, affirms:

> In the pre-Atlantic-slave trade societies in West Africa were made up of the nobility, the middle class and the commoners. The nobility provided political leadership and maintained a bond between the middle class and the masses. The ancestors

of African-Americans and African-Caribbeans left a rich legacy of checks and balances in government to prevent dictatorship, misuse of power and injustice. What we call the rule of law today has been embedded in their customs from time immemorial.[11]

My point is to substantiate that we as Africans were well-acquainted with self-government before arriving at America's ports. Our introduction to government and sovereignty occurred in Africa – Not America or Europe. So regardless of how great America is or ever becomes, nothing will ever alter or preclude the reality that we have been "disinherited" of our sovereignty as self-governing people.

There is a universe of conceptual difference between – Thinking that our ancestors *were* formerly "denied and deprived of freedom" in a past era of time, as opposed to – Knowing that we *are* currently "dispossessed and disinherited of our sovereignty" in this present era of time.

The first conception suggests something passé, since we obviously are no longer enslaved as chattel property. However the latter has far-reaching contemporary implications because, despite all our seeming progress, we have yet to regain the sovereign status that we once proudly held prior to enslavement. This means that we are functioning at an irrecoverable deficit by virtue of our acceptance of "Civil Rights" or any other *right* that is short of "Sovereign Rights."

Some would agree that slavery did deprive us of freedom, but they would argue that we are now free. Yes, we are "free" within the context that freedom is accorded by US law, but by no means are we a "sovereign people." Indeed we live in a sovereign nation. But the sovereignty of America has always belonged to White Americans of Anglo-European descent. Neither our past freedom received at emancipation, nor our present freedom of integration is predicated upon sovereignty. As I wrote in *Pawned Sovereignty*

America may be a melting pot of people, but it is not a melting pot of sovereignty. The sovereignty of Euro-Americans is an

7

indivisible substance that will never be sliced in pieces to share with others.

Over the last century, America has welcomed people of all of races, creeds, and colors to naturalize as citizens. Its citizens come from all over the world. But make no doubt about it, America is still a Western European nation and its sovereignty is the exclusive possession of Euro-Americans. Unless defeated in war, Euro-Americans will never allow their sovereignty to be diluted by anyone, including Black America.[12]

We do have plenty of company however. Multimillions of people in this world are free, without being sovereign. "Being free" is not the same as "being sovereign," which is why we still have a long road ahead to regain the most valuable of all properties confiscated through slavery … And that is our natural, rightful, God-given inheritance of sovereignty.

There's nothing honorable about having a foreign enslaver "emancipate" you and grant you civil rights and permission to vote, when in essence by birthright you are supposed to be sovereign in the first place. Otherwise, what difference does it make that we descended from kings and queens? Based on our current conditions, it should be embarrassing for us to even tell anyone of our lineages. If we truly originated from kings and queens, then it's time that we politically produce nothing less than a modern form of sovereignty to prove it.

People, Governments, & Consciousness of Sovereignty

Within the overall interplay of The Human Quest for Sovereign Powers, it is not incidental that we as Africans in America have not collectively waged a sovereign struggle. This is because the Euro-American establishment never intended for us to ever become sovereign again. And the necessary dosages of both brute force and psychological influences were exacted in stages over the centuries to ensure as much. As a result, we have developed a most peculiar psyche of freedom, wherein the concept and consciousness of sovereignty is not inherent to our political makeup.

More than ever the need now exists for us to explore and unearth every domestic and international aspect of sovereign rights and sovereign applications. Based on research conducted by Dr. Uhuru Hotep, author of *72 Concepts to Liberate the African Mind*, there are numerous definitions and forms of sovereignty being implemented worldwide.

In addition to the previous definitions, I apply three aspects and expanded definitions of sovereignty in this work that encompass: 1) The "People" who hold or pursue sovereignty; 2) The "Government" which exercises or abuses sovereign powers; and 3) The "Consciousness" that fuels a people and sustains the sovereign life of nations.

Nationhood requires functional inter-workings and strong but delicate balances between a People, their Government, and their Consciousness. Whenever serious breakdowns arise, counter-productivity will occur at minimum, and society and/or the government will face faltering repercussions of some sort. When all three components work compatibly as one, a nation will then have the best chances for heightened nationalism and sociopolitical cohesion. To better understand their functionalities and the need for balance, each component is briefly elaborated here in turn.

First, regarding "People," sovereignty foremost concerns a people's inherent and unalienable right to self-government without foreign influences or interferences. In other words, no group of people has the moral or legal authority to superimpose a government or political system upon another people without their willing consent.

To confirm this point, you'll find that the third sentence of the US Declaration of Independence (see Chapter 2) eloquently attests to, inherent "rights to self-government" on one hand and "consent of the governed" on the other. It is important to understand both sides of this "people/government equation," since all people in modern societies are under the political jurisdiction of some form of governmental *"Reign"* – Be it sove*reign*-rule or fo*reign*-rule.

9

Ordinarily, there's an inborn and oftentimes irrepressible nature within a people to pursue sovereign rule. To be dispossessed of sovereignty as we have, would be an unthinkable, unspeakable tragedy for most.

This calls to mind the tiny island nation of Kiribati that has a population of 100,000. Located in the middle of the Pacific, adjacent to the equator and International Date Line, its people have lived in relative peace for over 3,000 years in this tropical paradise. Now, because of environmental changes presumably attributed to "global warming," ABC reported that "the land is disappearing one inch at a time, as ocean waves slowly creep inland."[13]

Kiribati President, Anote Tong, believes the island will eventually get swallowed underwater, becoming uninhabitable by 2056. Speaking before the General Assembly at the United Nations in 2004, he said, "We don't know how much longer we're going to have it, [their island]," adding that his people would "become the first sovereign victim of manmade climate change."[14]

As some Kiribati citizens have already begun an exodus to other countries, "Tong believes there will be tens of thousands more who will want to relocate and challenge the future of his nation, and he knows that no sovereign nation has ever peacefully relocated intact." The unanswerable question he posed is, "What happens to our sovereignty?"[15]

Tong knows that if, or when, everyone disperses and gets absorbed into the populations of foreign nations, Kiribati natives would no longer retain their sovereign, self-governing status as an independent people. Unless they are able to reestablish a new sovereign domain, the greatest of sovereign calamities will befall them – They would become a landless people who would lose their Kiribati identity, thereby becoming "Politically Extinct" in a sovereign sense.

Maldives is looking into the same mirror of catastrophe, as rising seas from climate change are slowing sinking its stretch of 1,200 islands, located south of India.[16] The government is subsequently purchasing land to relocate Maldivians. In an article titled "Maldives Seek to Buy a New Homeland," President Mohamed Nasheed said they cannot stop climate

10

change so they will buy land elsewhere as an "insurance policy for the worst possible outcome." . . . India and Sri Lanka are possible locations because of "similar cultures, cuisines and climates. Australia is also being considered because of the amount of unoccupied land available."[17]

President Tong of Kiribati asked, "What will happen to their sovereignty?" I ask Africans in America, "What has happened to our sovereignty?" Will we one day succumb to being "Politically Extinct" in a sovereign sense too?

If the worst-case scenario occurs where the people of Kiribati and Maldives must vacate their homeland, and then the best-case scenario occurs where they successfully relocate to sovereign territories elsewhere, it would set contemporary precedents that could serve as international case studies for Africans in America to closely monitor for reasons to perhaps replicate. Or, it is possible that we could set a precedent first, with unique circumstances of sovereignty of our own.

This segues to the second component of sovereignty, which is "Government." A government's sovereignty is like a political currency that can vary in range and scale from limited forms like that of some Native Americans tribes, to absolute forms like that of the world's most powerful nations. This subject is further addressed in Chapter 7, along with the lesser-known form of sovereignty exercised by the Vatican (Holy See), which is also a sovereign nation.

With absolute sovereignty a government holds power and authority to control all consenting people, activities, resources, and territory within its borders, including airspace and surrounding waters within a certain radius. Sovereignty however, differs in practices and principles from country to country. Cuban sovereignty varies from Ethiopian sovereignty which varies from Finnish sovereignty. But all governments nevertheless are supposed to operate within the specificities of international laws of conduct and organized protocols of the United Nations that cover human rights, airspace, land, and seas.[18]

For example, governments with coastlines have the right to exercise territorial sovereignty into the sea for a "breadth up to a limit not to exceed 12 nautical miles" as agreed by UN members.[19] Foreign nations are allowed "innocent passage" on the waters and airspace of other nations with government authorization. In March 2007 Iran captured a British watercraft and detained 15 crewmen for 13 days, for what Iran claimed was "trespassing" on its sovereign waterspace.[20] According to a 1982 United Nations Convention on the Law of the Sea, which established rules governing all oceans and their resources, "Coastal States have sovereign rights in a 200-nautical mile exclusive economic zone (EEZ) with respect to natural resources and certain economic activities."[21]

I mention these particular laws because the Arctic will soon generate new headlines since its melting ice is making new sources of oil and gas available, along with new water routes that link the Arctic Ocean with the Atlantic and Pacific Oceans.[22] These new routes are expected to reduce ocean travel from New York to Singapore by thousands of miles.[23] Governments, including the US, are consequently jockeying for sovereign position to grabbag this emerging 21st-century oil boom.

A government's sovereignty also physically expands to its embassies in foreign countries. Embassy properties operate as recognized extensions of a government's sovereign territory and jurisdiction. In addition, "diplomatic immunity" provides legal protections from prosecution for high-level government representatives.

Diplomatic immunity was established in its modern form by the Vienna Convention on Diplomatic Relations in 1961. Ambassadors and other diplomatic officers ... have complete personal inviolability, which means that they may not be handcuffed (except in extraordinary circumstances), arrested or detained, and neither their property nor their residences may be entered or searched.

They enjoy complete immunity from the obligation to provide evidence as witnesses and cannot be required to testify. Family members of diplomatic agents enjoy the same privileges and immunities as do the sponsoring diplomatic agents.[24]

Sovereignty in many ways is like an international language and license of power that governments use to communicate and interrelate amongst themselves and on the worldstage, where *might* in many cases is unfortunately the prevailing yardstick of *right*.

Third, and most importantly to this work, sovereignty concerns the political and ideological "Consciousness" of a people. Sovereignty germinates as a consciousness that forms core ideals of nationhood that unify and impel a people to seek and establish self-government, along with their own authentic political and ideological self-identity. People who lack "Sovereign Consciousness" are bound to become "politically unauthentic" and find themselves parroting the words, ways, and positions of whichever sovereign power they reside under.

Part of establishing authenticity involves the development of *Doctrines*, *Documents*, and *Declarations*. These instruments serve to politically define a people, express their ideology, and legitimize their cause before the family of nations in the world. This not only garners respect and recognition from other governments, it also instills pride and patriotism in citizens.

Without "Sovereign Consciousness" in today's world where The Human Quest for Sovereign Powers reverberates globally, a people will not only find themselves *Doctrineless*, *Documentless*, and *Declarationless*, but also expendable and unable to employ self-solutions on their own political terms. In our case, the term "White Supremacy" is regularly used to describe the heavy-handed as well as the subtle injustices we experience as a body politic through legislations, attitudes, and practices of Euro-Americans. But is there really such a thing as "White Supremacy," or are we facing the dire downsides of our own political inauthenticity?

I contend that if we use the concept and consciousness of sovereignty as our political lens of interpretation, it will become clear that what we *perceive* as "White Supremacy," are in actuality, expressions and affirmations of "White Sovereignty." Why so? Because sovereignty, by definition and practice confers *"Supreme power* especially over a *body politic."*[25]

At issue therefore is not their "supremacy," but our own faulty political "frame of reference." A main reason we are so attuned to detect the "supreme" nature of Euro-Americans is because we are not attuned to detect the "politically unauthentic" nature of ourselves. If we simply updated our purview, it would become evident that the real problem is that we have yet to self-develop our own sovereign/supreme potentials.

Marcus Garvey was so correct in the early 1900s when saying, "Those who are not sufficiently able, not sufficiently prepared, will be at the mercy of the organized classes for another one or two hundred years."[26] If you think this government or society has finite solutions to our ever-growing difficulties, think again, because this government and society need cures themselves.

It is therefore no exaggeration to say that "Sovereign Consciousness" is indispensable to finding self-solutions to the manmade ills and obstacles we face. Our current integrationist consciousness causes us to think and act like a people content with being "governed by others," rather than thinking like a people who strive to "govern for self." Kwame Nkrumah, a founder of Pan-Africanism and the first president of Ghana said, "It is far better to be free to govern or misgovern yourself, than to be governed by anybody else."[27]

While we stand as spectators on the sidelines of sovereignty, hoping and protesting for Euro-Americans to "govern us better," others around the world are rushing at light speed to the forefront of The Human Quest for Sovereign Powers to stake and take their claims. Rather than expending more centuries of energy attempting to politically *reform* Euro-Americans of who they are, we need to *transform* ourselves into the political people we desire to be. Instead of thinking and believing that America holds all keys and answers, there's much more to learn from studying the history of sovereignty along with successful contemporary sovereign movements.

14

Sovereignty, Independence, Statehood

When you think about it, it's peculiar that America has always considered itself a "democracy," even throughout the duration that we were enslaved and segregated. How is it logically possible for a nation to practice institutionalized slavery, yet simultaneously be a democracy?

Well, for starters, Euro-Americans do not honestly factor in their inhumanities against us when they measure America's greatness or morality. Also, and more importantly, our relationship with them is not based on what I call "political mutuality." By this I mean that their freedom is not founded or contingent upon their relationship or association with us. Conversely, our freedom is entirely founded and contingent upon our relationship and association with them.

Perception may suggest otherwise, but the simple yet complex truth is that the "freedom" acquired by Euro-Americans after colonialism is politically dissimilar to the "freedom" we acquired after emancipation. There are widespread but unspoken political realities to this that affect race relations and prompt topics of discourse that this country needs to seriously address. To make full sense of this, you must first understand that there is a spectrum of different "Concepts of Freedom."

Euro-Americans have their particular orientation and concept of freedom that is predicated upon uncompromising international "pursuits of power" and lofty ideals of "self-government," via independence. When it comes to political power, they are a people who have historically regarded compromise and non-violence as signs of fear and weakness. Once they smell fear or sense weakness in a people (especially those who possess some type of resource they want or need), believe me, it won't be long before they begin feeling for "soft spots" to plunge political/capitalist daggers.

When examining their concept you'll clearly see that freedom for them has always consisted of nothing less than "Sovereignty, Independence, and Statehood." From the moment they fired the first muskets and cannonballs at the British during the Revolutionary War, they've been fixated with the singular quest for "self-rule and self-rule only."

Comparatively, America was a ragtag disorganized underdog of 13 measly colonial properties, waging a seemingly impossible war against an empire that was known to smash its adversaries. By all measurable indicators, their chances of victory were slim to none. Visibly, they possessed nothing close to the tangible resources, manpower, or military skills of the British. Logistically, their sovereign quest appeared unrealistic, even suicidal.

However, their *intangible* measures of heart and desire were grossly miscalculated and underrated. Little did the British realize that the sovereign convictions of the colonist outweighed all fears of Britain's military might. The fact that Euro-Americans carried out the blood-slaughter of their own relatives shows the limitless extent of their conviction. Considering that they killed their kin to seize sovereignty, what do you think they won't do to others to preserve it?

They weren't interested in civil rights or integrating with the British, or voting or having *minority* participation in British Parliament. Their sole aim was to establish a sovereign government and society with their own self-defined ideology. Anything short of this would have been deemed a disastrous defeat. Unlike with us, having full government control is not something optional to them – It's non-negotiable!

Civil Rights, Integration, Citizenship

Situated at the opposite end of this spectrum is the orientation and concept of Africans in America. Because slavery's physical and psychological damages were so extensive, our post-emancipation "Concept of Freedom" took an alternate course from that of Euro-Americans. We lacked all necessary power and resources to conceivably establish or control a government, and forming a society with our own ideology was impossible. Freedom for us therefore had nothing to do with "self-rule."

Based on all the hardships we experienced, it was considered a blessing and triumph just to "Not Be a Slave Anymore." Emancipated Black men were relieved to finally be free enough to not get whipped at whim or have slaveholders "borrow" their wives at night. But the physical, mental, sexual and psychological trauma did not end with emancipation. Fear, danger, and further inhumanities were constants for a full century thereafter.

The freedom agenda for the vast majority of those emancipated, entailed working long, hard hours for measly wages, while trying to stay safe from racial predators. By design of government policies and social practices, most could barely read, write, or count. In fact, being considered "bright" or "knowing too much" was a sure way to draw unwanted lynching attention. For survival, many had to "play it dumb" as a general rule of life. Unfortunately this was our orientation, even up until the mid-1960s for some.

Since that time, the former barriers have supposedly been dismantled. Because of civil rights, Africans in America have no second thoughts about whether we are free today. Meanwhile, a blunt reality that gets ignored is that we embrace freedom in ways that Euro-Americans outright reject.

Whereas their orientation to freedom is predicated upon self-government and international pursuits for power, Black America's orientation is predicated upon integration and domestic pursuits for equality. For them, the process to gradually achieve equality through legislation and nonviolence does not conform to their sovereign nature to seize power and exercise self-government. At the same time, Euro-Americans have determined that political independence is something that's non-applicable to us. This same twisted reasoning has been psychologically transferred and imposed upon the Black masses to the point where, we do not regard our lack of sovereignty as even a remote factor of our quandaries.

In stark contrast to the Euro-American concept which comprises "Sovereignty, Independence, and Statehood," our freedom has been limited to "Civil Rights, Integration, and Citizenship." If you seek to know the deepest cause of all racial inequities and sociopolitical disparities, look no further than the dissimilarities between these two varied "Concepts of Freedom."

This conceptual distinction is among the *most* consequential, yet *least* recognized source of all imbalances of power. In the final analysis, when the defining factors and features of each concept are compared and contrasted, the conclusion is inarguable that "Civil Rights" does not politically equate to the supremacy of "Sovereignty." "Integration" does not confer the autonomy of "Independence." And "Citizenship" does not bestow the liberties of having "Statehood."

By function and definition, "Civil Rights, Integration, and Citizenship" are political subcomponents that are legislated and regulated by those who hold supreme powers of "Sovereignty, Independence, and Statehood." With "Sovereignty, Independence, and Statehood," comes governmental authority to enact or repeal "Civil Rights, Integration, and Citizenship." This is a political fact of life that Black America needs to quickly come to terms with.

Distorted Self-Identity and Self-Relevance

Conceptual dissimilarities also spill over into other areas, including history. We have been conditioned with tendencies to insert ourselves into American history in ways that are altogether inaccurate, and at times ridiculous. What this does is provide the mainstream with a comfort-blanket to believe that we politically and historically have more in *common* than in *controversy* with Euro-Americans.

I say this not to stir racial conflict, but to show how we as Africans falsely relate to certain historical events that did not involve or directly apply to us. As a consequence, we've become increasingly out of touch with our true historical experience, thereby making us vulnerable to hero-worship events and people that abetted rather than eradicated inhumanities against us.

To be specific, take America's founding *Doctrines, Documents, and Declarations*. Neither the US Declaration of Independence nor the Constitution were written on our behalf or intended to include us. If anything, the fulfillment of both was largely accomplished at the expense of our humanity and in furtherance of ideals that we were forcibly denied. In addition, the majority of the signers went to their graves without the slightest compunction of guilt. Yet the pseudo-sacredness of these men has been shoved down our throats since elementary school.

My intent is not to challenge the words, or invalidate the ideals, or dismiss the universal appeal of America's *Doctrines, Documents, and Declarations*. Nor do I deny that Black America of today has received ancillary benefits thereof. I'm saying that the depraved conduct of the founders should be impugned no less than that of other corrupt leaders, be it Hitler of Germany, King Leopold II of Belgium, or P. W. Botha of South Africa. They all are "birds of a feather," whose atrocities qualify them equal space in the dustbin section of history.

Here's where the real problem comes into play. When we consume and adopt sterilized versions of US history, we contribute to a damaging psychology that distorts our "Sense of Self-Identity" and "Sense of Self-Relevance." It confuses our children of who they are in history and muddies the waters of our true relationship to Euro-Americans.

Questions we must ask and answer for ourselves are – Where exactly do the lines of demarcation begin and end with our political relationship with Euro-Americans? Are there any lines at all? Or is our political relationship with them perpetual with no end?

Life as we knew it during enslavement was totally attached to and filtered through Euro-Americans. Everything had to be authorized by them. So we basically lost all sense of "self," and we certainly had no sense of a "Political Self." This was typified by the "WE" analogy where a slaveholder would cough and the house-slave might ask, "What's the matter master, WE sick"?

Distortions of our sense of self today are no longer so severe that we'll ask if "WE sick?" But we nonetheless ascribe to false notions that "WE" share special historical and political bonds that permanently connect us to Euro-Americans; when in reality, no such bonds have ever existed. We are only attached to them as much as the political figments of our imagination presume us to believe.

This points to major distinctions within history and politics that it would benefit us to recognize and make Euro-Americans honor. What I mean by this is that we've been boxed into a position to go through life as though we have an inseparable "common history" with Euro-Americans. Two nations or two groups of people can have a "related history," but not necessarily a "common history."

In this regard, "common history" entails much more than nations or groups having a mere convergence of historical paths. To have "common history," people must experience history in ways whereby they supported the same side, positions, and outcome of a conflict. If their historical paths converged, but they experienced or supported opposing sides, positions, and outcomes, then they have a "related history."

For example, based on events and outcomes of World War II, Germans and Jews have a "related history" but they by no means share a "common history." You won't hear Jews narrate their encounter with the Third Reich in ways that portray a "common history" with Nazism. Nor do they attach themselves to the people and activities of Germany in ways that distort their self-identity as Jews.

There are points in history and politics where we too should understand where to draw such lines of distinction with our relationship to Euro-Americans. Michelle Obama took a lot of flak after saying she was "proud" of America "for the first time" in her adult life.[28] She ended up having to "clarify" her remark because, based on "political correctness," we are expected to always pretend that we share and experience the exact same sides, positions, and outcomes of history.

A clear example of our "related history" being confused with "common history" is found in the way the Revolutionary War is propagated. The popular belief is that "WE" won the war, and America subsequently became a democratic nation. But in reality our forefathers fought while enslaved; thereafter not receiving freedom or independence upon America's victory, but instead compounding their enslavement with 89 additional years of captivity.

Now that's real "Beef," as Mos Def and Talib Kweli would say, when you fight on the winning side of a war for independence – only to come out at the other end further enslaved – in a so-called "democratic nation."

Contrary to independence, we solidified their freedom by sacrificing our own. So by all logic and undistorted accounts, we lost. School textbooks present another version of the story. But if you remain or end up enslaved after fighting in any war, trust me, you did not win. By no stretch of imagination could "WE" therefore have won the Revolutionary War.

<><><><><><><>

Institutional Walls of Americanization

"Americanization" is a designation I use to refer to the ideological/ sociopolitical mold and belief system that constitutes the character and conduct of America as a nation. Think of it as a special designer-set of trademarked fingerprints that make Americans "American." As such, Americanization can be viewed as an Anglo-European "Process of Thought" that leads to a "Way of Life" which ultimately becomes a "Nature."

Once it becomes a "nature," its impact and damages are hard to self-detect and even harder to escape. Its idiosyncrasies are deeply ingrained and expressed in the outlooks, ethos, reasoning, and behaviors of government and society, thereby making it extremely difficult for those affected to objectively draw conclusions or view the world from any standpoint outside of an "American" perspective.

Americanization has its official beginnings in 1776 when the gauntlet was thrown down against Britain. As Africans, our official assimilation into Americanization began at emancipation; however the effects have been in full force from the time of our arrival. Since the government did not want us to ideologically "drift" away, no alternative to Americanization was realistically made available upon being emancipated. After centuries of exposure, Americanization has become just as much the "nature" of Blacks as Whites.

In a certain sense, Americanization for Africans has been a lot like being "institutionalized" as depicted in the prison movie, *The Shawshank Redemption*. One guy had been incarcerated for so long that rather than being relieved after being released, his "process of thought" caused him to constantly reminisce about his prison "way of life," thereby causing despondency to the point where he eventually committed suicide.

He'd become so mentally accustomed in "nature" to the locks and bars of prison, that he equated freedom to the routines and regiments of being restrained behind the "walls of incarceration." Other prisoners also had the same fears that they too would feel misplaced and unable to cope on the outside. Morgan Freeman played a character who described this unnatural attachment to prison as being "institutionalized," saying, "First you hate it. Then you get use to it. Then you can't live without it."

Similarly is our historical experience with the routines and regiments of Americanization. ... "First we hated it. Then we got use to it. Now it seems we can't live without it." We've been held in its political custody so long that it's difficult for some to fathom that meaningful realities exist outside the "Walls of Americanization." Like with *Shawshank* prisoners, this constrictive mentality becomes like a self-professed prophecy of doom that thwarts our intellectual capacity to imagine or create sovereign realities for ourselves.

However, the confidence gained from defeating the British caused the exact opposite occurrence in Euro-Americans, who believe that there's virtually no end to their greatness and self-importance. Another movie called *Glory and Honor* perfectly demonstrates the arrogant psyche that drives Americanization. Delroy Lindo stars as the real-life Black explorer Matthew Henson, who along with Commander Robert Peary became the first men known to reach the North Pole in 1909. In the movie, Perry is obsessed by the Euro-American spirit of Manifest Destiny to conqueror the Pole as a triumph for America.

Being typical of Euro-American males of his times, he was psychologically incapable of respecting Henson's intellect or humanity, and he thought even less of the Inuit (Eskimos) who accompanied them on expeditions. Unlike Henson, Peary never learned the ways or earned the brotherly trust of the Inuit, nor did he ever care to do so. He wanted to be the great White "leader" who everyone would admire and hail. He was so bent on proving how smart and courageous the ways of the White man were, that he foolishly dismissed the ancient Arctic survival skills of the Inuits. ... and he paid severely.

Against Inuit warnings and wisdom, Peary endangered everyone's life in the expedition by deciding to trek through inclement Arctic weather. The bitter cold nearly froze him into a human Popsicle, causing his frostbitten toes to snap off like dry twigs. Henson, at one point, had to physically carry Peary in his arms like a baby. Without Henson and the Inuits, Peary would have been dead-stiff by mid-movie.

You would think he would have thereafter been humbled and appreciative – but no, not Peary . . . not the almighty White man. He later went so far as to analogize himself as "God" and Henson as "clay."

Henson thought he knew Peary's depraved character well. But after Peary brought two loyal Inuit guides to Greenland in an effort to attract investors for their final expedition to the Pole, Henson witnessed a deeper level of depravity. When the guides unfortunately died of pneumonia, instead of giving them a respectful burial, Peary still had "money on his mind and his mind on money," so returned their loyalty by having them mummified and put on display in a museum Arctic exhibit, standing with spears next to a stuffed polar bear. When Henson saw it he nearly fainted.

Throughout the movie the message was clear – Peary didn't give a damn about Henson, while all that Henson ever wanted was due recognition of his earned value as a fellow explorer. That however was far too much for Peary to ever acknowledge. Never, not even once, did Peary recognize Henson's contributions to the success of their explorations, either in private or public. Because Peary controlled the funding, he operated as though Henson were invisible . . . as if he were doing Henson a favor by letting him tag along; when in fact he needed Henson.

To epitomize the arrogant psyche of Americanization, when they neared a day's reach of the Pole, Peary *ordered* Henson to remain behind so he could proceed alone to become credited as the "first man to reach the Pole." But in epitomizing the *Sovereign Evolution* that we need to embark, Henson outsmarted him. He awoke earlier that morning and proceeded to the Pole on his own volition, unbeknownst Peary. When Peary got within a few feet of the Pole, he strained to look through the wind-blown snow and to his astonishment, Henson was already there waiting for him.

Evolutionized Standard & State of Freedom

If you plant apple seeds, don't expect to harvest figs. Trees only produce fruits according to the nature of their seeds. To harvest specific fruits, you must plant corresponding seeds. Ralph Waldo Emerson wrote in his essay on *Compensation* that "the fruit is in the seed" and "the end preexists in the means."[29] In order to create specific effects you must initiate the necessary equivalent cause.

If Black America wants a Declaration of Independence, we must proclaim it. If we want a Constitution, we must write it. If we want a government, we must create it. If we want a specific type of freedom, we must self-establish and set in motion the corresponding political

24

mechanisms. And if we ever intend to accomplish any of these goals, we must resume the evolution that stalled once "equality" became our accepted Standard and State of Freedom back in the 1960s.

With each successive generation from emancipation until the civil rights era, there's been a collective and progressive evolution of Black political thought and action. But a destructive stagnation has since blocked this flow. It's as though we've reached an Evolutionary Endpoint, where little or no originality of political thought or action has occurred.

Too many Africans in America remain transfixed with the 1960s mindset when we were thankful to sit in the front of buses and eat in White restaurants. This is not said to ridicule the Civil Rights Movement, but rather to regard it as a building block – Not an endpoint. Just as sure as there was freedom for us beyond segregation, there is definitely freedom beyond integration.

Once the Civil Rights Bill of 1964 was signed, the appeasement produced gradual and increasing degrees of the destruction and stagnation that is now present in virtually every domain and endeavor of Black life, encompassing everything from gangs to government. Inner-city conditions have never been worse, with no relief in sight. Gang life and violence have escalated to the point where even infants and elders are targets. Ask any kid in these communities and they'll tell you that guns, drugs, dropouts and drive-bys are natural parts of everyday life. Some neighborhoods are so bad that you'd be safer at a corrupt cop convention than walking down the streets at night.

Destruction in these communities is further exacerbated by our political stagnation in government life where we've only had just 3 elected Black senators and 2 elected Black governors since Reconstruction. Despite our perceived political power, it's obvious from the deteriorating conditions of inner cities that Black politicians have no workable solutions to quell street ugliness.

Instead of seeing this as an urgent State of Emergency, there's a pervasive misassumption that the Civil Rights Movement has restructured government and society, so that (one day) American democracy will *equally*

25

do for the Black masses exactly what it has done for Euro-Americans . . . as long as we vote and conform to mainstream ways.

Being rooted in the 1960s model and mentality, our present political thinking and approach lacks capability to reach Evolutionary heights of analyses or conclusions to sufficiently address or resolve the complexities of today. The 1960s is a long bygone era. We live in a modern Political Dispensation like none before, with sophisticated challenges like none before, which require advanced political thoughts and tools like none before. Attempts on our part to apply outmoded thinking and approaches from the past only accelerate the plagues that stalk us.

Since the 1960s, America has changed drastically and the world has changed exponentially. There's no longer a Soviet Union or an East and West Germany. Look at what happened throughout Eastern Europe with the Balkan states. Consider all the ongoing political landscape changes in South America, in countries like Venezuela, El Salvador, and Chile. Arab nations now have internationally known reputations. China is launching manned spacecrafts. Iran is building and launching satellites and has a space research center in the making. Asian countries are economic powers, with a growing presence throughout Africa.

Do you realize that over 80 of the near-200 nations in the world were founded after we integrated in 1964? New governments have bloomed worldwide. Kosovo most recently seceded Serbia to join the ranks of nationhood in February 2008, with nodded support from the US government.[30] South Ossetia and Abkhazia however did not receive US backing in their sovereign quest to secede from of the Republic of Georgia.[31] View the following chart for a listing of sovereign nations since the Civil Rights Act of 1964.

Sovereign Nations Established Since the Civil Rights Act of 1964

From April 1964 to 1979: Tanzania, Malawi, Malta, Zambia, the Gambia, Maldives, Singapore, Guyana, Botswana, Lesotho, Barbados, South Yemen, Nauru, Mauritius, Swaziland, and Equatorial Guinea.

From 1970 to 1979: Tonga, Fiji, Bahrain, Qatar, United Arab Emirates, Bangladesh, the Bahamas, Guinea-Bissau, Grenada, Mozambique, Cape Verde, Comoros, Sao Tome and Principe, Papua New Guinea, Angola, Suriname, Western Sahara, Seychelles, Djibouti, Solomon Islands, Tuvalu, Dominica, Saint Lucia, Kiribati, and Saint Vincent and the Grenadines.

From 1980 to 1989: Zimbabwe, Vanuatu, Belize, Antigua and Barbuda, Saint Kitts and Nevis, Brunei, Marshall Islands, and Federated States of Micronesia.

From 1990 to 1999: Lithuania, Namibia, Yemen, Georgia, Croatia, Slovenia, Estonia, Latvia, Russia, Ukraine, Belarus, Moldova, Azerbaijan, Kyrgyzstan, Uzbekistan, Macedonia, Tajikistan, Armenia, Turkmenistan, Kazakhstan, Bosnia and Herzegovina, Czech Republic, Slovakia, Eritrea, South Africa, and Palau.

Since 2000: East Timor, Montenegro, Serbia, and Kosovo.[32]

Document 1. Sovereign Nations Established Since 1964

With the modern rise of Pan-Europeanism and the European Union, it's almost forgotten that up until 1914 most of Central and Eastern Europe was made up of 3 dominant empires: "The Hapsburg Empire comprised what are now Austria, the Czech Republic, Hungary, and Slovakia and parts of what are now Bosnia, Croatia, Poland, Romania, Ukraine, and more; The Romanov Empire stretched into Asia, including what is now Russia and what are now parts of Poland, Ukraine, and more; And the Ottoman Empire covered modern Turkey and parts of today's Bulgaria, Greece, Romania, and Serbia and extended through much of the Middle East and North Africa as well."[33]

From this unscrambling of empires came the modern demarcations of Europe, where "for the most part, each nation in Europe [has] its own state, and each state [is] made up almost exclusively of a single ethnic nationality. … The breakup of Yugoslavia was simply the last act of a long play."[34] As a consequence of The Human Quest for Sovereign Powers, the map of Europe is still undergoing national facelifts.

Why is this ethnic unscrambling important to know? Because we need to understand how the European world was shaped into its present sovereign formation. Most significantly, we need to know that unity among ethnicities is not exclusively predicated upon integration. Contrary to the popular political catchphrase of "bringing everybody together," it is natural, not racist for people to have governments that reflect their ethnicity.

As Africans in America however we have done the exact opposite of what European ethnicities have done. While they've been busy *unscrambling* themselves from empires, we've been busy *scrambling* ourselves into an empire.

Even though its vast territory was acquired through usurpation, America is not considered an "empire" in the traditional sense of rulership and conquest by sword. But in accordance with characteristics of a modern form of empire, it exercises sovereign control over a host of ethnicities and has expanded itself ideologically and commercially. It doesn't need to forcibly seize land anymore, because its hegemony exists no less. And this, according to Webster's, qualifies America as being an "Empire" since it is: "A major political unit that has a territory of great extent and a great number of peoples under a single sovereign authority."[35]

Obviously as an empire, the establishment delights and supports our perennial celebrations of civil rights, since it prospers politically and economically from our being psychologically stuck in the mud of the past. Nostalgia for the 1960s has in some ways blocked the flow of our sovereign potentials. Euro-American politicians will gladly lay wreaths at Dr. King's gravesite and make impassioned speeches every year to commemorate civil rights anniversaries. Until we wake up to the sovereign consciousness that has engulfed the globe like wildfire, we will remain scrambled into an empire, trapped as psychological prisoners of our antiquated political thinking.

Again, I am not belittling the people or progress of the 1960s. Let me reiterate that civil rights should be inherent and basic to the relationship between every government and society. Any government that a people must prod or protest for centuries in order to be treated civilly is not only disingenuous, but unworthy of loyalty.

To put the 1960s in proper perspective, understand that the Civil Rights Movement was a highly effective "collective movement" that remains unparalleled in action and results. At no point either before or after was Black America more unilaterally organized and mobilized for a common political goal. What has since occurred however is that the hard-fought achievements of the 1960s caused a mainstream complacency and belief that there's no longer need for *another* "collective movement" to fight for anything further.

But freedom is relative and comes in various states. The good thing of late is that mounting levels of socioeconomic deterioration in our communities are causing more Black people to see that new solutions are required. After all, things like voting disenfranchisement, intergenerational poverty, and ever-widening Black/White disparities in wealth, health, and housing can't be blamed on gangsta rap videos.

Recent responses have resulted in the *Millions More Movement* in 2005, followed by the *Covenant with Black America* in 2006, the *Covenant in Action* in 2007, and *Accountable: Making the Covenant Real* in 2009. The fact that millions of cross-segment Blacks feel the need for change, signals an apparent yearning for a State of Freedom that 40-plus years of integration has yet to avail. This verifies that there's a growing mass awareness that we are not as free or equal as integration would have us think, which subsequently suggests that Black people are becoming primed for continued Evolution.

To amplify what I mean by "continued" Evolution, let me quote Harriet Tubman, who said that she could have freed more slaves, "If they knew they were slaves."[36] In other words, she was dealing with a mentality of people who'd become so psychologically conditioned and accustomed to a repressed state that they were unable to relate to or envision life otherwise. But as for those who she did manage to "free," the question is: Were they really "free"?

Since freedom is relative and comes in states, they certainly were not free according to the standard we know today. Nevertheless, despite having no human or political rights to speak of, those who were emancipated *thought* they were free since they were no longer physically enslaved. Tubman herself exclaimed, "I looked at my hands, to see if I was the same person now that I was free. There was such a glory over everything; the sun came like gold through the trees, and over de fields, and I felt like I was in heaven."[37]

Evolution has politically cycled us a long distance since Tubman's days. None of us today would feel "like we were in heaven," if we were reduced to the limited State of Freedom that she elated over. That would be hell, not heaven.

Although we still remain accustomed to the 1960s Standard and State of Freedom, all of us would concur that the 1860s standard and state has definitely outlived its usefulness. So the very same freedom that our forefathers jubilantly embraced at emancipation is now altogether unacceptable.

In the same vein, throughout the 100 years following emancipation, successive generations lived in the purgatory of segregation, which was standard for those times. Although we would also object to such a state today, segregated Blacks nevertheless *thought* they were free. Once integration ushered in a new standard and state, the segregated freedom that many of us were born and reared into automatically became outlived of acceptability too.

As the political pendulum continues to swing nonstop, time and history deem it necessary for us to appraise our current Standard and State of Freedom to determine if the functionality of integration has also outlived its usefulness (at least for some of us). Could it be that integration has fulfilled the sociopolitical endpoints for which it was designed and intended? Perhaps a higher standard and state is needed to surmount the modern hurdles before us.

Sure, we now get paid for our labor and we are equal enough to needlessly die alongside Whites in an integrated military. Yes, civil rights and voting rights are necessary and valuable. Certainly, the playing field that emerged from the 1960s standard and state was monumental, and integration undoubtedly resulted in better jobs, increased wages, and higher positions.

But on the flipside, America as an empire was expanding commercially at the time, which in turn necessitated the need for a larger (corporate) labor force. In Economics 101 this supply/demand dynamic is called a "direct relationship." So, the more wealth our labor generates for US industries, the more our lives will proportionately improve in relative increments. The establishment therefore knew that it had to inevitably terminate segregation, not because of morality or justice, but for its own political and economic efficacy.

When White-owned Fortune 500 companies hire Black CEOs or appoint Black board members, it's questionable if they are acting from a standpoint of ethics, justice, or even qualifications. What is certain however is that they are driven by profit motives. Hiring Black executives and giving money to charitable causes like the Darfur crisis and the MLK Monument on the Washington Mall (which is tax-deductible anyway), guarantees White corporations a dependable flow of Black dollars and dominant market positions in return. And Black Loyalty

Similarly, this same tactic is used to guarantee our political loyalty. But despite all the many notable legislative and social reforms, integration has not sufficiently altered the disproportions in economics, the imbalance in political power, or the unprincipled nature of our relationship with Euro-Americans. According to Garvey:

> Prejudice of the white race against the black race is not so much because of color as of condition; because as a race, to them, we have accomplished nothing; we have built no nation, no government; because we are dependent for our economic and political existence. .... You can never curb the prejudice of the one race or nation against the other by law. It must be regulated by one's own feeling, one's own will, and if one's feeling and will rebel against you, no law in the world can curb it.[38]

If Africans in America are to progress unhampered and without strings, we must undergo a *Sovereign Evolution* to reach our next Standard and State of Freedom. Though this may seemingly run counter to our current political direction with the "bringing everybody together" philosophy of President Barack Obama, sovereignty is really part of the natural progression of our political Evolution. Let me explain by pointing out that Evolution moved us from slavery onto emancipation and segregation during Harriet Tubman's time. During Dr. Martin Luther King's time, the same forces of Evolution moved us from segregation to integration.

While each Evolution occurred during different eras, they were a continuum . . . Dr. King's objective to integrate was achieved *without* conflict or discredit to the work and legacy of Harriet Tubman. We exist today by virtue of a replenishment of philosophies and sequential Evolutions of predecessor movements and people – All of which compliment and build upon the prior achievements of each.

In similar fashion we can likewise continue this Evolution and achieve freedom beyond integration *without* conflict or discredit to the work and legacy of those who brought us this far. There is no discrepancy of principles or clash of agendas whereby we somehow dishonor Dr. King or Harriet Tubman if we open our minds to *Sovereign Evolution*. In fact,

[handwritten margin note: What About The BlACK Power Movement?]

the political requisites of these modern times demand that we carry their works and philosophies to the next level.

Inasmuch as every upcoming generation in a family is expected to exceed their parents' generation, the same applies politically to a people. If we have not yet figured out how to thrive better or interface with Europeans more soundly than leaders from the 1860s or 1960s, then something is wrong. This is not meant to insult anyone's past greatness, but rather to challenge us today to have a greater, not lesser sense of mission and responsibility. "We are moving from one state of organization to another, and we shall so continue until we have thoroughly lifted ourselves into the organization of GOVERNMENT," as Garvey declared. [39]

Where are the geniuses and original political minds of this age? We need men and women suited for the intricacies of these times, just as past leaders were suited for their times. We must produce a new breed of leaders and heroes for tomorrow's generations to study and hail. If we embrace the consciousness and ideals of *Sovereign Evolution*, monumental change and progress of no less magnitude than the Civil Rights Movement can potentially follow.

Personally, I happen to be the first in my family, of a long intergenerational chain stretching back to slavery, who can read and study for intellectual and philosophical pursuits. You too may be the first or second generation in your family with the same ability. Why is this point important? Because together, we possess the greatest collective intellect of all times to reexamine the past and self-shape the future in ways that previous generations were unable. We therefore owe an irrevocable obligation to all our forebears who were dispossessed of sovereignty. History is likely to judge us harshly if we fail to leave sovereign footprints in the sands of time.

Our biggest obstacle to a *Sovereign Evolution* may perhaps be the very obstacle that Harriet Tubman faced – The mindset that prevented the enslaved from realizing that they were actually enslaved. Hopefully, this psychological ghost from the past won't haunt the mindset and prevent present generations from realizing that our freedom can advance from "Civil Rights" to "Sovereign Rights."

A Sovereign Nucleus

Not all Africans in America will be open to sovereign ideals. That's understandable. However, a paramount reality that we all should acknowledge and never lose sight of is that – Those of us who seek to further embrace Americanization have just as much right to do so as those of us who seek to be free from it.

It's been repeatedly stated and agreed that we are not a monolithic people. So it's not expected that our total population would participate in a *Sovereign Evolution*. At the same time, this does not diminish the relevance or integrity of sovereignty as a pursuable ideal. What we must strategically realize is that, based on our historical circumstances – We have rightful political claims to both Americanization and sovereignty.

Nobody knows the exact breakdown of who is or isn't interested in exploring sovereign options. Based on my own empirical assessments, I am strongly convinced that a sizeable percentage of Blacks are receptive to sovereign consciousness right now, and a substantial more would be receptive once properly edified. But the immediate number is secondary, since it doesn't initially require millions of people to validate political movements.

Check history and you'll see that it's not uncommon for a small but influential nucleus to drive the entire thrust of consciousness for movements. In America it was only 56 men who signed the Declaration of Independence from which the revolution and independence ensued.

Ghana had the famous "Big Six" of Kwame Nkrumah, Obetsebi-Lamptey, Ako Adjei, Edward Akuffo-Addo, Joseph B. Danquah, and William Ofori Atta, who in 1957 spearheaded independence from

British colonialism.[40] Nkrumah said, "The best way of learning to be an independent sovereign state is to be an independent sovereign state."[41]

Photo 2. *The "Big Six"*

Kwame Nkrumah, Obetsebi-Lamptey, Ako Adjei, Edward Akuffo-Addo, Dr. J. B. Danquah, William Ofori Atta

In 1956 Fidel Castro originally had just 81 men, who over the next two years waged a successful guerrilla campaign from their stronghold in the Sierra Maestra mountains.[42] From this group evolved the present nation and ideology of Cuba.

In 1954 the Vietnamese won an "impossible victory" over the French, which stood as "A bitter lesson for the colonists – and later the Americans – about underestimating a determined country fighting for independence."[43] Conservative analysis and egghead commentator, George Will, wrote about the power of a sovereign nucleus in one of his columns, stating:

History usually is made not by majorities but by intense minorities. Remember 1917 and this from Richard Pipes' *The Russian Revolution*: "The Bolshevik triumph in October was accomplished nine-tenths psychologically: the forces involved were negligible, a few thousand men at most in a nation of 150 million."[44]

Although no officially structured nucleus currently exists among us, there's always been a presence of Africans in America who in spirit were/are more "African" than "American." Ever since the first ship left the shores of Africa in 1619, a special segment of our ancestors retained sovereignty in their bloodstreams. These men and women were not born to be reduced to an "ethnic minority" or to live under the authority of foreign people. Although a great number adopted Americanization for survival's sake, others mutinied, revolted, or led insurrections. Many were beaten to death for defiance. Some escaped and adopted Native American cultures. Others escaped and died from exposure to the elements. Or like Joseph Cinque and Prince Abdul Rahman, they returned back to Africa.

America tactically ignores this side of history, favoring instead to promote the impression that our struggle has been exclusive to the pursuit of equality and integration, not sovereignty and independence. . . . As though all Africans suddenly desired to join the Democratic Party as soon as their ship set sail. You don't read or hear proportional accounts of those who fought, died, and prayed to regain their sovereign freedom.

No one can accurately pinpoint this number either, but my senses tell me that there were immense yearnings (especially during the early stages) among Africans to return to Africa. Any other rationale seems illogical to me. Their resistance may not have always been visible or verbal due to high risks of death and mutilation, but resistance had to abide within them nonetheless.

Their sovereign blood hasn't drained dry over the centuries. Though mostly dormant and suppressed, it still flows pure in a present-day segment, embodied in aspirations. Up until now however, this segment has been unable to successfully do what nearly-200 other contemporary people have done – Develop functional ideological and political frameworks to transform our sovereign aspirations into sovereign realities.

As for skeptics who regard sovereign ideals as radical or divisive, I say two things. First, let me reiterate that aspirations of self-government do not necessarily clash with aspirations of those who prefer Americanization. Neither preference should be viewed as a counter-force to the other, or as *competing* rather than *complementary* ideals. It's really more a case of "both/and," not "either/or" because both can theoretically coexist in joint alliance and support of the other. In fact, this should be a mutually committed goal among us.

A prime example of "both/and" is found in Euro-America's relationship with the British. Historically, they are *one* people who formed *two* separate nations that are now united in cohesive political alliances. They are the same people by blood, yet politically, they possess two distinct sovereign identities. Individually they differ in politics and ideology, while together they represent two of the world's closest Western allies and strongest democracies.

If Euro-Americans hadn't undergone a *Sovereign Evolution* there'd be no America as we know it, and all people in America would have some sort of British-hybrid political identity. Despite bad blood in the past, Euro-American and British relations are now ironclad. Since they are living proof that coexisting is possible, we can similarly do the same. After all, we follow probably 99 percent of everything else Euro-Americans do.

In the event of our sovereignty being actualized, it would generate a two-way street of new options and opportunities that could not otherwise exist. Just like America and Britain, our shared benefits would uniquely advance our interests like no other bilateral relationship ever could. Furthermore, in future instances when the US government rears its ugly head of indifference again – á la hurricane Katrina – African Americans would have a sure sovereign ally to count on for guaranteed assistance.

Secondly, I say to skeptics and detractors to remember that before integration became popular and mainstream, it too was considered radical and divisive. In fact, for most of our days here we could not even speak openly about being equal to White folks. Up until the mid-1960s you could get lynched for professing ideas about equality and integration. With this being true, the vast majority of Black people did not dare publicly participate in civil rights activities. But in private and in their hearts, this same "silent majority" wanted change even though they never took a public stand.

Was our pursuit of civil rights *wrong*? Of course not! Yet, not only was integration considered wrong; it was also a crime. But that did not stop a relatively minute and unafraid nucleus of courageous men and women from spearheading the movement for civil rights. And today in retrospect we adore and regard them as giants to be emulated.

In advancing this same point and reasoning a step forward, I ask you – Would our pursuit of sovereign rights be *wrong*? Of course not! But you can believe that, like civil rights of yesterday, our sovereign rights of today are bound to be contested by this government for the same selfish reasons.

Sovereignty is commonly regarded as controversial by ruling governments that take political and economic advantage of ethnic or minority groups in given societies. The British too thought it was a bad objective when sovereign ideals took hold of Euro-Americans. Once a sovereign nucleus formed, the days of unearned privileges were thereafter numbered for the British.

Those of us with sovereign aspirations do not have to search far for successful precedents of a Sovereign Nucleus, Sovereign Evolution, or Sovereign Coexisting. We have them all right here in our midst. Never forget, however, that long before this country existed, and long before Europeans ever set foot in Africa, sovereign structures existed throughout Africa. Thus, our single greatest challenge this century is not to overcome the likes of racism, or election frauds, or so-called White Supremacy, but rather to rejoin The Human Quest for Sovereign Powers to reclaim our disinherited sovereignty.

"The very idea of the power and the right of the People to establish Government presupposes the duty of every Individual to obey the established Government."

President George Washington

"In individuals, insanity is rare: but in groups, parties, nations and epochs, it is the rule."

Friedrich Nietzsche, German Philosopher (1844-1909)

"It can be stoked by anger or fear – but equally by pride or love. Nationalism, ever adaptable, stands as the most enduring 'ism' of modern times."

Paul Starobin, Journalist

"Every emancipation has in it the seeds of a new slavery, and every truth easily becomes a lie."

I.F. Stone, Journalist (1907-1989)

2
Governments, the Governed, and the Ungovernable

Governments and Societies: Clash or Cohesion?

Most people probably do not give much daily thought to the subject of "Government and Society." We all know that citizens comprise societies which governments govern, but the two are not always mutually conjoined in shared interests. Just as governments and societies cohere and converge in some areas, they also clash and conflict in others. This is because government is not society, and society is not government. Although members of societies comprise governments, a government's structure and policy directions can still be adverse to particular interests of certain society members.

Awareness of the inter-dynamics between "Governments and Societies" is prerequisite to any successful *Sovereign Evolution*. This includes having academic, political, and institutional understandings of the makeup and functionalities of both, since a people could not otherwise gain control of either. But because we've been reared to accept a "minority" description of ourselves, the idea of "control over government and society" hasn't ranked high on our list of priorities as Africans in America. Our focus has rather been to assimilate and fit as neatly possible into the already-established folds of government and society, without causing status quo annoyances that could hinder our acceptance.

But at this stage in our history, we need to understand the conceptuality and formation of governments and societies as being products and symbols of sovereignty. Among other fundamental factors, I'm referring to the capacity of ideals and institutions, along with the required caliber of leadership that goes into nationhood, thereby making it possible for a people to create and control a government and society that reflect their true nature and core values.

This chapter therefore delves into sociopolitical bridges and breakdowns between *Governments*, the *Governed*, and the *Ungovernable*. Hold on though. Before anyone gets revved up to raid storefront windows of HD TVs, you should know that being "Ungovernable" does not infer anarchy or a license to loot for personal gain. In a political context, it refers to acts of "De Facto Sovereignty" where people "act as if" they already legally and officially possess sovereignty.[1]

When government injustices and indifferences exceed tolerance levels, people have resorted to *de facto* acts to collectively function to the fullest degree possible "as if" they are sovereign. *De facto* acts are carried out for various reasons, but with some common denominators wherein people begin to regard their sovereign rights as primary to the politics and policies of others. They believe that no other people can or will govern their interests better than themselves. They also share in courage to not relent, knowing that *de facto* acts are necessary for self-preservation in today's political jungles where the strong is known to politically cannibalize the feeble.

Today's world brims with different sorts and levels of political breakdowns between governments and societies. Events in places like Myanmar, Taiwan, Iraq, Palestine, Sudan, Chechnya, Georgia, and Kosovo typify some of the more intensified struggles. When society prevails, a government will change its policies and/or representatives. Or, in extreme cases, governments can be toppled and replaced, then ushering a new era of sovereignty for a people.

Instances occur when new governments are formed in the aftermath of coups, and depending on the circumstances, some established governments will refuse to recognize or hold diplomatic relations with such governments. The US government does so with governments that it deems to be evil or undemocratic, as in the case of Iran, Cuba, North Korea, and Somalia.

Although the US government is known for holding other governments to strict standards of democracy and human rights, its relationship with Africans in America has been far from exemplary. As we've scrapped and clawed for basic human rights, it seems as if the goalposts are moved each time we gain political ground. Yet, we've been politically conditioned to wake up each morning saluting US government authority, as though it's mandatory that we honor an authority that historically has not reciprocated in upholding its responsibilities in return. The fact that we were formerly enslaved accounts for why we did so in the past. But pause momentarily and ask yourself this very important question – What exactly makes us obligated at present to recognize and obey US government authority?

Because of conventional thinking, this question may seem ridiculous to some. But when you understand the true source and nature of a government's authority, juxtaposed to the rights of the governed, this becomes a long overdue question with answers and ramifications that can potentially shatter-to-pieces what we've come to know and accept as "government authority."

As Africans in America, we know firsthand that governments can legislate and violently enforce immoral laws and practices. Although segregation laws no longer exist on paper, we periodically receive messages through events like Katrina and Jena to remind us of who is boss. Our political clarity of *de facto* acts and being *ungovernable* can therefore hold great bearing on whether we will further permit the US government to continue its jurisdiction over our 21st-century political affairs. As we begin, take note of the following definitions from Webster's (the italics are my own):

Government: The *continuous exercise of authority* over and the performance of functions for a political unit: The complex of political institutions, laws, and customs through which the function of governing is carried out: A *small group of persons* holding simultaneously the principal political executive offices of a nation or other political unit and being responsible for the *direction* and *supervision* of public affairs. [2]

Society: A *voluntary association* of individuals for common ends: An organized group working together . . . because of *common interest or beliefs*: An enduring and *cooperating social group* whose members have developed organized patterns of relationships through interaction with one another: A community, nation, or broad grouping of people having *common traditions, institutions, and collective activities and interests*.[3]

Let me add that governments are intangible. You can't physically see "governments." You do see the people who form and control governments, and you do see the effects of the policies from people who operate governments. But you don't actually see "governments."

Also, contemporary governments are commonly formed and sustained through bloodshed, corruption, and abuse of the governed. Some governments conduct relations and engage in clandestine affairs that its citizens may never know about. Sometimes nefarious activities are known, but not publicly discussed by citizens due to fears of reprisal.

Though government can be dirty and unscrupulous business, that serves "a small group" in disproportion to the masses, attempts are frequently made by governments to avoid having information and ideas circulate in society that promote unfavorable impressions of their policies or image. This is because it benefits governments far more than the governed, when society believes that strong, mutually binding relations exist between them. Governments therefore keep political instruments like nationalism, propaganda, and indoctrination at their disposal, to use whenever necessary to maintain loyalty, allegiance, and patriotism in societies.

As a society, Americans have always been led to believe that the US government "represents" the interests and ideals "of the people, for the people, by the people." What stands out conspicuously however, is that the word "represent" does not appear anywhere in the preceding definition of government.

By virtue of what is *not* stated, it's seems safe to conclude that by definition, governments "do not represent the people." Rather than being representative of the people, modern-day institutions of governments have mutated over the centuries into what Webster's accurately designates as, "a *small group of persons* who *exercise continuous authority over the direction and supervision of public affairs*."

Relationships between governments and societies have become complex beyond what citizens typically know and learn in high school civics classes. To quote Thomas Paine on this matter:

> Some writers have so confounded society with governments, as to leave little or no distinction between; whereas they are not only different, but have different origins. Society is produced by our wants, and governments by our wickedness . . .
>
> Society in every state is a blessing, but government, even in its best state, is but a necessary evil; in its worst state an

intolerable one; for when we suffer, or are exposed to the same miseries by a government, which we might expect in a country without government, our calamity is heightened by reflecting that we furnish the means by which we suffer.[4]

Just in case you're unfamiliar with Paine, he was a premier thinker of his times who provided much of the intellectual substance to America's independence movement. His work raised America's philosophical/ political bar, by phrasing sovereignty in a language that ordinary folks could easily relate to. His political "School of Thought" was not only central to Euro-Americans gaining *de facto* clarity to become *ungovernable*, it remains central to the political psyche and spirit of the US government.

Paine's revolutionary pamphlet *Common Sense* took early Americans by storm. According to *Britannia*, "The publication of The Declaration of Independence by Thomas Jefferson which was signed by 56 delegates was no doubt influenced by the publication of Thomas Paine's *Common Sense* written in July 1776."[5] Though originally written specifically to and for Euro-Americans, *Common Sense* has current applicability to Africans in America and repressed people worldwide. It somewhat serves as a companion guide that lends political credence to this work because, if you can understand the sovereign principles he advocated for Euro-Americans, you should equally understand the same principles in parallel to our plight.

On a deeper level with modern governments in general, there are swarms of international influences exerted upon politics and policies that supercede politicians. The majority of governments operate within sophisticated structures of neocolonial-like relationships under Western powers. Not only are governments co-opted and compromised in the process, unseen forces and factors hover behind the scenes. Officials who visibly perform government functions are not necessarily the true source from which power emanates.

Furthermore, because of the greed and economic nature of today's world, most major industries and all natural resources are monopolized by relatively small circles of individuals and corporations. Wealthy plutocrats and international institutions wield influence that can at times strong-arm the passing of self-serving policies and legislation that negatively impact governments and societies.

Countries in effect have two governments – One is *comprised* of the politicians you see who supposedly "represent the people." The other is *devised* by those you don't see who operate the international and fiscal strings of control. Absent these monetary channels, a government would find itself isolated from the world's major financing mechanisms, thereby endangering itself to potential economic collapse. As governments face pressure to conform to these influences, societies are affected in turn.

Even though governments should not bend or twist society to conform to their ways, people worldwide find themselves having to "drink the Kool-Aid." In some countries the process is blunt and bloody, causing epic clashes between government and society. In others the process occurs gradually over time, so that in the end people aren't even aware that they've been politically or psychologically manipulated.

The US Patriot Act, which grants the government authority to secretly read your love letters in the mail and rummage the likes of your medical and library records, is part of a gradual process that is currently bending and twisting Americans to "drink the Kool-Aid" of policies that benefit the government more than the governed. Despite widespread complaints that it violates civil liberties, invades privacy rights, and strips the public of constitutional freedoms, its provisions are still enforced and will not be retired anytime soon. If anything, the Patriot Act is subtly paving a path towards a future with increased degrees of martial law.

[Bush] claims he can designate any American an "enemy combatant." For those under that suspicion, he claims the right to wiretap them without warrants, arrest them with charges, detain them without lawyers, torture them without judicial review, and hold them until the war ends. He also says that neither the

Congress nor the pubic has any right to review his decisions, or to gain access to the papers that he chooses to keep secret.[6]

No group of people in modern history has arguably been politically or psychologically bent and twisted to serve a government and society more than Black America. Over and over we hear that "you can do or be anything you want in America." Don't be fooled because at the core of Americanization are Anglo-European principles and practices of government and society, primarily designed to accommodate them first. But as I wrote in *Pawned Sovereignty*:

> The ideal function of any form of government is to establish a nondiscriminatory political, economic, and social apparatus to satisfy the needs of its citizens. If people need clean drinking water, better healthcare, or greater political voice, the duty of the government is to help facilitate the means to acquire these ends.
>
> As the self-professed "government for the people" and "leader of the free world," the US government is not exempt from serving the rightful needs of the people it once enslaved and segregated via democracy.[7]

Since governments and societies do not always intersect on vital issues, people can live under a "democratic government" and still have need to take *de facto* acts to institute a new government. Just because a government calls itself a "democracy" doesn't mean that the needs and interests of a people will be aptly satisfied. In *Common Sense*, Thomas Paine wrote the following rudimentary account of how a society evolves to necessitate and form a compatible government:

> In order to gain a clear and just idea of the design and end of government, let us suppose a small number of persons settled in some sequestered part of the earth, unconnected with the rest;

they will then represent the first peopling of any country, or of the world. In this state of natural liberty, society will be their first thought. . . . Thus necessity, like a gravitating power, would soon form our newly arrived emigrants into society.

But as the Colony encreases, the public concerns will encrease likewise . . . This will point out the convenience of their consenting to leave the legislative part to be managed by a select number chosen from the whole body, who are supposed to have the same concerns at stake which those have who appointed them, and who will act in the same manner as the whole body would act were they present. . . . That the ELECTED might never form to themselves an interest separate from the ELECTORS, [and] they will mutually and naturally support each other, and on this, (not on the unmeaning name of king,) depends the STRENGTH OF GOVERNMENT, AND THE HAPPINESS OF THE GOVERNED.[8]

People who comprise "the governed" must know that neither governments nor societies are permanent or unchangeable fixtures. Whenever any government fails to meet basic human requirements, society should band together knowing that governments are manmade institutions that can be reshaped or remade if necessary. Ralph Waldo Emerson observed:

In dealing with the State we ought to remember that its institutions are not aboriginal, though they existed before we were born; that they are not superior to the citizen; that every one of them was once the act of a single man; every law and usage was a man's expedient to meet a particular case; that they all are imitable, all alterable; we may make as good, we may make better. Society is an illusion to the young citizen. It lies before him in rigid repose, with certain names, men and institutions rooted like oak-trees to the centre, round which all arrange themselves the best they can. But the old statesman knows that society is fluid; there are no such roots and centres, but any particle may suddenly become the centre of the movement and compel the system to gyrate round it. . . ."[9]

Emerson's analysis is relatable to Africans in America, in that, this society "existed before we were born" and the government has historically acted "superior" to us as "citizens." Euro-American "names, men, and institutions are rooted like oak-trees to the center" of US government and society, so we have always had to "arrange ourselves around them as best we can." Most importantly however, he mentions that "society is fluid" and that "there are no such roots or centers."

Almost 200 sovereign nations exist at present. But if there's one repeated or predictable message of history, it is that – World orders and world powers do change hands. Regardless of size, power, or influence, no nation is undefeatable and no government lasts forever. Time has atrophied the longevity and invincibility of every nation and empire thus far. The Holy Roman Empire lasted 963 years; the Babylonian Empire 717 years; and Ancient Greece 454 years.[10]   Since America isn't the Kingdom of God, the forecast of world history has likewise predestined an impending expiration date.

<><><><><><><>

Nationalism Versus Propaganda

To ensure success and longevity, governments must invest in "points of views" to steer public opinion and sustain confidence among the governed. One way to advance and protect such investments is to infuse strong and steady dosages of nationalism within and throughout society, thereby making the governed more prone to support the principles, practices, and policies of the government.

"Nationalism" is defined as: "Loyalty and devotion to a nation; a special sense and consciousness within people, causing them to exalt their nation above all other nations, and place primary emphasis on promoting their culture and interests as opposed to those of other nations."[11]

To a great extent, nationalism grows from the mixed ideologies (political/economic/religious) that governments adopt, be it democratic or fascist; capitalist or communist; Judaic or Buddhist, etc. Citizens are then influenced or even at times impelled to accept ideologies in varying increments until society is largely in one accord.

Once nationalism is firmly implanted and handed down from generation to generation, societies can blindly accept traditions and beliefs which may or may not be true. It is not unusual for governments to profess standards and values that are plainly inconsistent with reality. Journalist Paul Starobin wrote in an article titled "Us and Them: The Fires of Nationalism in a War-Torn World" that "… The appetite for nationalism arises from the natural desire of peoples linked by culture and other bonds to share a mythic story about themselves."[12]

Throughout history, nations have exalted themselves with overly exaggerated perceptions of their greatness and morality. Expressions of nationalism have also led to encroachments and devaluing of the cultures and humanity of others. Unfortunately, this has triggered countless international controversies and even military conflicts.

Domestically, the overpowering reach of governments is also known to chastise and brutalize citizens and groups that rub against the grain of nationalism. In Turkey in 2006 a government official was arrested for "chewing gum" while laying a wreath at a monument honoring the country's "revered founder" Kemal Ataturk.[13] He was formally charged with "insulting Ataturk's memory." In Ecuador an environmental activist from the US was deported in 2007 for "violating national sovereignty" after assisting police in seizing two tons of illegally fished shark fins. President Rafael Correa stated that he would not "allow any foreigner to come and tell [Ecuadorians] what to do.[14]

Nationalism in America is spread so thick that it stretches from church pulpits to professional sporting arenas, where teams have the US flag sewn on uniforms. Tributes are paid to war at some sport stadiums with recordings of bomb blasts over the PA system to simulate the national anthem lyrics of "the bombs bursting in air." Sometimes military jetfighters even fly overhead. Every "7th Inning Stretch" at Yankee Stadium in New York, a rendition of "God Bless America" is played to the patriotic delight of the crowd.

All of this is great for patriotism. But a thin line divides the promotion of patriotism and nationalism from veering into danger zones of propaganda, where societies are misled to accept falsehoods and misconceptions. In mainstream America the word "propaganda" is not used or associated with government or society. But watch what draws applause and what makes headlines during RNC and DNC Conventions or after a presidential address, and you'll see propaganda in the making.

During his 2004 "State of the Union Address," President George W. Bush stated: "Our founders dedicated this country to the cause of human dignity, the rights of *every* person, and the possibilities of every life."[15] Why is this propaganda and not nationalism? Because based on its deeds and contrary to its creed, America was not founded on the rights of *every* person, but rather the rights of *some* persons. Despite being inaccurate, phrases like these are commonly broadcasted by government and echoed loudly throughout society. Leave it to Euro-Americans and you'd be swayed through propaganda to think that ideals of justice and human rights originated from (of all people) their (slaveholding) founding fathers.

Society has become intoxicated by popular buzzwords and catch phrases like "Equality," "Truth and Justice for All," and "Fighting for Freedom" . . . What I call the sweet-sounding "Language of Liberty." This well-scripted language that comes from America's *Doctrine, Documents,* and *Declarations*, provides a smokescreen that shields immoral US government conduct.

America's inverted sense of justice and morality is analogous to a man who *nobly* sets out to build a hospital. But due to the lack of resources he *ignobly* robs a bank, and in the process he ends up injuring and murdering innocent people. He then uses the stolen money to build a wonderful state-of-the-art hospital, and even treats some of those he injured along the way. Although the hospital may be a good thing, it would be inaccurate to profess that the hospital was (as Bush said of America) founded on "human dignity." The hospital (like America) was founded on "human indignity."

Indoctrination: "In" the "Doctrine" of a "Nation"

A political cartoon appeared in newspapers depicting the familiar finger-pointing Uncle Sam caricature. But instead of the familiar slogan "Uncle Sam Wants You," the caption read: "Be A Loyal American! Stop Knowing Things We Don't Want You To Know."[16] Considering the turbulent state of domestic and international affairs, the issue of our "loyalty" to America and questions about "things the government do not want us know" are more relevant than ever.

Like propaganda, "Indoctrination" is not a word that America associates with itself, because again, this is supposedly a "free country." Although the notion seems far fetched, indoctrination is not something that only happens in "foreign countries" under despots and dictatorships. Degrees of indoctrination exist wherever any government and society exists.

Though it may infer brainwashing and mind control, "Indoctrination" comprises three words: *In, Doctrine,* and *Nation.* As I established earlier, all nations have doctrines, as well as documents, and declarations. By definition, a "Doctrine" is merely "something that is taught."[17] All societies are thusly impacted by sociopolitical ideals that are taught. As such, when people are "Indoctrinated" they simply learn and adopt the traditions, ethos, and ideals of their nation. By believing and conforming to what is taught, people are thereby *In* the *Doctrine* of their *Nation* – Hence, "Indoctrination."

Dr. Ahati Toure of Delaware State University, who is the author of *John Henrik Clarke and the Power of Africana History*, pointed out at a conference that a simple illustration of indoctrination is found in the historical dates that are etched into the minds of people in various societies. Americans, as he noted, have affinities to dates like 1492, 1776, and September 11th, all of which are indelibly indoctrinated into thoughts. Dates that are significant to people in other nations, do not rank alongside these dates that Euro-Americans have declared significant.

On the surface it may not appear that indoctrination in America is of the same mind-altering magnitude as in *other* nations. It's easy to see from afar what appears to be indoctrination in foreign countries, but it's not so easy to detect right under your nose in your own country. From the outside looking in, certain ways and behaviors of foreign countries seem strange to Americans, and vice versa.

The wild stage performances of the Rolling Stones are viewed as "freedom of speech" here "*in* the *doctrine* of the *nation*" of America – But not so "*in* the *doctrine* of the *nation*" of China, which of course has its own *Doctrine*, *Documents*, and *Declarations* to authenticate themselves. The Stones' 2006 show in Shanghai was censored by the Chinese government even though some fans paid over a $600 ticket price to see raunchiness.[18] More of the same clamor over free speech occurred at the 2008 Olympics in Beijing.

NBA star LeBron James and his Nike commercials are big hits here in America, but his "Chamber of Fear" commercial, where he defeated a cartoon Chinese kung fu master, was banned in China.[19] Though regarded as "just" a commercial here, the Chinese government felt it insulted China's "national dignity," and "goes against rules that require ads not to contain content that blasphemes national practices and cultures."[20]

Indoctrination in America doesn't turn people into beady-eyed zombies who follow commands on prompt. In Black life, however, indoctrination ranges from simplistic to extreme . . . Simplistic, as in having barbeques every 4th of July or enjoying Ray Charles' soulful patriotic rendition of "America the Beautiful." Extreme, as in being voluntarily airlifted across the globe to fight and possibly die in a war for dubious reasons – While at the same time, New York police unload and then reload gun-clips to shoot unarmed Black men up to 50 times, like target dummies at a shooting range.

Generally, nationalism and indoctrination are used for good, to strengthen patriotism. But they can be used to induce the governed to serve ulterior agendas of a government. If for example the US government decided to reinstate another draft tomorrow, the same young Black men that policemen kick for exercise and shoot for target practice, would be *ordered* to "fight for freedom" if their draft number popped up.

In this is so-called free country, 18- to 25-year-olds are not free from being conscripted to kill or be killed in the military. This alone should make young Black men question if they are really as free as indoctrination seems to suggest, especially since, by law, all males in this age bracket must register with the military Selective Service to be on call, just in case the government gets in the mood again for drafting.[21]

Another questionable aspect of freedom involves traveling, since your passport is not "your passport." You don't "own" it. It's owned by the government which can confiscate it, or restrict or prevent your travels. Read the fine print to see that your passport is "THE PROPERTY OF THE UNITED STATES GOVERNMENT. IT MUST BE SURRENDERED UPON DEMAND . . . " If travel bans are enacted, you'll be prosecuted if you dare think you are "free enough" to visit those places, even your own native homeland.

The formal process of indoctrination trickles at grammar-school level, and then rushes like a tsunami by the time students reach the university level. Middle school students in Caldwell NJ were given homework to "write a catchy slogan and a poster advertising why slave labor was the best way to run a cotton plantation. [22] Following is an actual copy of the assignment.

Middle School Slavery Assignment

Lap of Luxury: You have recently inherited a lot of money from your dear old aunt who passed away. Along with the cash from her estate, you have also become the owner of a large and fertile tract of land near Charleston, S.C. You have determined that the most profitable course of action is to build a plantation for the purpose of growing cotton. You have also established that slave labor is the only way of running your plantation without catastrophic personal and financial ruin. However, your dear aunt also has two sisters who may veto your plans if not properly convinced, and then withhold your inheritance from you. Mrs. Chomko and Mrs. Rutzler, your aunts, must be persuaded that slave labor is the best choice, because they are from the North and aren't sure that they agree with slavery. Keep in mind that your aunts have moral as well as financial questions about your decision to use slave labor.

Your job: Create an advertisement that will convince your aunts that your idea is the best course of action.

First, create a list of the pros and cons of using slave labor. Then use the ideas from your list to create an advertisement that you plan to run in the newspaper, where your aunts will see it. You are hoping that your ad will be sufficiently persuasive that, upon seeing it, your aunts will give you the green light to begin building your new home.

Your advertisement must contain:
1. A catchy slogan (or name) for your plantation.
2. At least three reasons why slave labor is the best idea.
3. Reasons why your plantation won't be financially sound if it doesn't use slave labor.
4. Illustrations.23

Document 2. Middle School Slavery Assignment

Two Black university professors expressed concern only that the subject matter seemed "too advanced" for middle schoolers. One said it was a "great way to teach the students. . . . It is important for students to understand both sides," while the other said he didn't have a problem "teaching the past through several lenses."[24] This shows that even the most educated and seemingly most intelligent of us, are too drunk with indoctrination themselves to protect children.

The assignment reflects an overall greater problem, which is that American history is generally taught as though there is a "side" or "lens" to slavery that precludes its ignorance and immoralities. Do students also make "catchy slogans and posters" for the *other* side to September 11th or the *other* side to the Jewish Holocaust? Students learn to incontrovertibly condemn terrorism and Nazism, with no room for alternative views or discussions. However, when it comes to slaveholders there's always room for debate.

Sure, slavery had a host of economic "sides" because profiteering was the purpose. But yet the establishment never wants to admit the commercial scale or magnitude of slave labor. This assignment was not about teaching "the economic relations between slave labor and national development," but rather to indoctrinate students to learn to rationalize what otherwise would be indefensible conduct of both government and society.

Just as we need to monitor indoctrination at grammar schools, the same holds true at universities. While America is nose-deep wallowing in its own political excrement in Iraq and anxious to bomb Iran and Syria, the US military is lurking around Historically Black Colleges and Universities (HBCU), lying in wait to inveigle students to enlist, under the pretext of GI benefits, home loans, further education and leadership skills.

The Navy funded the Tavis Smiley Group in 2007 for a "Talented Tenth HBCU Tour," where Smiley conducted interactive discussions on "the characteristics of successful role models," while the navy hosted "special sessions" on how leadership skills are developed in the navy.[25]

The name is a spin-off of the "Talented Tenth" concept coined by Dr. W. E. B. DuBois, referring to the top 10 percent of the Black intelligentsia.

With all the violence and other distractions that keep our youths from attending college in the first place, we don't need to ambush them once they get there with military violence disguised as leadership. After escaping death and influences of street gangs, they don't need indoctrination to join another kind of gang.

Based on our historical experience and knowing what we know about this government's love of blood and political insincerity, it's time we self-produced new forms of leadership and statesmanship at HBCUs. Rather than participating in wars and having the military lecture our students on reckless belligerence disguised as leadership, we should innovate special curriculums of diplomacy to teach our youngsters how to prevent and end wars . . . Isn't that more in line with what Dr. King would want? *The government threatens to withhold funding to institutions that dont allow military recruitment on campuses*

As much as universities are supposed to engage students in critical thinking and objective scholarship, a survey at 50 top schools determined that 40 percent of students said professors "frequently commented on politics in class even if it was outside the subject matter."[26] This survey, conducted by the American Council of Trustees and Alumni, also found that 31 percent "felt there were some courses in which they needed to agree with a professor's political or social views to get a good grade."[27] It goes on to say:

> Traditionally, clashes over academic freedom have pitted politicians or administrators against instructors who wanted to express their opinions and teach as they saw fit. But increasingly, it is students who are invoking academic freedom, claiming biased professors are violating their right to a classroom free of indoctrination.[28]

Written records of our fight against indoctrination predate emancipation. Back in 1827 John B. Russwurm and Samuel Cornish

56

published the first Black newspaper in the US in New York, called the *Freedom's Journal*. The first editorial began with the lines: "We wish to plead our own cause. Too long have others spoken for us."[29] Roughly a full century later Marcus Garvey emphasized the same importance of having our own doctrine in an editorial titled "Ours the Right to Our Doctrine," where he wrote:

> We must inspire a literature and promulgate a doctrine of our own without any apologies to the powers that be. The right is ours and God's. Let contrary sentiment and cross opinions go to the winds. Opposition to race independence is the weapon of the enemy to defeat the hopes of an unfortunate people. We are entitled to our own opinions and not obligated to or bound by the opinions of others.
>
> Let no voice but your own speak to you from the depths. Let no influence but your own raise you in time of peace and time of war. Hear all, but attend only that which concerns you.[30]

Another century has nearly passed since Garvey's editorial, and we are still no less indoctrinated and still do not posses our own *Doctrine*, *Documents*, and *Declarations* to authenticate us. Some might disagree, but if we did not adhere to being "*in* the *doctrine* of this *nation*," it would have been impossible for us to have assimilated this far into this dominant European society. And after undergoing centuries of uncalled-for subhuman treatment, we certainly would not have prioritized integration at the top of our "to-do list."

<><><><><><><>

Converted by Time & Made for Society

A well-accomplished 40ish Black female attorney once told me about a White couple who'd adopted an infant Chinese boy. By the time he turned

12, she said she found it "strange" to see someone Chinese who doesn't speak Chinese or have any cultural sense of being Chinese. She felt the boy was somehow being "deprived" of expressing and experiencing his true "Chinese identity." What I found strange was how she could not relate the parallel when I questioned the same of Africans in America adopting the foreign culture, foreign language, and foreign political identity of Euro-Americans.

Though she considered herself "African-American," she spoke no African language and lacked knowledge of African cultures, traditions, and history. Unlike the sad sentiments felt for the Chinese boy, she didn't personally feel "deprived" of anything African. When I asked her to explain the difference, her reasoning was based on "time" . . . That being Americanized is not strange for Africans because "we've been here for so long."

Thomas Paine addressed this same issue of time from the standpoint of British ways being imposed upon the colonies, writing: "Perhaps the sentiments contained in the following pages, are not *yet* sufficiently fashionable to procure them general favor; a long habit of not thinking a thing *wrong*, gives it a superficial appearance of being *right* and raises at first a formidable outcry in defense of custom. . . . Time makes more converts than reason."[31] (Italics my own).

He's conveying the point that when people are exposed to particular thoughts, beliefs, and customs long enough, they can become inclined to regard them as true and right, even if false and wrong. Though certainly "converted by time," Africans in America are no less strange in this Western society as Chinese people are. Besides, unlike the Chinese, the physical and psychological conditioning we forcibly endured to fit into this society was not only tragic, but un-Godly.

Time can indeed persuade people to accept sociopolitical conditions, but time does not justify immoralities nor make wrong conditions right. Margaret Fuller put it this way, saying: "Man is not made for society, but society is made for man."[32] Societies, in other words, ought be constructed to serve the needs and interests of the people – Not the reverse. To take

Paine and Fuller's reasoning a step further, let me say that "Societies should make governments, governments should not make societies." Part of our difficulty as a society is that we never made a government – we conversely were made by the US government.

While no group of people has the right to violate or seize the sovereignty of another, the grinding effects of time and traditions can seemingly normalize the dissolution of a people's sovereignty. The real harm of being "converted by time" and "made for society" is when truth and history are revised to make people accept oddities and conditions that they otherwise would reject.

Remember in the old cowboy movies when a little White boy or girl got captured by Indians, and how after being "converted by time," they started thinking and acting like Indians? In some episodes the boy became so converted that he even fought against White people, or the girl would fall in love and have a baby with an Indian male . . . Man oh man, was that a terrible calamity within the storyline.

A happy ending would be when they were rescued and reunited with White society. Remember the soft music and how emotionally touching the scenes were as they re-converted to their "true identity" again? It probably made you teary-eyed when the rusty-haired boy finally took off that *savage* feathered headdress and put on a neatly pressed Calvary uniform, or when the girl discarded those dreadful *squaw* clothes and put on a pretty petticoat.

Photo 3. Native Americans "Before" Enrollment at Hampton Institute First
Class of Native Americans "Before" Enrollment at Hampton Institute, Hampton, Va. 1878
Back row left to right: Laughing Face, an Arikara; White Breast, a Mandan; Carries
Flying, a Blackfoot Sioux; Man Who Looks Around, a Mandan; and Sioux Boy,
an Arikara. Second row, left to right: Sharphorn, tribe unknown; Walking Cloud,
a Hunkpapa Lakota (Sitting Bull's Tribe; One Who Hoots When He Walks, a
Hunkpapa Lakota; White Wolf, an Arikara. Seated: Long Arm, a Gros Ventre.
(Courtesy of Smithsonian Institution, National Museum of Natural History, National Anthropological
Archives)

The above photo shows a real-life group of Native Americans in
1878 prior to enrolling at Hampton Institute (now Hampton University)
in Virginia, where I happened to have graduated. As part of "converting"
them to be "made for society," they had to cut their hair and change
their native clothes to make themselves *appear* more European. Though
America may profess diversity, this establishment has ways to marginalize
people who don't look or act "Western." The following photo shows the
same group after being institutionally raped of their cultural identity.

Photo 4. Native Americans "After" Enrollment at Hampton Institute First
Class of Native Americans "After" Enrollment at Hampton Institute, Hampton, Va. 1878
(Courtesy of Smithsonian Institution, National Museum of Natural History, National nthropological
Archives)

But it's not over yet. Officials at Hampton University now prohibit
male and female MBA business students from wearing braids or locks.[33]
Perms, s-curls, straightening combs, and conks however are acceptable,
along with any other harmful or unnatural product to chemically induce
African hair to *resemble* European hair. Braids nevertheless represent an
African tradition of hair style that's not only naturally suited for our hair
texture, braids are also too ancient to be dated. If braids emanated from
European traditions, you can be sure they would not be frowned upon in
society or banned at an institution of higher learning.

As a result of being "converted by time," there's a certain variety
of Africans in America who'll say they are neither African nor African-
American. They refer to themselves as "Americans." However, being
"American" is a "political designation" of citizenship that has nothing to
do with the ancestral origin of who you are. You are who you are, based
on ancestry – Not politics. Whether anyone likes it or not, those of us who

are here via the consequences of the slave trade are African by blood and heritage.

Although time may convert people to accept foreign ways and cultures, the essence of who they are by blood and heritage can never be altered by politics or geography. Even if we are here a million years from now, we will still be Africans by ancestry. And no matter how thoroughly we convert or how many miles we march in protest, it won't alter the fact America is a European nation . . . Not in geography, but in government, politics, and society.

If you doubt that America is Europe, just take a look and you'll see dominant signs and indicators of Europe all around. Start with laws and the Constitution. Laws represent the governing spirit of a nation. In this country there's a prevailing European thought process that guides and impacts those who practice, interpret, and enforce laws. Pick up a law book and note the language of the laws. It is so thick with Old English phraseology and European thought, that some students fail law courses and some can't pass the BAR because they are unable to grasp sense of the language. Read some opinions of the Supreme Court and take note of their peculiar sequence of wordings. If you study law it's guaranteed your mind will be drenched and indoctrinated to the core with Europeanized thought.

Watch the world/evening news on CBS, NBC, and ABC for further evidence of Europe. Try this for experiment. . . . While stories are being previewed at the start, click your remote quickly back and forth between the three networks. You'll find that they regularly cover the exact same stories, mostly in the exact same order, using almost the exact same words, phrases, and footage. Except for different "human interest" stories at the end, the stations are verbatimized carbon copies of each other, and their anchors are like windup mannequins who all speak with the same cadences and intonations.

It doesn't matter which channel you watch because mainstream media all report the same things and reach the same conclusions anyway. This tells you that "media" and "journalism" and what is considered "news" is being managed and officiated by central sources. Otherwise, it would be literally impossible for CBS, NBC, and ABC to be so routinely synchronized. Based on the coverage and slants, it's clear that every second is used to communicate European interests and ideals. Pundits and media personalities don't just *report* news, they *determine* news. They don't just *discuss* issues, they *create* issues . . . All of which are then perceived as realities by society.

Because of the same controls and influences, it shouldn't have surprised anyone that Don Imus was fully resuscitated back to radio-life soon after the loud public outcry from Black society for his offensive comments (that included Black "hair") about Black women on Rutgers University's basketball team. Protest chants of "Imus Must Go" came to fruition as he went from one multimillion-dollar radio contract to another, where he now boasts of more viewers, listeners and affiliates.[34] If we "punish" him any more, he'd be able to buy WABC where he now works.

Also, pay attention to the disparities in media notoriety given to individuals. John H. Johnson for example, the founder of Johnson Publishing, died during the same week as ABC anchorman Peter Jennings. Granted, Jennings was counted among the best broadcast journalists, but mainstream media gave him inordinately more coverage, even donning him on the August 22, 2005 covers of *Newsweek* and *People* magazines.

Johnson Publishing however, is a legacy. *Ebony* and *Jet* have a combined worldwide circulation of over 2.4 million and readership of nearly 22 million.[35] Johnson's bio states that in 1982 he became the first Black person on *Forbes* list of "400 Richest Americans," and as a philanthropist he'd just gifted $4 million to Howard University. Overall, his personal and business success would have been phenomenal even if he hadn't battled societal obstacles of his times.

To be fair, Jennings' bio states that he won 16 Emmys and many other distinguished awards. But pound for pound, in terms of lasting impact in the world – Peter Jennings, with all due respect, was no John H. Johnson. Johnson did what few men (Black or White) ever do . . . Built a renowned institution that will thrive worldwide well beyond the years he lived on earth. Yet, Jennings still received the lion's share of media coverage.

But this is America and America is Europe, which is also why the media and society show far more concern for missing White women and children. When they go missing, chances are much greater that the story makes national headlines and receives coverage over extended periods. And if the woman is considered attractive, oh my goodness, the story really enlarges in sensation.

With missing Black women and children, you can forget it. They're lucky to make national news once . . . Especially anyone with a name like Shaquanna or Latisha. Black females aren't as newsworthy because their stories lack *Snow-Whiteness* appeal to capture empathy from the greater Euro-masses who regard rail-thin White women with keen facial features as the advertised standard of feminine beauty. So, just like in the old cowboy movies, there's a dire sense of urgency and tragedy when such a woman comes up missing in this society that was "Made for Europeans."

<> <> <> <> <> <> <>

Politically Subjective "Rights" and "Wrongs"

When it comes to war, a government's political positions tend to subjectively sway society. Through nationalism and indoctrination, governments have historically lured citizens to support and participate in wars and malicious acts of all sorts. When a government launches aggression against other nations or members of its society, innocent people are bound to suffer and generations can sometimes be scarred indefinitely.

How is it possible that governments have amassed unchecked powers to blend and blur the lines separating the moral from the immoral, sometimes causing otherwise decent people to repress and participate in military attacks against innocent people? Well, governments and leaders do not generally engage in hostilities with the mindset that their nation is politically or morally *wrong*. They do so with a nationalistic belief that they are *right*.

Greek philosopher Plato taught this political lesson around 400 BC. Karl R. Popper (1902 – 1994), who was a noted political philosopher, said that Plato: "Perceived and presented himself not only as the brilliant architect of the political framework of his Ideal State, but as a great moralist, as well. The rulers of his city, based on his theory of the Philosopher King, were suited to maintain that role in perpetuity only by virtue of their innate superior grasp of the nature of Truth, Wisdom, and Goodness."[36]

At the same time, Plato acknowledged that governments must lie, writing that: "It is the business of the rulers of the city to tell lies, deceiving both its enemies and its own citizens for the benefit of the city. . . . Lies are necessary if your herd is to reach perfection; there need exist arrangements that must be kept secret from all but the rulers if we wish to keep the herd of guardians really free from disunion."[37] A specific type of lie that Plato cites relates to war and the general tendency of governments "to justify their existence by saving the state from its enemies – a tendency which must lead, whenever the old enemies have been successfully subdued, to the creation or invention of new ones."[38]

War, however, can also stir up ambivalences in societies. In America, for instance, it was considered highly unpatriotic to be anti-war at the onset of the war in Iraq. So, people who regarded the war as immoral would say they "support the troops, but not the war." That's like saying you condemn the devil but not the works of his demons. There is no subjective middle ground or splitting-of-hairs when it comes to morality and war. In this case, the same troops that these people "support" are, in effect, engaged in immoral conduct that results in maiming and murders of innocent people.

Interestingly, the *New York Times* uncovered in April 2008 that the Pentagon has an "information apparatus" that uses television analysts "to generate favorable news coverage of the [Bush] administration's wartime performance."[39] Not only are some paid $500 to $1,000 per appearance, some also have business ties to more than 150 military contractors in Iraq, either as lobbyists, senior executives, board members or consultants.[40]

When historians write their nation's war history, they likewise do so with subjective moral leanings. Over time, subjectivity can morph into gospel truth as successive generations are reared with such beliefs. French author Jean Cocteau (1889 – 1963) wrote, "History is a combination of reality and lies. The reality of history becomes a lie. The unreality of the fable becomes the truth."[41]

International positions on political rights and wrongs are not always based on truth or morality, but sometimes on a government's allegiance with its allies. For instance, because of the US government's coziness with the former apartheid government of South Africa, Nelson Mandela and all other ANC members were on America's "Terrorist Watch List" as late as mid-2008, requiring them to have "special permission waivers" to visit this country.[42]

Was the ANC wrong, and can South Africans be considered "terrorists" for being *ungovernable* and fighting against apartheid in their own country? Well, the answer depends on whichever government or individual you ask. Obviously, based on its allegiance to the Boers, the US government's position was that the ANC was wrong, that the ANC was a terrorist organization. Depending on an individual's personal and political orientation, they too are prone to substitute truth and morality for subjective beliefs of rights and wrongs.

International conflicts are not always clear to decipher. Propaganda can sometimes be so concentrated that it's difficult to separate fact from fiction, rights from wrongs. Both China and Taiwan believe they are politically and morally right regarding Taiwan's pursuit of sovereignty. The same is true with Israelis and Palestinians with disputed territories. And of course, all the warring factions in Iraq (the Shiites, Sunnis, Kurds and the US) believe they are politically and morally right.

After Hezbollah kidnapped some Israeli soldiers in 2006, a complex military skirmish hit a height of subjective rights and wrongs among Israel, Hezbollah, Lebanon, Syria, Iran, and the US. Most interesting were the accounts of victory from all sides after the United Nations brokered a ceasefire.[43] Hezbollah claimed victory even though the Israeli army significantly disabled its military capabilities and bombed parts of Southern Lebanon into dust and sky-high piles of rubble.

Syrian President Bashar Assad said, "The Middle East they [the Americans] aspire to . . . has become an illusion. . . . We tell them [Israelis] that after tasting humiliation in the latest battles, your weapons are not going to protect you – not your planes, or missiles, or even your nuclear bombs."[44]

Iranian President Mahmoud Ahmadinejad saluted Hezbollah for hoisting "the banner of victory" over Israel."[45] "God's promises have come true," he said. "On one side, is corrupt powers of the criminal US and Britain and the Zionists . . . with modern bombs and planes. And on the other side is a group of pious youth relying on God."[46]

It's peculiar how the end result of wars and events can determine how people and nations are viewed in history. An African proverb tells us: "Until the lion has his historian, the hunter will always be the hero." Politically so, it seems that the overriding historical distinctions between right and wrong, heroes and terrorists, are determined largely by propaganda and which side wins the conflict in question.

If Marcus Garvey had been successful with his nation-building initiative, he would be renowned today as the founder of an African republic. Since his movement was derailed, he's subjectively regarded in this society as a misfit who bucked against what is just and moral. Consequently, he is allotted very limited space on the pages of mainstream US history, even though objectively speaking; he arguably qualifies to sit at the table reserved for 20th-century political giants.

Being that the US overthrew Saddam Hussein, he will forever be labeled a despot in American history, and all Iraqis resistors will forever be painted with a broad brush as terrorists, insurgents, and enemy combatants. But are they really? Call them whatever you like; no one, however, can deny that US forces are a "foreign army," so it's not a head-scratching mystery why various segments of Iraqis (not just the resistors) have long detested US soldiers and private security firms on their sovereign soil.

Yes, civil and sectarian strife also rages, and Iraqi agencies and administrators have been attacked too. But the resistors regard the institutions established by way of "foreign influences" as being puppeteered. Hence, they believe they have every right to be violently *ungovernable* in the face of foreign occupation. And in substantiating this belief, the Iraqi resistance proved much tougher than US war planners ever anticipated. Their mercurial ways of urban warfare tell me that cadets at West Point will need revised textbooks for many semesters to come.

Iraqi resistors will never accept America's presence as a "fight against terrorism" or a "fight to spread freedom." Conversely, US soldiers have fueled a deep sense of obligation within young Iraqis to uphold what they feel is the honor of their land, by driving out foreign invaders. Without doubt, Americans would do no less under similar circumstances.

At no point in history would the US government have ever complied with foreigners on US soil who attempted to *right* its political *wrongs*. Be it slavery, segregation, or any other injustice they've committed, Euro-Americans would be ferociously *ungovernable* and fight with never-ending resistance before allowing the military or political influences of any foreign government to stain the fabric of US sovereignty.

Iraqi resisters surely will never gain credibility in US or Western history books. But, say they were to be successful in ridding US soldiers off their soil and establishing their own political structure. Such men would then be recorded in contemporary Iraqi history as patriots, heroes, and freedom fighters – Certainly not terrorists, insurgents, or enemy combatants.

Subjective views of war and the castigating of foes are not something new. Take for instance, British accounts of America's "Revolutionary War" for independence in 1776. Unlike Americans who refer to the war as a "revolution," the British called it a "rebellion." Those who America proudly refers to as patriots and heroes are regarded by Britain as radicals and seditionists who committed treason against the king and sought to divide the Empire.

High-schoolers in America won't read detailed accounts of the many colonists who thought it was a "sin" to revolt against a king, or that after the first Continental Congress, George Washington wrote, "No thinking man in all of North America desires independence."[47] Or that Benjamin Franklin "Cautioned against a break with the mother country, for despite its unkindness 'of late,' the link was worth preserving."[48] Or that at one point "The majority of the colonists opposed independence, or at least, were not willing to fight Britain to gain it."[49]

Had the British been victorious, America's founders would have gone down in history as insurrectionists who defied authority. If it were today, the founders would be rounded up like "enemy combatants" and imprisoned somewhere like Guantánamo, wearing flip-flops and orange jumpsuits with hoods over their heads. Based on the war's outcome however, to disparage any of the founders is like committing political blasphemy and historical heresy. The official position is that the founders were *right* and the British were *wrong* . . . End of story.

Following however is an excerpt from a *New York Times* book review of *Rough Crossings: Britain, the Slaves and the American Revolution,* by Simon Schama, which provides perspective into a rare side of the war – The side experienced by enslaved Africans.

In New York, black loyalists were justifiably fearful that the British would renege on the promise of freedom — and that their former masters would steal into the city and reclaim them. Among the terrified former slaves was Boston King, who had escaped his master in South Carolina and put as much distance as he could between his family and "the Americans."

Imagine how history would have unfolded had we lost the Revolutionary War and been brought to heel by His Britannic Majesty, King George III. Instead of being revered as founders, George Washington, Thomas Jefferson and their compatriots could well have been marched to the gallows and forgotten. British propagandists would have churned out a mythology much like the one American schoolchildren are force-fed today — but with the national roles reversed. The British monarchy would be depicted as the champion of liberty, with the rebels cast as agents of republican chaos and tyranny. The lesson would no doubt focus on the contradiction cited by Samuel Johnson, who inquired pithily of the Americans in 1775: "How is it that we hear the loudest yelps for liberty among the drivers of Negroes?"

"Rough Crossings" focuses on the black American role in the Revolution and, most particularly, on the tens of thousands of slaves who fled to British lines after Lord Dunmore issued a proclamation in November 1775 offering slaves from rebel plantations freedom in return for service to the crown. ... If nothing else, Schama's portraits of black loyalist fighters should provide Hollywood with fresh ideas about how to depict this war. Screenwriters will find prime material, for example, in the black guerrilla fighter known as Colonel Tye, who escaped from his master in New Jersey, survived the epidemics that ravaged Dunmore's Ethiopian Regiment in the Chesapeake and returned North to haunt the patriot outposts that were reachable from the British stronghold of New York.[50]

There's an interesting contrast between Euro-America's rise from colonialism and our rise from enslavement and segregation. Although the British were their blood relatives, Euro-Americans still declared them enemies. However, in mainstream US history books you won't read accounts of Euro-Americans being cited as our enemies. In the recording of 246 years of slave history, Euro-Americans took careful measures to not portray or allow themselves to be portrayed as enemies, oppressors, or any other unfavorable term.

It is not incidental that they framed themselves in history as "slavemasters," not "enemies." Psychologically, there are big differences between the two because, whereas you *follow* your master, you *fight* your enemies. *Enemy of African Sovereignty & Independence*

As "masters" and through attrition, Euro-Americans were able to psychologically validate themselves and Americanization as standards that we should politically desire and abide. The success and long-term impact of this is interesting as well, because it would be highly politically incorrect today to use terms like "enemies" or "oppressors" to refer to slaveholders or the US government at that time. Yet it is acceptable and appropriate to say "slavemaster."

There are however, countless examples of one-time enemies becoming allies. It happens all the time. Japan, Viet Nam, and Germany were all recent enemies of America who now are allies, and in no way is it political incorrect to identify them as past enemies. But in order to psychologically contain us as sovereign subjects, it is strategically important to this establishment that we do not examine history through any type of political lens that would classify Euro-Americans as enemies of the past . . . "Masters," yes; "enemies," no.

<><><><><><><>

Are All Men Really "Created Equal?"

Equality is a concept that this establishment has "politically pimped" to its advantage for centuries. I say this because our relationship with Euro-Americans lacks "political symmetry" of power, where authority and influence in government and society are equally managed and controlled between us. Equality has never meant or involved the equal sharing of power or a ratable redistribution of wealth. Being integrated with them has had the sociopolitical effect of making us more "like" them, instead of "equal" to them.

The origin of the notion of equality is rooted in the popularly highlighted phrase of the Declaration of Independence – "We hold these truths to be self-evident, that all men are created equal." But being "Created

Equal" is arguably the most misunderstood expression in the document and perhaps the most misconstrued concept in American politics.

Much has been revised or swept under the rug when it comes to the "intent" of America's founding fathers, which has resulted in a huge gap between the perception and reality of who and what the Declaration of Independence represents. Remember that *Doctrines, Documents,* and *Declarations* are instruments that in part define, express, and authenticate the sovereignty of a people. Therefore, before the content and intent of any historical document (whether written in America or elsewhere) can be accurately understood, you must take at least 3 considerations into account: 1) Who wrote the document and who they were writing to; 2) Why and for what purpose the document was written; and 3) What the pervading politics and circumstances were at the time.

Answers inform us that the Declaration of Independence was: 1) Composed by all White males (most of whom were slaveholders and early subscribers of taxonomy) and addressed to King George III and the British government; 2) The purpose was to proclaim political secession; and 3) Euro-Americans were colonized at the time, while Africans were enslaved and considered subhuman by the same Euro-American people who sought to achieve the very freedom they in turn denied to Africans.

Yet, there's this misleading contemporary revision that the Declaration of Independence politically incorporates and speaks for Africans in America too. This has caused us to misread between the true lines of the intent of "We hold these truths to be self-evident that all men are created equal."

Beware and be aware however, whenever hearing this phrase quoted in isolation, because being "Created Equal" does not stand alone as an ideal unto itself.

Being "Created Equal" is a subcomponent to the document's central message to "Dissolve the Political Bands" that connected Euro-Americans to the British. The true context of being "Created Equal," as expressed within the document is not an advocation to profess "equality" as a sociopolitical ideal for "all men" in the world. Nor did the founders intend for future generations in America to "perfect an imperfect Union" as you may hear people now say in relation to Obama's presidency. All of this is a revision of the document's original intent and purpose.

"Created Equal" strictly concerns the rights of Euro-Americans, as it expressly states, to: "Assume among the powers of the earth, the *separate* and *equal* station to which the Laws of Nature and of Nature's God entitle them." "Created Equal" is about the Euro-American quest to attain "Sovereign Equality" with world governments – Not promote "Integrated Equality" for African Americans at some future date in time.

With this in mind, review the first two sentences in the following portion of the document. (Italics are my own.)

THE DECLARATION OF INDEPENCENCE
In Congress, July 4, 1776

THE UNANIMOUS DECLARATION OF THE THIRTEEN UNITED STATES
OF AMERICA

When in the Course of human events, it becomes necessary for one people to dissolve the political bands which have connected them with another, and to assume among the powers of the earth, the separate and equal station to which the Laws of Nature and of Nature's God entitle them, a decent respect to the opinions of mankind requires that they should declare the causes which impel them to the separation. – We hold these truths to be self-evident, that all men are created equal, that they are endowed by their Creator with certain unalienable Rights, that among these are Life, Liberty and the pursuit of Happiness. – That to secure these rights, Governments are instituted among Men, deriving their just powers from the consent of the governed. – That whenever any Form of Government becomes destructive of these ends, it is the Right of the People to alter or to abolish it, and to institute new Government, laying its foundation on such principles and organizing its powers in such form, as to them shall seem most likely to effect their Safety and Happiness. Prudence, indeed, will dictate Governments long established should not be changed for light and transient causes; and accordingly all experience hath shown, that mankind are more disposed to suffer, while evils are sufferable, than to right themselves by abolishing the forms to which they are accustomed. But when a long train of abuses and usurpations, pursuing invariably the same Object evinces a design to reduce them under absolute Despotism, it is their right, it is their duty, to throw off such Government, and to provide new Guards for their future security.

Document 3. Declaration of Independence

Realizing that other nations would assess the validity of their declaration, they wrote in the very first sentence that: "A decent respect to the opinions of mankind requires that they should declare the causes which impel them to the separation." So, in presenting their case, they used the phrase "All Men Are Created Equal" as part of a strategic appeal to "mankind" to proclaim their "equal entitlement" to the same sovereign rights as their sovereign contemporaries.

In the final analysis, "Created Equal," has absolutely nothing to do with integrationist sentiments or civil rights ideals of equality as historically espoused and sought after by Africans in America.

I'm convinced that many of us know this truth in our hearts, as was evidenced in the profound clash of viewpoints at the 2006 State of Black America Forum, when Minister Louis Farrakhan challenged the timing and historical relevance of Tavis Smiley's *Covenant With Black America*. After calling it "impotent" the Minister impugned the government's trustworthiness, and then quoted Dr. Martin Luther King's metaphor that Black America might be "integrating into a burning house." Contrary to Dr. King's position that we should "be firemen," he concluded that if God set America ablaze because of endemic injustices, then who are we to try to extinguish the flames?

The atmosphere was never the same as subsequent panelists had little space for middle ground, since defending the *Covenant* on one hand meant rationalizing (to a degree) America's flagrance on the other. I say that the cause of the "burning house" is the Machiavellian nature of Euro-Americans, and therefore the flames can only be extinguished through their volition to change – Not through our increased participation or commitment to Americanization.

But beyond the *Covenant* and all the verbal sparring at the forum, the point I wish to advance was cloaked and conveyed in the split applause of audience members – Which attests to the reality that not all of us accept integration and equality at face value. In fact, an ABC poll in October 2008 found that only 11 percent of Black people believe that America has reached racial equality.[51]

If Africans in America are to ever benefit from the true intent of being "Created Equal," then we too (just as Euro-Americans did) must become *ungovernable* and exercise *de facto* acts as a means to attain "Sovereign Equality" in the world – Not march decade after decade in

75

hopes for a form of "Integrated Equality" that has thus far proven to be politically nonexistent.

Government Legitimacy & Consent of the Governed

This chapter opened with the question: What makes Africans in America obligated to recognize and obey the authority of the US government? Ask yourself as well: What exactly is it that legitimizes any government to govern over a society? In answering these questions, I've concluded that America's political authority over Africans in America is more "self-ordained" than legitimate.

To eliminate any confusion, let me emphasize that I'm not challenging the US government's legitimacy as an institution. That's an altogether different subject. What's at issue here, is the government's "source of legitimacy" to exercise perpetual political jurisdiction over all past, present, and future generations of Africans in America.

Much can be learned about the Euro-American interpretation of a government's legitimacy by studying the following 15 words of the third sentence in their Declaration of Independence which state that: "Governments are instituted among Men, deriving their just powers from the consent of the governed." According to their own words, the true litmus test of a government's legitimacy is measured in terms of the "Consent of the Governed."

I'm sure "Consent of the Governed" was resonating through his mind when Patrick Henry said: "My political curiosity, exclusive of my anxious solicitude for the public welfare, leads me to ask who authorized them [the framers of the Constitution] to speak the language of 'We the People,' instead of 'We the States?'"[52] The distinction he's making here is important because "States" connote the government, while the "People" connote the governed. He is therefore alluding to the principle that government authority must emanate from the consent of those who are being governed, not from the powers of State amassed by a government.

If Henry (being a founder and beneficiary of Americanization) had concerns as to who authorized the framers to speak "as the people," then we as an outskirt segment should be doubly concerned . . . Especially since, as facts will later show, we never had any representatives sign any formal document with Euro-Americans, whereby we ever "Consented" to any form of their political jurisdiction.

Just because a government was founded and has passed legislation as far back as 1776, does not necessarily mean its authority is legitimate or that the governed has consented. It is the "will of the people" that is primary – Not the longevity, not the political strength, not the military might of a government.

Thomas Jefferson backs me up on this, saying: "The will of the people is the only legitimate foundation of any government."[53] Garvey held a similar perspective, saying: "Government is not infallible. Government is only an executive control, a centralized authority for the purpose of expressing the will of the people. . . . Before you have a government you must have the people. Without the people there can be no government. The government must be, therefore, an expression of the will of the people."[54]

Part of the reason we've overlooked the true implications of these 15 words is because indoctrination makes us believe that the Declaration of Independence represents us too. However, a central truth during our enslavement that we must come to terms with is that – Even though all government policies and acts may have affected us, not all government policies applied to us.

This particularly pertains to the Declaration of Independence, because with it, Euro-Americans achieved sovereignty and set political standards for themselves – Not for us. As a consequence, their domestic struggle against unjust government powers ended, while ours reached a new beginning. Rather than liberating us too, Euro-Americans used their newfound independence to impose far greater injustices upon us than those they had surmounted.

The real beauty of this document is that it establishes a bona fide precedent that justifies *de facto* acts sovereignty. Personally, I feel that no other ideal in this document holds more present-day applicability to Africans in America than our right to dissent. Opposite "Consent of the Governed" is "Dissent of the Governed," as expressed in the fourth sentence of the document which speaks to the rights of a people to "Alter or Abolish" a government and "Institute New Government . . . Whenever any form of Government becomes destructive . . . to Life, Liberty and the pursuit of Happiness." The unedited translation of this is that: "The Governed reserves the inalienable right to become *ungovernable* through *dissent* and *de facto* acts of sovereignty."

To avoid dissent and illegitimacy, a government's policies and practices must intersect at crucial points with "Consent of the Governed." Otherwise, a government's authority can be challenged at minimum, and disrupted or dismantled at most. History abounds with examples of breakpoints in civil embattlements where societies refuse to comply with governments.

Again, South Africa comes to mind, where the Boers usurped power and established a European government on African territory, against the will and consent of African people. Although Western governments supported the "self-ordained authority" of the Boers, the UN General Assembly passed resolutions condemning the Boer government, including one in 1976 that characterized it as "illegitimate."[55]

During the days of Charles de Gaulle, France's population was 40 million. Upon refusal of French society to accept his "certain idea of France," he retorted with a humorous but telling remark, saying, "A nation of 360 cheeses cannot be governed."[56] In other words, because of varied and expanding worldviews, there are tipping-points in societies that cannot be exceeded even by governments with "ordained authority."

Maybe I'm wrong, but I think the US government has exerted "self-ordained authority" over Black America for so long, that it has distorted its calculations of what it can impose upon others. It consequently is learning the hard way from the Iraqis that not all cultures and societies in the world want to watch romp-shaking on MTV, eat hot wings at KFC, or even get a scholarship to MIT.

Ronald Reagan once jokingly said something that underscores America's "self-ordained authority." People say a variety of things, like "testing 1-2-3," while making microphone checks prior to speaking. Reagan made a radio microphone check in 1984 by saying he had "signed *legislation* that will outlaw Russia forever. We begin *bombing* in 5 minutes."[57]

His attempted humor reveals an enduring trait of violence and "self-ordained authority" in Euro-Americans that has proven far more fatal than funny. Note that he said he "signed legislation." Ever since 1776 after signing the Declaration of Independence, they've gotten so comfortable and accustomed to signing people and systems in or out of existence that they've power-tripped into believing that whenever they sign a document, it becomes a political absolute, like Pharaoh or Caesar – "As it has been written, so shall it be done."

But the signing and bombing process in Iraq has become way more complicated and costlier than anticipated, and securing the Iraqi "Consent of the Governed" has become lethal beyond expectation. Never did the US government imagine the nightmare that Iraqi society would *dissent* to its authority and become *ungovernable*. Their hope now is that Africans in America will remain too loyal to ever *dissent*, and not sovereign-minded enough to ever become *ungovernable*.

<><><><><><><><>

Emancipation "Dictation," not "Proclamation"

Some might believe that the *Emancipation Proclamation* solidified both Black America's freedom and America's legitimacy to govern us. But it is unjust and unheard of for a people to undergo centuries of enslavement with the outcome resulting in the offenders being rewarded perpetual authority to govern over those they enslaved.

Without exemption, no government has the right to enslave others . . . Period. All sane and civilized people would morally agree with this truth. From this truth, you can then reason and deduce that if enslavement did occur, the offending government has no right to self-authorize legislation in the aftermath to confer power upon itself to decide the political fate of the people it unlawfully enslaved.

This truth pertains all the same to the US government, which likewise had no right to enslave Africans or anyone else. Furthermore, if slavery was in fact "over" after emancipation, then Euro-Americans should not have had any authority whatsoever to institute permanent government over successive generations of the people it unlawfully enslaved.

Our ancestors who were supposedly freed by the *Emancipation Proclamation* should have therefore had both the right and the option to be free *from* US government authority – Not inextricably subjugated to it forever.

That's only fair, logical, and reasonable. Or, are we to accept the farce that Euro-Americans are so politically angelic that they can criminally enslave us on one hand, then compensate themselves on the other with unending government authority, of which we are legally bound to honor? If there were such a thing as "White Supremacy" I guess this would be it. Whatever you wish to call it, the "self-ordained authority" that precipitated from this document still unfolds until this very day.

Freedom, by definition, means to be "extricated" from a source of difficulty, not "integrated" into it. To purport that we were emancipated, yet simultaneously obligated to remain under authority of the very government responsible for our enslavement, is among the greatest political misconceptions of modern times.

The *Emancipation Proclamation,* in effect, marked the advent of "Ownership Transferal," as ownership of Africans changed from private to public. Whereas slavery entailed "private ownership" of Africans as chattel property of individuals, emancipation entailed "political ownership" as citizens of the federal government. Ownership was essentially confiscated from individuals as private property and then transferred peremptorily to

80

the government as taxed citizenry. Iron shackles were replaced by fetters of political control.

Don't get me wrong – Emancipation was a step forward by Abraham Lincoln's administration. But the issue here concerns the government's pre-lack of legitimacy and post-lack of authority. Slavery is a universal crime that lacks all legitimacy from start to finish and everywhere in between. At no point within the duration do governments or slaveholders gain rights of legitimacy or authority.

The passing of time does not decriminalize a crime or the criminals. If anything, the persistent committing of a crime magnifies, not minimizes the crime or the criminals. If anything, 246 years of enslavement confirms the US government's illegitimacy. So in this regard, Abraham Lincoln had no more legitimate authority to Americanize us than George Washington had to enslave us.

Yet, it is assumed that the US government somehow inherited legitimacy somewhere along the way, and further assumed that all descendents of the enslaved magically desired Americanization. It would be unpardonable on our part to allow Euro-Americans to politically fling us around to this past extent without addressing and correcting matters at present with sovereign reckonings.

Part of this reckoning concerns validating the political premise of our relationship. Correct me if I'm wrong, but from what I've read and observed in world history, wars and conflicts are resolved through some form of OFFICIAL AGREEMENT(S), based on bilateral (trilateral, etc.) terms of accord, approved and signed by ALL parties involved. For example, the British and Euro-Americans jointly signed the 1783 *Treaty of Paris* which ended the Revolutionary War and recognized America's independence.[58]

Tell me, where is the original OFFICIAL BILATERAL AGREEMENT signed jointly by representatives of our forefathers and the US government, wherein we ever agreed to anything, especially terms of "perpetual surrender" of our sovereignty? Is it hermitically encased in break-proof glass, guarded by 24-hour armed security like originals of the US Constitution and Declaration of Independence?

We have no such document or collective agreement with Euro-Americans that validates a bilateral relationship or treaty that binds us to uphold. And no, the *Emancipation Proclamation* is not BILATERAL, nor is it an AGREEMENT. When all the emotions and glorifying of the times are put aside, you'll find that it is a UNILATERAL document, signed only by Lincoln and his secretary of state, William Seward. It does not circumscribe any agreed political terms between the two parties concerned.

Technically, it could very well be called the "*Emancipation Dictation*" because, being unilateral, it was just as much of a "dictate" as any other slave document or declaration passed previously. No voice of consent was either sought from or given by our forefathers. No diplomatic interactions occurred. No political or economic amends were negotiated for gross damages or power sharing.

Following is a copy of the *Emancipation Proclamation*. You'll see its failure to include input from the people it claims to "free." Under no just and moral circumstances can the ideals, concerns, and demands of the 4 million "emancipated" people in question be entirely disregarded or spoken for by others … Especially by the offending government. Kwame Nkrumah once said that "Freedom is not something that one people can bestow on another as a gift. They claim it as their own and none can keep it from them.."[59] As much as abolition was the right thing, this document in essence exerts authority *without* "Consent of the Governed."

EMANCIPATION PROCLAMATION

BY THE PRESIDENT OF THE UNITED STATES OF AMERICA
A PROCLAMATION

WHEREAS, on the twenty-second day of September, in the year of our Lord one thousand eight hundred and sixty-two, a Proclamation was issued by the President of the United States,

---

containing, among other things, the following, to wit:

"That on the first day of January, in the year of our Lord one thousand eight hundred and sixty-three, all persons held as slaves within any State or designated part of a State, the people whereof shall then be in rebellion against the United States, shall be then, thenceforward, and forever, free; and the Executive government of the United States, including the military and naval authority thereof, will recognize and maintain the freedom of any such persons, and will do no act or acts to repress such persons, or any of them, in any efforts they may make for their actual freedom.

"That the Executive will, on the first day of January aforesaid, by proclamation, designate the States and parts of States, if any, in which the people thereof, respectively, shall then be in rebellion against the United States; and the fact that any State, or the people thereof, shall on that day be in good faith represented in the Congress of the United States, by members chosen thereto at elections wherein a majority of the qualified voters of such States shall have participated, shall, in the absence of strong countervailing testimony, be deemed conclusive evidence that such State, and the people thereof, are not then in rebellion against the United States."

Now, therefore, I, ABRAHAM LINCOLN, President of the United States, by virtue of the power in me vested as Commander-in-chief of the Army and Navy of the United States, in time of actual armed rebellion against the authority and government of the United States, and as a fit and necessary war measure for suppressing said rebellion, do, on this first day of January, in the year of our Lord one thousand eight hundred and sixty-three, and in accordance with my purpose so to do, publicly proclaimed for the full period of one hundred days from the day first above mentioned, order and designate as the States and parts of States wherein the people thereof, respectively, are this day in rebellion against the United States, the following, to wit:

Arkansas, Texas, Louisiana, (except the parishes of St. Bernard, Plaquemines, Jefferson, St. John, St. Charles, St. James, Ascension, Assumption, Terre Bonne, Lafourche, St. Mary, St. Martin, and Orleans, including the city of New Orleans,) Mississippi, Alabama, Florida, Georgia, South Carolina, North Carolina, and Virginia, (except the forty-eight counties designated as West Virginia, and also the counties of Berkeley, Accomac, Northampton, Elizabeth City, York, Princess Ann, and Norfolk, including the cities of Norfolk and Portsmouth,) and which excepted parts are for the present left precisely as if this Proclamation were not issued.

And by virtue of the power and for the purpose aforesaid, I do order and declare that all persons held as slaves within said designated States and parts of States are and henceforward shall be free; and that the Executive government of the United States, including the military and naval authorities thereof, will recognize and maintain the freedom of said persons.

And I hereby enjoin upon the people so declared to be free to abstain from all violence, unless in necessary self-defense; and I recommend to them that, in all cases when allowed, they labor faithfully for reasonable wages.

And I further declare and make known that such persons, of suitable condition, will be received into the armed service of the United States to garrison forts, positions, stations, and other places, and to man vessels of all sorts in said service.

And upon this act, sincerely believed to be an act of justice warranted by the Constitution upon military necessity, I invoke the considerate judgement of mankind and the gracious favor of Almighty God.

In witness whereof, I have hereunto set my hand and caused the seal of the United States to be affixed.

Done at the city of Washington this first day of January, in the year of our Lord one thousand eight hundred and sixty-three, and of the Independence of the United States of America the eighty-seventh.

By the President: ABRAHAM LINCOLN
WILLIAM H. SEWARD, Secretary of State.

Document 4. Emancipation Proclamation

Similar to the Declaration of Independence, there's a deceptive sneakiness to this document that's been passed off as the goodness and humanity of American democracy. Although slavery eventually ended in the process, Lincoln's objective in issuing the proclamation was not to end slavery. Abolition was secondary to the proclamation's value as a "military instrument" to help the North win the Civil War and preserve the Union.

Proof of this has been confirmed in remarks by a most unlikely but well-accredited source – President Barack Obama. His intent however was certainly not to challenge the government's illegitimacy, he was rather constructively criticizing the duplicitous nature of both Lincoln and the document. Here is his quote to *Time* magazine:

I cannot swallow whole the view of Lincoln as the Great Emancipator. . . . As a law professor and civil rights lawyer and as an African-American, I am fully aware of his limited views on race. Anyone who actually reads the Emancipation Proclamation knows it was more a military document than a clarion call for justice.[60]

Considering that so much emotion and splendor have been historically staked to this document, the fact that Obama (being as middle-of-the-road as he is) publicly defined it as a "military document" validates my point that we have been beguiled to think of this document as something other than the "dictate" that it really is. This lends further weight to our need to examine the political basis of the US government's authority to govern us.

He stopped short of drawing any analyses or conclusions, legal or otherwise, on the implications of how this "military document" applies (or non-applies) to present generations of Blacks. But at minimum it is disingenuous of the government to have generations of Black people thinking that the *Emancipation Proclamation* is a symbol of our freedom, when factually it is none of the sort. Now that we know, it's time to psychologically unshackle ourselves from this and other levels of bondage, as Dr. King similarly commented during his last address to the Southern Christian Leadership Conference (SCLC) in August 1967, saying:

> Psychological freedom, a firm sense of self-esteem, is the most powerful weapon against the long night of physical slavery. No Lincolnian emancipation proclamation or Johnsonian civil rights bill can totally bring this kind of freedom. The negro will only be free when he reaches down to the inner depths of his own being and signs with the pen and ink of assertive manhood his own emancipation proclamation.[61]

In summation, the US government has undeservedly benefited for centuries from millions of Africans in America who never had the means to *dissent*. Like the *ungovernable* mindset that Euro-Americans developed through the Thomas Paine "School of Thought," we too must know that we have every right and every reason to consider *de facto* acts of sovereignty. W. E. B. DuBois accurately assessed government and society during his times by saying: "The problem of the 20th century is the problem of the color line …"[62] I assess during these times that: "The core issue of the 21st century concerns our just and legitimate rights to sovereignty."

<>< ><>< ><>< ><>

"All successful men have agreed in one thing, - they were causationists. They believed that things went not by luck, but by law; that there was not a weak or a cracked link in the chain that joins the first and last of things. A belief in causality, or strict connection between every trifle and the principle of being, and, in consequence, belief in compensation, or, that nothing is got for nothing ..."

Ralph Waldo Emerson

"An old error is always more popular than a new truth."

German Proverb

"Higher ideas and a better way of life cannot properly be defined unless one has a contrasting, flourishing manifestation of the progress achieved outside of the confines of what is termed 'a society based on higher ideals.' It is the same with moral values and principles."

Ben Ammi, Author of *God the Black Man and Truth*

3
Un-Sovereign People Pay
Un-Sovereign Consequences

The "Global Golden Rule"

In gauging the psychological climate of race and regard for African humanity after emancipation, you'll find that slavery ended in 1865, while the *American Society for the Prevention of Cruelty to Animals* (ASPCA) was founded a year afterwards in 1866. This says something very troubling and foretelling about American democracy, because as African humanity entered the throes of a full century of lynchings and legalized segregation, society was simultaneously astir protecting the rights of dogs and cats, trying to pass legislation to criminalize the "mistreatment of animals."

When you understand this parallel in time and events it explains today's psychological climate in society where dogfights and other animal-related stories plaster daily headlines, while there's a simultaneous yawn of apathy and shrug-of-the-shoulders attitude over the widespread murders and warehouse incarcerations of Black youths.

In August 2005, the *People for the Ethical Treatment of Animals* (PETA) went as far as to launch a tour called the "Animal Liberation Campaign," displaying photographs that compared abused animals to enslaved and segregated Blacks. It had "twelve panels juxtaposing pictures of violence against black people and animals. One panel showed a black civil rights protester being beaten at a lunch counter beside a photo of a seal being bludgeoned. Another set of photos juxtaposed two lynched black men with a cow hanging in a slaughterhouse."[1]

If you've noticed, people nowadays love to be seen and photographed with pets. This somehow is supposed to convey that a person is "humanized." Homeless people however, scatter the streets of every major city, even sleeping in frigid temperatures while at the same time 42 percent of Americans sleep in bed with animals.[2] Financially, America's pet industry clears $41 billion in annual revenues, exceeding the entire Gross Domestic Product of all but 64 countries in the world.[3]

I'm not against pets or suggesting that pet owners should house the homeless. I'm spotlighting a centuries-old trait in order to make the larger point that – If government and society's concerns for animals were ratably translated into genuine concerns for democracy and humanity, there'd be little racism today and there would have been no slavery or segregation yesterday. It's little wonder that while Black people were perishing in New Orleans during hurricane Katrina, the *Human Society* was busy rescuing animals instead.[4]

Katrina's fallout left many wondering how "something like this" could have happened in America. Well, history shows that moreso than any other country in the world, America is the perfect and most probable place for "something like this" to happen – especially considering that, within the last 400 years, it's only been since 1964 that we've been free from what essentially could be termed "legalized government tyranny." Politically so, the sum total of the government's depravity exceeds in great measure the sum total of its decency.

Never had there been a more precise time since Reconstruction where Africans in America were immediately needful of emergency government assistance than during Katrina. At that very moment, the government had an opportune chance to prove its genuineness and sincerity, beyond legislation on paper and lip-service from podiums. But true to its history of neglect and indifference, the government not only failed miserably on all accounts, it did so without visible shame or remorse.

Being a so-called "Christian" nation, Euro-Americans supposedly practice the "Biblical Golden Rule" of "Do unto others as you would have them do unto you." But politically there's another rule, a superceding rule that was witnessed firsthand by the world during events of Katrina. This rule is what I call the "Global Golden Rule" of contemporary politics, which states that – "Un-Sovereign People Pay Un-Sovereign Consequences."

Though many sociopolitical lessons can be gleaned from Katrina, it seems that the lesson of this proverbial rule has gotten obscured amidst all the wartime propaganda and partisan politics that have since monopolized the news. Africans in America are not alone however. The "Global Golden Rule" generally applies worldwide wherever people live under governments that they do not control, since holders of sovereign powers commonly advance self-indulgent agendas at the human expense of others.

Contemporary history cites example upon example of Un-Sovereign People who pay Un-Sovereign Consequences at the hands of others. ... Just ask the Dalai Lama. He'll tell you all about how Tibetans pay Un-Sovereign Consequences to the Chinese government. Aboriginal Australians pay Un-Sovereign Consequences to the Euro-Australian government. Palestinians pay Un-Sovereign Consequences to the Israeli government. Chechnyans pay Un-Sovereign Consequences to the Russian government. The Kurds pay 3-way Un-Sovereign Consequences to the Turkish, Syrian, and Iraqi governments.

Illustrations 1. "Meddle Winners"

© 2008 Courtesy of Adam Zyglis, The Buffalo News, and PoliticalCartoons.com

Sometimes, Un-Sovereign Consequences are non-life-threatening and paid for incrementally over the long term – like having *your* history excluded from being taught in the very public schools where *you* pay taxes for *your* children to attend. Sometimes, Un-Sovereign Consequences are life-altering and paid for calamitously – Like Katrina or the Sharpeville and Soweto Massacres in South Africa. Nevertheless, Un-Sovereign People are bound to incur the inevitabilities of Un-Sovereign Consequences in some form at some point.

Euro-Americans know the "Global Golden Rule" from both ends of the spectrum, since they once paid Un-Sovereign Consequences to Britain and they now exact the same upon us. What's bewildering, is that we've become so accustomed to paying Un-Sovereign Consequences that we know in our hearts that it's just a matter of time before we'll pay another round … It's only a question of when and what the costs will be.

Katrina's winds and waters exposed an irony and duality that encapsulates the historic paradox of the Black Experience in America. …

While one group of Blacks was dying unnecessarily paying Un-Sovereign Consequences from Katrina in the Gulf of Mexico region, another group was dying unnecessarily paying Un-Sovereign Consequences fighting for Iraqi sovereignty in the Persian Gulf region. Among the greatest of Un-Sovereign Consequences that a people can ever pay, is to fight and die to establish or defend the sovereignty of others, when they do not possess sovereignty for themselves.

Katrina: "Let Them Eat Cake!"

Newsmagazine shows on TV occasionally conduct sociological experiments that gauge a sense of today's psychological climate of race. Using hidden cameras, a Black and a White person with similar educational and financial backgrounds are sent to the same places to interview for a job; rent an apartment; and purchase a car. In some cases the Black person is more financially secure with higher education.

Like clockwork the same occurrences repeat – the Black person is discriminated against at the job interview; given the runaround or even declined at the rental office; and jacked-up at car dealerships with higher prices and interest rates. Comparably, the White person is given more preferences, courtesies, and amenities. Time after time, again and again, this happens over and over. Although this doesn't happen all the time in society, it happens frequently enough to confirm that racism does exist.

Just as interesting as the findings in these experiments, are the reactions of people after discovering they've been exposed on hidden cameras. Some start wiggling words around to explain themselves with "flimflam talk." Some try to make you think "you didn't *really* see what you *actually* saw." Some put their hands over the lens and say things like, "this is private property, get out of here and get that camera out my face, Buddy, before you get arrested."

Despite the unfiltered reality shown by these hidden cameras, some people still find it hard to accept that such things are not untypical.

What's even harder for some is to recognize that a political extension of this same psychology and sociology reared its ugly head during Hurricane Katrina.

Anyone who claims that race does not factor into federal and national politics is either naïve or practicing deception. Racism is a fixed sociopolitical reality that in the case of Katrina had deathly consequences. Though the government and others flatly deny this, it's unrealistic to disassociate the indifference captured during experiments by hidden cameras, from the indifference captured during Katrina by live cameras. Not to mention the sights and scenes captured by Spike Lee's cameras in the documentary *When the Levees Broke*.

Secretary of State Condoleezza Rice dismissed race at her first post-Katrina press conference by harping emphasis on being "American." Although she did acknowledge that mostly "poor" Blacks were victimized, she then rationalized by saying, "It's so hard to watch pictures of any *Americans* going through this. . . . Nobody wants to see *Americans* suffer. . . . That *Americans* would somehow, in a color-affected way, decide who to help and who not to help, I just don't believe it."[5]

Someone should help her "believe it" by reminding her that she and millions of us were born into a segregated society with a "color-affected" government that decided all issues on a "color-affected" basis for nearly three-and-a-half centuries. "Color-affected" decisions have played a role in every Un-Sovereign Consequence we've paid thus far.

Former Congressman Tom Delay's (R-Texas) reactions to the televised images of Katrina were eerily similar to people caught by hidden cameras. Four days after the hurricane, *MSNBC* journalist Lester Holt mentioned to Delay in an interview that most victims were poor Black people. He then asked Delay, "When you look at this . . . what does this say about where we are as a country?"[6] Using the wiggle-flimflam technique, Delay blathered, "What it tells me is that we're doing a wonderful job and that we're an incredibly compassionate people."[7]

Holt responded, "I don't think anybody argues the compassion and the outpouring we've seen. I'm specifically referring to those people

93

who are looking into our cameras saying 'Help us.' . . . They are mostly poor, they are mostly Black, they are mostly left behind."[8]   DeLay then applied the technique to make us believe "we didn't *really* see what we *actually* saw" by casting blame on Holt, saying with visible agitation, "I know you're trying to make an issue out of this."[9] He then reverted to repeating the "wonderful job" script.

DeLay represents a prevailing political psyche and system that not only hinders but endangers Black people and African interests. Here was an obvious situation where the entire world was watching frightening, live, continuous coverage of dying and destitute people needing urgent rescue. . . . Yet there he was, wholly detached, sitting comfortably on his feathery perch, spouting political nonsense on behalf of people who he will never personally encounter face-to-face in the snooty circles of his life.

If you didn't know better, you could have easily mistaken Katrina footage for scenes from some poverty-stricken nation, ruled by a ruthless dictatorship that didn't care about its people. DeLay's remarks added the full complement of a rich, arrogant, out-of-touch official, unaffected by human sufferings. His aloof comments bring Marie Antoinette to mind, whose privileged life in the French ruling-class made her so detached that when told of peasants who were starving and didn't have bread, she allegedly responded, "Then Let Them Eat Cake!"[10]

On Day 5 of the aftermath, President Bush did a "fly-by" to New Orleans with some officials and added his "Eat Cake" attitude at a press conference. While over 35,000 people were in-the-thick of distress and duress, rather than condemning, he complimented Federal Emergency Management Agency (FEMA) director, Michael Brown, saying "Brownie, you're doing a heck of a job."[11] At that point, officials in attendance (with rolled-up sleeves) roundly applauded. Why their shirtsleeves were rolled is a mystery, since the only physical labor they performed was to lift high-priced silverware to eat gourmet foods aboard Air Force One.

Before knowing that he was actually the FEMA Director, when I first saw Brown on TV he impressed me as a shaken person who'd just been rescued. His dereliction, mishandlings, and padded resume warrant more than just his voluntary resignation, where in his private life I'm sure he makes more money than each of the people he forced to "Eat Cake." At minimum, he should be indicted and prosecuted on hundreds of counts of manslaughter and criminally negligent homicide.

Of course Bush thought Brown was doing a "Heck of a Job" while flood waters simultaneously claimed Black lives in the process. Katrina was just a recent episode in a long continuum of African deaths and inhumanities linked to water. Dating back to the Middle Passage in the early 1600s, slavetraders did a "Heck of a Job" transporting Africans across the Atlantic waters while uncountable millions perished.

Up until the mid-1960s the U.S. government also did a "Heck of a Job" enforcing kangaroo-legislation that prohibited us from drinking or venturing near so-called "white water," which was a punishable offense that could result in mutilation and/or being hanged. We weren't allowed to make bodily contact with "white water," but that never deterred policemen from doing a "Heck of a Job" hooking up fire-hoses to blast us like rag-dolls with the same water they childishly forbade us from touching. So yes, Bush was 100-percent right in his job assessment and public tribute to Brown. Indeed, the government's legacy of making us pay Un-Sovereign Consequences has been a real "Heck of a Job."

Controlled Chaos Drill

Among the most tragic of all circumstances is that Black America has no independent political power to hold anyone accountable for anything that happened during Katrina. Though I do not write from a "conspiracy theorist" viewpoint, I do say that the federal government may have perhaps been conducting a political lab test or Controlled Chaos Drill for future knowledge and possible implementation in event of a war or revolution.

The armed security; the depravation of food and medicine; the horrid living conditions; the forced transporting of people from the

Superdome to the Astrodome – All have suspicious overtones of what could happen if Blacks or any other ethnic group got carried away with having "rights" and decided to rebel or incite some form of "civil uprising." According to the *Associated Press*:

> Several hundred evacuees claimed that police from suburban Gretna blocked them as they tried to flee New Orleans for safety on Sept. 1.
>
> Many of the evacuees, who had been stranded at the New Orleans convention center without food and water, said they were told to cross the bridge to be evacuated from the city. But Gretna police confronted them on the bridge and forced them to turn around.
>
> Gretna Police Chief Arthur Lawson has acknowledged that his officers fired shots into the air during the blockade in an attempt to quell what he described as unrest among the evacuees.[12]

For naysayers, it's a big mistake to underestimate what this establishment will or will not do, especially during these terror-tensed days of war where America does not comply with any set or standard rules of engagement. History bears proof that certain segments of Black people have always been expendable and experimental anyway ... as verified in the Iran-Contra Scandal in the 1980s when the CIA secretly funneled weapons to Iran and funded Nicaraguan rebels, while flooding Black communities with crack cocaine.[13] And let's not forget the Tuskegee Experiment.

Another suspicious act is the government's refusal to secure and allocate monies and resources pledged by foreign governments and organizations. Sources from the international community pledged $854 million in cash and oil for Katrina relief. But according to an *MSNBC* report, 20 months afterwards, most pledges had not even been collected and only $40 million in resources had been distributed.[14]

Whether you believe it or not, Katrina has given this establishment a clearer firsthand sense of what it takes to control America's urban streets; contain potential rowdy masses; and convert sports stadiums into prison concentration camps.

Katrina also served as a barometer that tested the 21st-century threshold of what "Black leaders" are willing to take. Considering that the government got away clean with being so unresponsive on such a massive scale, it's almost a given that it can virtually get away with doing just about anything to us with impunity. True, there's been no shortage of complaints and protests, but still, no one has been held liable. The establishment continues to sleep well at nights, knowing that today's mainstream Black leaders have a near-endless trust for the government and a near-limitless tolerance for injustice.

<><><><><><><>

After-the-Fact Concerns

Despite the government's obvious sloth and neglect, Black America resumed "business as usual" shortly after Katrina. Except for those directly impacted, it seems the Black masses have gotten sucked in by the government's "political theatrics" beginning on Day 5 after Katrina – After all the lives were lost and all the damage had been done!

You have to be alert and on guard these days because theatrics now seem to be part of ongoing efforts to divert our attention away from all the other Un-Sovereign Consequences we pay. Notice closely and you'll detect a cunning pattern of government outpours of "After-the-Fact Concerns" for crimes and injustices committed decades ago. According to USA Today:

> The FBI has reopened investigations of about a dozen decades-old suspicious deaths [as of February 2007] … amid a Justice Department focus on cracking unsolved cases from the

nation's civil rights era. The high-priority cases, described as numbering between 10 and 12, are among an estimated 100 that investigators nationwide are looking at as possible civil rights-related murders."[15]

This reopening of cases gives the impression that "times are changing," but in most instances the suspects are either dead or near death. Emmett Till, for instance, was murdered back in 1955 and the White defendants at the time were freed in a fixed-court decision by an all-White jury. After 49 years the government staged concern and reopened the case in 2004, but no one was indicted and the main defendant was already dead.[16]

Medgar Evers was assassinated in 1963 and the government staged concern 31 years later in 1994.[17] In the end, the state of Mississippi convicted a scraggly, bug-eyed, senile-like dude who looked like a hungry 101-year-old hillbilly who had never been in a room with electricity. In August 2007 a 72-year-old former Ku Klux Klansman was sentenced to three life terms for kidnapping and murdering two Black teenagers in Mississippi, 43 years earlier in 1964.[18]

After criminally conducting decades of covert biological warfare that purposely exposed Black men to syphilis in the 1930s in the aforementioned Tuskegee Experiment, 60 years later the government staged concern by "apologizing" in 1997.[19] But the intent of this experiment was deliberate; the "research" was already complete; and the damages were long done.

More than 50 years after the fact, the government, under the Clinton administration, decided in 1997 to decorate 7 Black veterans with Medals of Honor for their "heroic acts" during World War II.[20] The medals were so much after-the-fact that 6 of the 7 recipients were deceased and had to be awarded posthumously.

To get one-upmanship on Clinton's theatrics, Bush awarded the Congressional Gold Medal (the highest civilian honor) to the few surviving Tuskegee Airmen for their 1940's bravery. At the ceremony he feigned being emotionally choked-up while saluting them, saying he wanted to "help atone for all the unreturned salutes and unforgivable indignities" they endured during their service.[21]

> Although the stellar combat record of the 2,000-member unit played a large part in persuading President Harry S. Truman to desegregate the military in 1948, the full government recognition that many Tuskegee Airmen say they've been expecting for decades did not come until today [March 29, 2007].
>
> At 1 p.m. in the Capitol Rotunda, most of the roughly 200 surviving pilots, navigators and support troops of the Tuskegee Airmen will line up to receive the nation's highest civilian honor, the Congressional Gold Medal.[22]

Militarily, Euro-Americans have always portrayed themselves as being braver and smarter than we are. Declassified "Military Performance Reports" from World War II describe Black soldiers as "unsuited for combat" and spoke of "black cowardice."[23] Tuskegee Airman Sgt. George Watson commented: "The U.S. government said Negroes, as they called us back then, had smaller brains than whites and could never fly an airplane in combat."[24]

Although Euro-Americans have relied heavily on Black servicemen in each conflict since the Revolutionary War, that still didn't deter them from subjecting us to Un-Sovereign Consequences all the same. Even the Nazis questioned Black soldiers during WW II as to why they would fight under the command of people who disdained our humanity.[25]

After-the-Fact Concerns have now even reached back to slavery. Ever since February 2007 when Virginia legislators passed a resolution to apologize for slavery, New Jersey and state legislators in Georgia, Maryland, Missouri and Tennessee have also considered apologies.[26] In July 2008 the U.S. House of Representatives even passed a resolution to apologize for "wrongs" against our ancestors "under slavery and Jim Crow segregation laws."[27] At this rate, if we're lucky, maybe by early next century the federal government might get around to apologizing for its contrivances during Katrina. The *Associated Press* reported that:

> Revelations about the past are pushing some people to think about race in America in new ways. Plus, echoes of racial bias remain all too obvious, and politicians may be grasping for new ways to show concern.
>
> Generations after the civil rights movement began, African-Americans generally remain poorer, less educated and more likely to be in prison than whites.
>
> Many historians, political scientists and public policy experts argue that this is rooted in blacks' unhealed wounds for slavery, combined with widespread tactics during the century or so that followed to keep blacks from equal education, jobs and housing.[28]

2005 marked a monumental year for After-the-fact Concerns. In August 2005 a posthumous pardon was issued to Lena Baker. She was executed by electric chair after being convicted in 1945 by an all-White jury of men, for killing a White man who "held her in slavery and threatened her life."[29]

Forty one years to the date, an 80-year-old former Ku Klux Klansman was convicted of manslaughter in 2005 for the 1964 murders of three civil rights workers (Schwerner, Goodman, and Chaney) in Mississippi.[30] Also in 2005 the government offered a $25,000 reward for tips to the 1951 murders of civil rights activists Harry and Harriette Moore, whose home was bombed as a gift on Christmas day.[31]

Then in September of 2005 the U.S. Postal Service joined the act to stage its concern by issuing 10 postage stamps commemorating the Civil Rights Movement. The U.S. Senate also jumped in the ring and issued a limp apology for turning a blind eye to a full century of lynchings that were never investigated. From 1900 to 1950 the Senate failed to pass any of "over 200 anti-lynching bills introduced to Congress" that would have made lynching a federal crime.[32]

Lynching was used as a weapon to "reinforce the prevailing racial power structure" that targeted "Blacks who had achieved a degree of success or conveyed a sense of self-worth"[33] Data complied by Tuskegee University determined that about 5,000 people were mob-lynched between 1880 and 1960 with complicit silence from the federal government.[34] Former Senator Mary Landrieu of Louisiana said, "There are still Americans who refuse to believe that this happened, that it happened on the scale that it did."[35]

Senate approval was also given in 2005 for Rosa Parks to lie in state in the Capitol Rotunda; an honor usually reserved for presidents, soldiers, and politicians.[36] Not only was she was the first woman to receive this honor, Bush also signed a bill to make her the first Black person to be memorialized with a statue inside the Capitol building's Statuary Hall.[37]

But that wasn't all ... The "Rosa Parks Act" was also introduced in 2005 so that Parks, along with "civil rights activists and others convicted of laws that enforced racial discrimination during the Jim Crow era would be eligible for a pardon from the state of Alabama."[38] Even though this is supposed to be "great news," stop and ask yourself if all of this is really progress or appeasement?

One thing that stands out is the curious timing of all these honors and investigations, in relation to the bottomless pit of fiascos and failures in Iraq. Suspicion tells me that these gestures could be aimed to tighten the psychological bolts to keep us believing that "America really cares about us," when in reality the objective is to retain our patriotic loyalty during these critical war times. It seems like a chess move to preempt questions (like those raised by the Nazis) as to why we continue to fight wars abroad when we still have tons of unresolved issues right here, as Katrina and Jena attest.

During a heated House Judiciary Committee Hearing on Jena in 2007, Congresswoman Sheila Jackson Lee was rightfully angry about the federal failure to step in when the infamous noose was first discovered on the "Whites Only" tree at the high school in Jena, Louisana.[39] But since it took until 2005 for the Senate to condemn a century of thousands of lynchings with nooses, certainly the act of hanging one noose would be viewed as "minor" by the Senate, albeit "major" to us.

There's also an underlying sovereign arrogance to all of this, particularly the legislation for pardons. I say this because if America was a true democracy, Rosa Parks and others would not need pardons because they wouldn't have ever had reason to protest for civil rights, because the government wouldn't have ever had racist policies. So the whole notion of issuing "pardons" is really a human and political insult, since it was government that was wrong – Not Rosa Parks and other civil rights activists.

If any pardons are to be considered, it should be us making the determination of whether the U.S. government qualifies for our "pardons" – Not the other way around. For Euro-Americans to give pardons to civil rights activists is the political equivalent of going to dinner with a man who knowingly stole your wallet, and then you thank him after he pays the check with your money. But so-called "Black leaders" seemingly lack the sovereign intuitions to even understand the sense of this point.

Marcus Garvey said, "There is always a turning point in the destiny of every race, every nation, of all peoples ..."[40] If Black leaders cannot see the need for a sovereign "turning point" after Katrina, then it's understandable why they are gratified to receive "pardons" from a government that is itself blood-guilty of the civil rights crimes and violations. We don't need political pardons *from* this government; we need sovereign powers *for* ourselves.

<><><><><><><>

The Un-Abolishable "N-Word"

Genesis, the first book of the Bible, provides allegorical account of man's commission to "name and define all things." This charge of dominion over words, definitions, and language ties an enduring spiritual dimension to the sociopolitical components of sovereignty. Whether you believe it or not, those who define words and terms are in effect exercising a spiritual form of power.

All words are not created equal. Some have strategic values and definitions that can be used to insult, empower, or exploit individuals as well as entire nations. Whosoever holds sovereign powers over a territory also has subsequent access to regulate words and concepts, along with the potential to make or reshape thoughts, perceptions, philosophies and doctrines. Within the vast history of Un-Sovereign People Paying Un-Sovereign Consequences, man has probably warred over words and doctrines just as much as territory and resources.

Each year Webster's adds a variety of new words to its dictionary. "Linguists say the words and phrases we used over the last 12 months will give historians a snapshot of what the world was really thinking and talking about. ... The [2004] election inspired people to look up 'incumbent,' 'electoral' and 'partisan,' while the war in Iraq inspired queries for 'insurgent' and 'sovereignty.'"[41] Interestingly, "sovereignty" ranked 9th on Merriam-Webster's "Words of the Year" in 2004.[42]

Certain criteria are used before a word qualifies for the dictionary; one of which is common usage. If "bootylicious" is used long enough and frequently enough by enough people, it too will eventually be added. The Editor-in-Chief of Oxford American Dictionary commented that adding words is a "sensitive task" because language is a "battleground."[43]

Out of this same vein of sovereign variables and controls came the originally vile "N-Word." All the present controversies and verbal sparring over its redefined use by hip hop have much wider and more serious implications than society is led to believe, because the N-Word, like a hangman's noose, does not exist in isolation. Inasmuch as *cutting* down the "Whites only" tree at the Jena high school did nothing to resolve the deeper racial issues reflected in the symbolism of nooses, *cutting* the N-Word from the vocabulary will do nothing to resolve the deeper issues that it symbolizes.

Trying to abolish it because it is an "ugly word" or telling young people "Don't say it," is like advising them to hide under the bed to escape the raging flames of a fire. Why? Because based on the nature and severity of the issue, the solution is not that simplistic.

To begin unraveling the intricacies of the N-Word, it's important to understand that there are some general, yet complex societal, political, and psychological aspects to this word that have purpose and bearings which long predate U.S. history. Regardless of who's being enslaved or who's doing the enslaving, certain features are elemental to the process for captors to gain and maintain control over captives. Specific among them are strict controls over words and language, and in our case – controls over music too.

Because of Britain's past colonial feats and America's present global influence, English is spoken in virtually every corner of the earth. This dominance has fostered the notion within circles of Euro-American culture that English is the most intelligent and the most intelligent-sounding language in the world. To speak another language, especially like African languages or even Spanish as spoken by Puerto Ricans and Mexicans, ostensibly infers a "lesser intelligence" in this imagined hierarchy of languages.

Language is not only culturally significant; the "official language" of every nation is politically significant. Have you ever observed how language is politically applied in government-to-government talks and negotiations? When some world leaders visit the White House or the United Nations, they'll speak their native tongue even though they may speak English fluently. Translators interpret back and forth, as leaders jostle and posture through diplomatic use of very choice words.

In a political and cultural showdown to counter the prevalence of English in Iran, President Ahmadinejad issued a "presidential decree" in July of 2006. All government agencies, cultural institutions, newspapers and publications were ordered to use words deemed more "appropriate" by the Persian Academy, which is Iran's "language regulating body."[44] Modified Persian words now "replace foreign words that have crept into the language, such as pizzas. ... The academy has introduced more than 2,000 words as alternatives for some of the foreign words that have become commonly used in Iran, mostly from Western languages."[45]

Understanding the power derived from defining and controlling language, it becomes clear why we weren't allowed to read or write during slavery, nor speak any language other than English. In fact, we weren't even allowed to hum to ourselves. Humming tended to make slaveholders uncomfortable because they didn't know the *words* behind the hum ... Here lies the initial source from where influence and controls over our music come into play.

It's no secret that musical sounds and vibrations affect the human mind in transforming ways. Why do you think blowing the bugle is integral to military culture? ... Certainly not for entertainment, but rather to ignite "mental charges" in troops, as well as to communicate definitive messages like reveille (assembly, up and at-um) and taps (lights out, solemn times). Troops immediately and instinctively know what to do and how to mentally respond whenever hearing any of these "sound messages."

Certain sounds can shatter glass. Others can rupture eardrums. Some are audible only to dogs, or dolphins, or other animals. "Music soothes the savage beast" is not just a saying; it's a scientific fact that music can have calming effects on wild animals. Science has also shown that plants can grow larger, greener, and healthier when exposed to soft music and pleasant-toned words. So it's accurate to conclude that words and sounds can stimulate both positive and negative impulses.

Even more so than humming, the sounds and vibrations from African drums made Europeans extremely uneasy and fearful, as depicted in old, ignorant African-set movies like *Trader Horn* in 1931. Europeans have always known that the drum has culturally and historically meant more to us than just a musical instrument; it's been a cultural and esoteric means of communication that they could never understand, yet in secret they admired our ingenuity. Samuel Morse's dot and dash beats of his 1867 Morse Code is nothing more than a technical-offshoot of the dateless science of African drum-beating.

Knowing that we had encoded rhythms to announce everything from childbirths to war-alerts, slaveholders prohibited us from even casually tapping our feet and fingers, fearing we might covertly send out signals to "Uprise." Don't ever underestimate why Americanization made it necessary to disconnect us from African sounds, music, and languages. It's not by accident that our once-powerful awareness and control over words and sounds have devolved to the point where some music and lyrics today have become degenerative, perverted, and perhaps even satanic – All under the guise of "entertainment" and so-called "Freedom of Speech."

The fact that White males control the multibillion-dollar revenue streams of every genre of our music is not based solely on economics alone, and definitely not because they love rap and hip hop. You better recognize that the same nervousness of "Uprisings" related to drumbeats and humming during slavery, has kept White men's attention closely attuned to the words, sounds, and vibrations of Black music all throughout history.

This accounts for why "positive rap" doesn't get played or promoted nationally in mainstream markets like songs that glorify "pimps and playaz." Rappers in general can freestyle positive lyrics on various topics. But, in order to "get signed" by major labels, rappers will tell you they must conform to "unwritten rules of the game" which dictate that lyrics must be hardcore, homoerotic, misogynistic or urban. (Just so you'll know, "urban" doubles as an industry euphemism for the N-Word).

Jumping on young rappers about content is the easiest route for Black leaders to take. But they are not nearly as quick to jump on White corporations and execs who sign the checks that finance the industry. Acquiring loans and business financing have always been difficult for us as a people in general. It hard enough for young Black males to get a good paying job, so forget about being "financed." But look at all the money floating around to fund and promote counterproductive Black music. This tells you that the financiers are central to the problem. After all, the music industry isn't being secretly funded by the Russians or promoted from caves by the Taliban. It's all orchestrated in broad daylight largely by White men who work in tall buildings in LA and New York.

Furthermore, only a handful of mega-companies control entertainment media, and only a few degrees of separation lie between them in ownership. Viacom, which owned CBS until splitting in 2006, is the same company that paid the salary of Don Imus at CBS Radio.[46] Viacom owns BET, which we all know specializes in airing content that helps fester all of the N-Word ruckus. Mainstream people and corporations make a lot of loot and have a vested interest in the N-Word's perpetuity, yet Black leaders have not adequately held their feet to the fire of accountability.

Most rappers are *discovered* in their teens or early twenties. Of course they are easily swayed to make millions by saying or doing anything. Let's be real. They are young, so we cannot fault them entirely. Besides, Black America as a whole has fallen "psychological prey" to a sophisticated commercial process that profits annually in the trillions from our optimism to live the "American Dream." Heck, for the kind of money some young rappers make, there are 50-year-old men and women who would lineup for miles in a blizzard to sign a million-dollar contract to make "booty videos."

Within the apparatus of democracy and capitalism, some Black leaders do exactly to adults using politics what some rappers do to youngsters using entertainment ... Promote hopes and lifestyles that have thus far been unattainable for masses of Blacks.

The similarities don't end there. Both get well paid to appear before cameras to recite pre-rehearsed words that ultimately serve White interests more than our own. And just as rappers can't "get signed" if their lyrics don't comport with industry scripts, Black leaders won't "get air-time" on television if their lyrics veer from the repetitive standardized jargon of Republican or Democratic scripts. Black leaders don't control politics any more than Black rappers control the music industry. They all go along for the ride and make their livings operating as subsets within the larger systems controlled by Euro-American males.

But just as rappers can freestyle positive rhymes, some Black leaders speak truths that don't meet script-approvals of either party. Such people are usually banished into social exile and removed as far as possible from "in-crowd events" and national TV cameras until they learn to conform better. Harry Belafonte for instance was a lieutenant and right-hand man of Dr. King, and is now a well-respected international figure. But when he expressed Free Speech that was critical enough to boil Bush's blood, he got "uninvited" to Coretta Scott King's funeral after Bush decided to make a political appearance at the funeral.[47]

As a side note, this establishment does not televise, reward, or commingle with people who pose "unauthorized" public challenges to its power or polices. It tries to punish them. So be leery whenever a so-called Black leader *seemingly* poses challenges, yet they keep popping up everywhere on TV. You can be sure that they have ties to DNC or RNC sources from which they financially benefit.

Let me emphasize that the concept of "Free Speech" entails much more than making CDs to say whatever you want about women and life in the hood. The essence and original intent of Free Speech is about having the freedom to publicly criticize the government and express views of "political liberation." Making rap songs that "casualize" gang-bangin' against ourselves isn't Free Speech – It's "Counter-Free Speech" because it reaps predatory profits for White execs who capitalize from misfortunes among those of our people who need "political liberation" most.

Being an Un-Sovereign People, we've always had definite limitations to Free Speech. From studying the "Conquest Notes" of earlier captors, it's always been known to Euro-Americans that all successful captors must be able to effectively manipulate language to their advantage, since language is directly linked to thoughts and perceptions. Words emit emotions. Words prompt visualizations. There are sensory interconnections between the words we speak and the thoughts we think.

Remember in the movie *Roots*, how Kunta Kinte was strung-up and barbarically lashed until he finally recanted and surrendered to calling himself "Toby" instead of "Kunta?" Logic might suggest that since we were debased as "less than human" during slavery, it would seem that slaveholders wouldn't give a damn what our names were or what we called ourselves. ... No, No, No!

Captors cannot afford for captives to communicate in unfamiliar languages or have unfamiliar names. Captors must maintain control over the language of captives or else they risk losing psychological control of them. Nebuchadnezzar exemplified this Biblically by changing the names of Hananiah, Mishael, and Azariah to the more familiar Shadrach, Meshach, and Abednego (Daniel 1: 6, 7). He also exercised musical control (Daniel 3: 5 - 7).

Relying on their "Conquest Notes," it was clear to Euro-Americans from the onset of slavery that *all* "Kunta Identities" had to be countered, dismantled, and destroyed. Beatings like Kunta's, not only aimed to stop the person, but also aimed to prevent all others from keeping their African identities and communicating in African languages.

According to traditions that are still practiced in contemporary cultures, African names are known to relate aspects of things like character, ancestry, and history. Slaveholders had no idea of the meanings or messages conveyed through African names, but they knew that African names encompassed much more than just "a name" in the European sense of names. They also knew they could never fully enslave a "Kunta Identity" since they weren't the originators who created or defined it, nor did they have any control over what it represented.

By contrast, Euro-Americans had every bit of control over everything that a "Toby Identity" represented. "Toby," then, for all intents and purposes of conquest, was not just designated as a common or conventional European name. On a deeper level, "Toby" was part of a systematic means to psychologically reduce and recreate "Kunta Identities" into *images* and *likenesses* that could ultimately be fully domesticated.

Within the power dynamics of language and definitions, "Toby vs. Kunta" represented two diametrically opposed "sovereign constructs," vying in a spiritual and ideological struggle of life or death, where the "winner takes all."

There could be no peaceful coexisting of sovereign identities since "Kunta" was anchored to a fixed sovereign nature and fixed sovereign manhood that had to be deconstructed entirely in order to fit the new sociopolitical skin of "Toby." This forced act to transfigure "Kunta Identities" into "Toby Identities" ranks among the greatest of all Un-Sovereign Consequences we've paid at the hands of Euro-Americans.

Interestingly, as another side note, for this very reason of opposing "sovereign constructs" you won't find Jewish people walking around the earth naming themselves "Adolph." Unlike us, they don't fit the skin and they've never accepted any images or likenesses of the people who debased their humanity. Maybe you have, but I've never encountered or even heard of another person surnamed "Hitler."

Names matter. Definitions matter. Language matters. Doctrines matter. So it's not by strokes of happenstance that we were collectively labeled with a host of pejoratives, including the N-Word, which like "Toby" encompasses more than just a mere name. No other term has had an equivalent and enduring racist impact. Segments of society still cringe at its mention as if hearing fingernails scraping a chalkboard.

Though originally used by Whites to dehumanize us, the current use of the N-Word by Blacks in camaraderie fashion is not new. Neither is it the only appalling word or trait that lingers from the remains of slavery. Sorry if anyone gets offended but, as unwise and unhealthy as it is, some Black people still happily eat chitlins … Not by force and not by need of survival as in times past, but because they've been intergenerationally conditioned via the horridness of enslavement to actually *enjoy* it. They'll tell you in a minute though that, "they don't eat *anybody's* chitlins."

Chitlins and the N-Word are among the ugliest remnants of the bottom-most worst of our history. Yet both have endured to the point where chitlins are categorized as "soul food," and the N-Word has been embraced as a "term of endearment."

Recently there's been a big push from different quarters to ban it. "Since white comedian Michael Richards [the Kramer character on Steinfield] repeatedly used the N-Word and referred to lynching in a rant, lawmakers in several cities have passed symbolic moratoriums on the racial slur once used by slave owners."[48] In Detroit at the 2007 NAACP Convention, thousands gathered at a "symbolic funeral" of the N-Word with the pageantry of a horse-drawn carriage transporting a casket adorned with a black wreath.[49]

It's wonderful that some people are emotionally motivated to abolish it, but unfortunately that's impossible in this day and age. The N-Word didn't just appear out of nowhere for no reason, so it won't just disappear into nowhere because of appeals from people who don't even say it themselves anyway. Attempting to ban it is as futile as trying to ban handguns. Neither is possible because both are endemic factors that make America the corrupt nation that it's been from inception.

Contrary to the way it may seem on the surface, the N-Word is not a "Black issue" that relates to us alone. Some might depart company with me here (if not beforehand), but I contend that it reflects unanswered issues of race and hypocrisy that prod Euro-Americans to examine *themselves* in ways that they find politically and psychologically uncomfortable.

For the establishment, the N-Word's pervasiveness is like a spreading rash caused by its own doing that's so far been untreatable. It's an unwanted reminder that American democracy is tainted in ways that contradict all the grandiose ideals this government pretends to portray as a model for the world to follow. For Blacks, the N-Word's profitable commercial use is a lasting lash of the slaveholders' whip of control and ownership. Its profuse street use is an unresponded "cry for rescue" from our youth that requires action beyond lecturing them with civil rights stories from yesteryear.

There's a general hesitancy in the mainstream to search beneath the surface of the N-Word, knowing it will unveil loads of dirty political and psychological laundry that's been piling up unattended for centuries in America's basement. I assert that within this dirty laundry is evidence that the "N-Word" is inseparable from "Toby" in function and intent, though different in design and perception.

Yes, the "N-Word" certainly stings more than "Toby," but each was meant to deconstruct our sovereign nature just as much as the other. Each misidentified and equally shackled us captive to a psychology and a world of words and definitions that we as Africans still do not control.

Think about it for a moment … Originally and undoubtedly, we were no more a "Toby" than we were a "N-Word." From a sovereign standpoint, both were initially humiliating and neither was honorable. So, in sovereign terms of analysis, just because we've become accustomed to being called "Toby" doesn't make it any more right or any less denigrating than being called the "N-Word."

In fact, when you ingest all of this from a sovereign perspective, our "Kunta ancestors" who resisted domestication, would have probably regarded being called "Tobies" as more dehumanizing than the "N-Word." I say this, not because they would have ever defined themselves as "N-Words," but because "Toby" signified "establishment approval," while the "N-Word" signified "establishment disapproval." Being the resistors that they were, our "Kunta ancestors" were not the least bit concerned about receiving Euro-American approval.

Through time and attrition however, our forebears were mentally conditioned en masse to not only seek approval, but to confusingly associate *approval* with *progress*. This mindset paved a pathway to arrive at our present sociopolitical destination where we've been psychologically habituated to: 1) Discard "Kunta," 2) Embrace "Toby," and 3) Detest the "N-Word."

Embracing "Toby" unavoidably led to forsaking our sovereign identities, leaving us susceptible to become Negroes, Colored folks, or whatever other slapstick label Euro-Americans determined. Against all odds however, youngsters of hip hop culture are now shaking the once-sturdy foundation of centuries-old psychology and definitions.

For them also, approval is not equated with progress. Rather than *detest* the N-Word according to norms, they deliberately *embrace* it – In effect, disassociating themselves from conditioned norms, unconcerned about establishment approval. For the civil rights generation, this seemingly slaps the face of all the liberties they've fought so hard for.

But the N-Word itself is not the real problem. It rather is an emblematic reverberation of longstanding unresolved issues that present-day civil rights advocates should regard as even harder slaps in the face. The N-Word is emblematic of all that is politically and principally wrong and unjust with the historic relationship between Black and White America … Emblematic of all that's economically and socially wrong and unjust with America's historic development as a nation … Emblematic of all that's spiritually and morally wrong and unjust with all the Un-Sovereign Consequences we've historically paid as an Un-Sovereign People.

You cannot expect to close your eyes and wish away the N-Word, while failing to resolutely deal with the realities that caused its effects. However, there are immutable, inescapable laws governing this universe that will eventually and inevitably balance all scales of injustices. In this regard, the N-Word serves as a living omen to remind America that "all is not well with this democracy" since justice remains outstanding for its human rights abuses.

In attempt to cover its tracks and pretend that "all is well," America is on a big "political correctness" kick. There's now a strict checklist of words deemed "racially offensive." Whereas recently we were powerless to do anything if a White person used a bullhorn to shout the N-Word from the steps of the White House, these days they'd face reprimands of sorts if they are overheard whispering it from the steps of their own house.

At the height of slavery up until the 1960s, it was inconceivable that the N-Word would one day become a term that could jeopardize the careers of Euro-Americans (especially public servants and political officials) if they got caught saying it. But now they've painted themselves into a corner with a ticking time-bomb. The very word they authored and used for centuries to humiliate us has become the very word that they better not say. That's right, they "better not say it" if they want to keep their jobs or hold elected office.

Conversely, we can say it with near-impunity. The irony of this is unlike any other in our history and relations with them. Bearing in mind that we've always been on the blunt receiving end of language being used as a weapon, there's no other word in the entire English language that we have independent leverage over like the N-Word.

Youngsters of hip hop culture seize full advantage of this by saying it publicly without any reservations or apologies. Call it ignorance or whatever else you like. However, I say that the real ignorance lies in the failure of older generations to understand our youngsters, along with the underlying causes that fuel the hostilities that they unleash against each other. The real ignorance is that upcoming generations are being devoured by the streets in unparalleled numbers while we stand unequipped to respond.

I expect that my sovereign assessments of the N-Word will be dismissed as unfounded and inaccurate by the mainstream. Meanwhile, street conditions are steadily worsening and our youngsters are becoming more unprotected and unruly beyond contemporary remedies. This lets you know that mainstream assessments have verifiably missed the mark of accuracy. So it's really only a matter of time anyway before "enough is enough" and sovereign assessments will begin to make practical sense to broader circles of Africans in America.

There have to be definitive answers to explain and most importantly to correct the defiant, violent behaviors that have reached the family doorsteps of us all. Since conventional approaches have fallen short, let me then assert another level of sovereign assessment for consideration ... Could partial explanation of the nonconformity of our youths involve an unrecognized link to our "Kunta ancestors" who personified resistance in the past?

Perhaps there's an overlooked historical continuity that's worthwhile examining because, just like our "Kunta ancestors" who never conformed to Americanization, maybe some of our youngsters today weren't "born to conform" to be "Tobies" either. After all, in truth, we really aren't "Americans" by blood or heritage anyway. So, maybe their

114

rebelliousness reflects a confused refusal of Americanization, in lieu of not having a sovereign alternative. Maybe their nonconformity could ultimately be a good thing, in that we're seeing a predestined reemergence of our "Kunta Identities" in the form of youngsters who (like their daddies) don't fit the un-sovereign skin of "Toby."

You cannot summarily rule out the influence or spirituality of our ancestors who never wholeheartedly embraced or converted into "Tobies." Throughout the generations, some skillfully faked conformity as a means to ensure personal and genetic survival, and to preserve semblances of our African spirit and nature. Until this day, Black families have oral histories that remind us of our African past. So we have always been spiritually linked to our African roots and ancestors in ways that aren't written about in textbooks or featured on the nightly news. Take a tour to slave dungeons like Elmina or Cape Coast in Ghana and you'll better understand the spirit and links I'm referring to.

Another unseemly link to our African past is found in the wide popularity of "ethnic names" given to our children today. Based on the primordial charge given to humanity in Genesis to "name and define," these names could be indicative of inborn desires to finally regain our lost dominion over the words used to define who we are. Sure, some names sound funny and may not even have meanings, and most may not even be African at all. But what is certain is that the names are intentionally *meant* to sound "Un-European."

Likewise, the popularity of the N-Word is intentionally *meant* to be antithetical to Euro-American convention. In this regard, the N-Word has become likened to an "identity" that our youngsters independently claim and control alone, without oversight or influences from anyone other than themselves. In a certain sense, it is akin to a feature of their own self-styled brand of nationalism, substituted to fill the void from being disemboweled of our original sovereign identities.

Of course our youngsters cannot articulate this in detail on this level. Neither can they internalize or interpret history efficiently enough to understand and navigate around all the built-in booby-traps of

Americanization ... which partially explains why they fight each other over trivialities instead of fighting collectively for sovereignty.

I'm convinced however that through their aggressiveness and unruliness, many of our young men are seeking *Sovereign Evolution* without consciously knowing it. They may not academically understand sovereignty, but they are still men. And as such, like all other men, they too yearn just the same to amass and express power in the world. Good, bad, or indifferent, this happens to be the nature of men. But in our case as men, power is always exerted over us by Euro-American males. Here's how author and publisher Haki Madhubuti commented on the frustration of this: "Men run the world, and now understand that you are not one of the men running the world, and layer on that, that men you don't like are always telling you what to do."[50]

A clear historical perspective that youngsters must gain is to know that the same warrior-like toughness and lack of fear that they now misdirect against each other, were considered *attributes* of "Kunta" when used to resist domestication. Nothing is therefore intrinsically wrong with being "gangsta," if properly harnessed and applied towards nationalism and sovereign good. Ironically though, these once-honorable attributes have now become a modern curse of self-inflicted miseries and murders that make young Black men their own worst enemy.

At the same time, a perspective that elder generations must gain is to realize that, if we were a sovereign people (as we rightfully should be), some of these same seemingly unreformable thugs who are castaways of society, could be diplomats in our government and ranking officers in our military, who represent and protect our freedoms and way of life. Many are would-be heroes if given sovereign ideals to believe in and fight for. Since they shoot and kill each other and are prepared to die over what essentially is street pettiness, imagine if their same level of commitment was dedicated to sovereign causes.

All the blame for their aberrant behaviors begins with us who are the elders. Why? Because we are their parents, and in the final analysis, children basically do a combination of two things – What parents *make* them do and what parents *let* them do.

Bill Cosby or no Bill Cosby, the reality is that they have not failed us. We rather have failed them. We owe our youngsters a sovereign form of political and spiritual leadership that they need and deserve ... Leadership that can redirect their warrior nature and anchor them to a sovereign-sense of mission and identity. Otherwise, it's fairly certain that throughout this 21st century we will remain an Un-Sovereign People who Pay Un-Sovereign Consequences, while the N-Word and all its emblematic outgrowths will remain un-abolishable.

<><><><><><><>

"Of all the enemies to public liberty war is, perhaps, the most to be dreaded because it comprises and develops the germ of every other. War is the parent of armies; from these proceed debts and taxes . . . known instruments for bringing the many under the domination of the few. . . . No nation could preserve its freedom in the midst of continual warfare."

President James Madison

"So long as governments set the example of killing their enemies, private individuals will occasionally kill theirs."

Elbert Hubbard, Author (1856-1915)

"For 50 years, it has been constantly repeated to the inhabitants of the United States that they are the only religious, enlightened, and free people. They see that up to now, democratic institutions have prospered among them; they therefore have an immense opinion of themselves, and they are not far from believing that they form a species apart in the human race."

Alexis de Tocqueville, French Statesman and Author (1805-1859)

4
The Cloak of Exceptionalism

Origin of Exceptionalism

America as a nation is devised by means of ideology as opposed to "Ethnonationalism," which is the "notion that the members of a nation are part of an extended family, ultimately united by ties of blood."[1] US citizens are not unified through common ethnicity, but rather via virtue of common creeds and political ideals. To be "American," according to the *US Foreign Policy Encyclopedia*, is "not a birthright but the willingness to believe in a certain set of political and social principles and values."[2]... Which is why foreigners that naturalize as US citizens, must study to be indoctrinated with Jeopardy-like questions about Americanization and its ideology.

America grew to become a hodgepodge of ethnicities in part to meet its labor needs for economic expansion. Originally however, this nation was founded on Anglo-European ethnicity. "For substantial stretches of US history, it was believed that only the people of English origin, or those who were Protestant, or white, or hailed from northern Europe were real Americans."[3] As Jerry Z. Muller wrote in *Foreign Affairs* magazine:

> Projecting their own experience onto the rest of the world, Americans generally belittle the role of ethnic nationalism in politics. After all, in the United States people of varying ethnic origins live cheek by jowl in relative peace. Immigrants to the United States usually arrive with a willingness to fit into their new country and reshape their identities accordingly. Within two or three generations of immigration, their ethnic identities are attenuated by cultural assimilation and intermarriage.
>
> Americans also find ethnonationalism discomfiting both intellectually and morally. . . . And ethicists scorn value systems based on narrow group identities rather than cosmopolitanism. But none of this will make ethnonationalism go away.[4]

From its inception, the self-grandiosity of ideals and actions of Americanization drew questions of inter-European concerns and controversies that still linger in some forms today. As early as the latter 1700s the question of "What is an American?" was posed in a book, *Letters from an American Farmer*, by J. Hector St. John Crevecoeur. In his 1997 book *American Exceptionalism: A Double Edged Sword*, Seymour Martin Lipset took his turn at trying to answer this question, writing:

> Born out of revolution, the United States is a country organized around an ideology which includes a set of dogmas about the nature of a good society. Americanism, as different people have pointed out, is an "ism" or ideology in the same way that communism or fascism or liberalism are isms. As G. K.

119

Chesterton put it: "America is the only nation in the world that is founded on a creed. That creed is set forth with dogmatic and even theological lucidity in the Declaration of Independence.

Other countries' senses of themselves are derived from a common history. Winston Churchill once gave vivid evidence to the difference between a national identity rooted in history and one defined by ideology. . . . Churchill said that as far as he knew, the Communist Party was composed of Englishmen and he did not fear an Englishman. In Europe, nationality is related to community, and thus one cannot become un-English or un-Swedish. Being an American, however, is an ideological commitment. It is not a matter of birth. Those who reject American values are un-American.[5]

The US government is on constant high alert for the slightest hints of "un-American" beliefs and behaviors within society. Once it detects any signs of what it regards as "un-American" tendencies, it immediately uses its intelligence agencies to surveil suspected individuals or groups. To insulate its borders from influxes of "un-American" influences, the government even established a controversial *House Un-American Activities Committee* (HUAC) in 1938 that investigated alleged disloyalty and subversive activities of citizens and organizations.[6]

Early into the process of defining and expressing their American-ness, Euro-Americans began to acquire what would become a lasting sense of special uniqueness that – America as a nation and Americans as a people, were somehow politically and culturally above and better than all others. This attitude and belief led to the phrase and field of study known as "American Exceptionalism." The *US Foreign Policy Encyclopedia* states that:

"American Exceptionalism" is a term used to describe the belief that the United States is an extraordinary nation with a special role to play in human history; a nation that is not only unique but

120

also superior. Alexis de Tocqueville was the first to use the term "exceptional" to describe the United States and the American people in his classic work *Democracy in America* (1835–1840), but the idea of America as an exceptional entity can be traced back to the earliest colonial times. . . . Many scholars of the belief in American exceptionalism argue that it forms one of the core elements of American national identity and American nationalism.

The ways in which US foreign policy is made and conducted are influenced by the underlying assumptions that Americans hold about themselves and the rest of the world. Like most nations, the United States has a distinctive pattern of policymaking that is determined by unique aspects of its national culture.

Two main strands of exceptionalist thought have influenced US foreign policy. One is that of the United States as an exemplar nation, as reflected in ideas such as the "city upon a hill." . . . The other, often more dominant strand is that of the missionary nation, as represented by the ideas of "manifest destiny," "leader of the free world," "modernization theory," and the "new world order."[7]

Various views and interpretations of American Exceptionalism have been posed over the centuries. Being that the US abandoned Euro-styled feudalism and aristocracy, early intellectuals suggested that America was Exceptional because it was a "New World" that was not a political or territorial extension of Europe. Though this was a visionary view that probably did not philosophically compute with typical settlers at the time, it seems to have formed the basis of thinking for wanton ways to take hold of the concept.

In more modern times, the term was accepted in a broad sense to refer to the US as the only industrialized country that did not have a significant socialist movement or Labor Party, which then grew to include

America's policies on the likes of private property rights, religious tolerance, free-market capitalism and democratic rule.[8]

Another Exceptional factor (though not mentioned in customary characterizations), is America's near-350 years of uninterrupted slavery and segregation that resulted in a scale of economic enormity that has yet to be recognized or quantified in political or commercial terms. Without this Exceptional advantage, America could not have accelerated beyond the pace of ordinary development of other nations as it originally did.

Superimposing Exceptionalist Beliefs

Exceptionalism and Americanization are inseparable. Embracing Americanization automatically spawns the espousing of degrees of Exceptionalist beliefs. Although centuries of Americanization have conditioned Africans in America to believe in Exceptionalism, Crevecoeur's erstwhile question of "What is an American?" requires 21st-century answers that must take sovereign considerations into account.

Yes, all of the near-40 million of us are supposed to be "US citizens," but are all of us truly "American" at heart? . . . Especially given the fact that being American "is not a matter of birth," but rather an "ideological commitment," as British Prime Minister Winston Churchill alluded.

Our assimilation into Americanization is analogous to having someone selfishly and deliberately poke you in both eyes (enslave you) to impair your vision as a means of advancing their own interests (become sovereign). They then force you to buy overpriced eyeglasses from them (make you struggle for civil rights) to ostensibly compensate you for the sight-damage they inflicted. Finally, they not only convince you to appreciate your limited sight, but also to praise the glasses. Reality should tell us however, that we originally had two perfectly healthy eyes. If it weren't for us being purposely poked in the first place, we wouldn't need glasses for our impaired vision. We would possess our own natural, God-given sovereign vision.

But the superimposing of Exceptionalism prevents us from internalizing this higher reality, causing us instead to accept and allow circumstances that we ordinarily would and should reject outright as "abuses of government" and "deviances of society." At the same time, Exceptionalism causes Euro-Americans to rationalize their abuses and deviances whenever they appraise America's history and conduct in comparison to other countries. Following are a few quick examples of what I mean.

Shortly after the death of PLO Chairman and Nobel Peace Prize winner Yasser Arafat, I heard a Palestinian say during a panel interview that "Arafat is the George Washington of the Palestinian struggle." Wow, what in the world did he say that for? Being that Arafat was counted among the world's terrorists by America, the Whites on the panel erupted with fury at the comparison. Objectively so however, Washington's hands were far bloodier than Arafat's. Washington in fact established the political precedent for America's newly instituted government to officially endorse and enforce human rights abuses, of which remnants still remain. Yet as Africans in America we are expected to shun Arafat and honor Washington.

Another example occurred during a 2007 presidential debate when Senator Christopher Dodd responded to an earlier comment of Barack Obama who said that, as president, he possibly would send US troops to Pakistan to hunt terrorists even if the Pakistani government disapproved.[9] Dodd rebutted that "General Musharraf [Pakistan's former president] is no Thomas Jefferson . . . but he's the only thing that stands between us and an Islamic state."[10]

Of course Obama had to play along, despite knowing that millions of Africans were enslaved under Jefferson's two administrations. Exceptionalism made him keep mum even though Jefferson's inhumanities exceed hands-down whatever charges Dodd could possibly prove or allege against Musharraf. However, the deciding difference here is that Euro-

123

Americans do not factor in their inhumanities against us when determining the greatness or morality of their own. Exceptionalism makes them believe they can "forgive themselves."

Oh, by the way, according to a November 5, 2008 report by Carl Cameron on *The O'Reilly Factor*, GOP sources felt that a major campaign weakness of Gov. Sarah Palin was that she was unfamiliar with and unable to effectively express Exceptionalist language.

A similar Jefferson contrast was made by New York Times correspondent Tom Friedman on the *Imus* morning radio show. As he talked about Shiite leader Grand Ayatollah Ali al-Sistani, a photograph of the turbaned, full-bearded Ayatollah appeared on-screen. After Imus jeered the Islamic cultural "look" that Ayatollahs tend to have, Friedman then chimed in: "Jefferson doesn't come to mind."[11]

In other words they were insinuating that the ruffled shirt, powdered hair "look" of Jefferson projects qualities of humanity that the Ayatollah lacked. As an American, when viewing the two photographs side-by-side, you are supposed to see Jefferson as an honorable kind-natured Christian, while al-Sistani is to be seen as a foreboding Islamic figure that conjures thoughts of violence and distrust.

Don't get me wrong; from a Euro-American perspective Dodd, Imus, and Friedman were all simply exhibiting loyalty to Americanization and their founding fathers; which is understandable. But as Africans in America we must be mindful that we do not share the exact same historical background as they do. In this case, once we separate truth from perception, the reality is that the dehumanizing of our forefathers traces to people who "look" like Jefferson, not like Ayatollahs. Again, don't get me wrong; I'm not promoting a congeniality or popularity contest. I'm simply illustrating how Exceptionalism gets smashed in our face.

I can go on to cite how America champions itself as the world's standard-bearer of human rights. Yet former FBI director J. Edgar Hoover, who was a confirmed enemy and witch-hunter of civil rights, has the lavish $126.1 million FBI headquarters named in his honor.[12] And to top matters off, Black tax dollars helped build and now help fund this building.

Any attempts to remove his name however, would be just as futile and controversial as trying to get the government to chisel out and replace some of the faces atop Mt. Rushmore.

As in the earlier illustrations of "common history" vs. "related history" and how heroes and rebels are determined by the winners of conflicts, the same holds true with Exceptionalism. Since we are an African people who integrated into an already sovereign European society, we find ourselves paying tribute to heroes, holidays, and history that would make no logical sense without the hypnotic sways of Exceptionalism. But to publicly raise this issue would quickly earn you the "un-American" label and qualify you for surveillance.

Both Exceptionalism and Americanization can only stand minimum-intensity critiques before depths of contradictions and sensitivities are reached that Euro-Americans do not want to acknowledge or address. Americanization is propagated as such an Exceptional ideal, that those who question or challenge its faults and discrepancies have historically been ostracized, criminalized, and even murdered. Malcolm X aptly called it a case of being "victims of democracy."[13]

Political/Religious Exceptionalism

Although Exceptionalism permeates all levels of life, this work focuses on Political, Religious, Military and Economic facets. Each has distinct characteristics, even though you will see that they all interlock and overlap in ways that make them inseparably one. At core, each has a common unquenchable thirst for wealth and resources that knows no bounds.

The puritanical overtones and heavy infusions of religious influences are also not incidental. Exceptionalism in general proliferates through a religious pretext that assumes that America has a uniquely favorable relationship with God. Wherever you find Exceptionalism, you'll also find a Protestant fervor that has largely been irrepressible. As stated in the *US Foreign Policy Encyclopedia*:

> Throughout American history there have been repeated claims that the United States is the promised land and its citizens are the chosen people, divinely ordained to lead the world to betterment. This notion goes back to the very beginnings of colonization. The New World was regarded as a virgin land upon which its new inhabitants could attempt to perfect society through social, political, and religious experiment. Americans have been charged by God with the task of reforming themselves and the world – they are a redeemer nation. The United States is thus guided by the invisible hand of God, and American actions are the result of divine will.[14]

In the following *Joint Resolution* (Public Law 97-280), the US Congress proclaimed 1983 as the "Year of the Bible" and further purported that "The Bible, the Word of God, has made a unique contribution in shaping the United States as a distinctive and blessed nation and people," and that "deeply held religious convictions springing from the Holy Scriptures led to the early settlement of our Nation."[15]

PUBLIC LAW 97-280 - OCT. 4, 1982

Public Law 97-280 96 STAT. 1211 (97th Congress)

Joint Resolution

Authorizing and Requesting the President
to Proclaim 1983 as the "Year of the Bible"
Whereas the Bible, the Word of God, has made a unique contribution
in shaping the United States as a distinctive and blessed nation and
people;
Whereas deeply held religious convictions springing from the Holy
Scriptures led to the early settlement of our Nation;

Whereas Biblical teachings inspired concepts of civil government that are contained in our Declaration of Independence and the Constitution of the United States;

Whereas many of our great national leaders --among them Presidents Washington, Jackson, Lincoln and Wilson --paid tribute to the surpassing influence of the Bible in our country's development, as in the words of President Jackson that the Bible is "the rock on which our Republic rests;"

Whereas the history of our Nation clearly illustrates the value of voluntarily applying the teachings of the Scriptures in the lives of individuals, families and societies;

Whereas this Nation now faces great challenges that will test this Nation as it has never been tested before; and

Whereas that renewing our knowledge of and faith in God through Holy Scripture can strengthen us as a nation and a people: Now, therefore, be it Resolved by the Senate and House of Representatives of the United States of America in Congress assembled, That the President is authorized and requested to designate 1983 as a national "Year of the Bible" in recognition of both the formative influence the Bible has been for our Nation, and our national need to study and apply the teachings of the Holy Scriptures.

Approved October 4, 1982

LEGISLATIVE HISTORY-S.J.Res.165:

CONGRESSIONAL RECORD, Vol. 128 (1982):

Mar. 31, considered and passed Senate.

Sept. 21, considered and passed House.

Document 5. PUBLIC LAW 97-280 - OCT. 4, 1982

This resolution represents the modern continuity of long-held Exceptionalist beliefs that God made a covenant with the Pilgrims and

Puritan settlers of New England, who "regarded the North American continent as a promised land where a new Canaan could be built as a model for the rest of the world."[16] "The pilgrims thought God had given the United States as a gift for furthering their belief, and a place where they (could) be safe from persecution. . . . As the nation matured, that mindset fit with the 19th-century American belief of Manifest Destiny, the notion that western territorial expansion was the inevitable mission of the nation."[17]

Exceptionalist religious beliefs are not new or unusual in world history. "Americans are hardly the only – or the first – people in the world to assume God favors their country, their cause, and their leaders. Previous world powers thrived (and eventually declined, historians say) on that conviction."[18]

Somewhere around 350 B.C., Greek philosopher Aristotle said, "A tyrant must put on the appearance of uncommon devotion to religion. Subjects are less apprehensive of illegal treatment from a ruler whom they consider god-fearing and pious. On the other hand, they do less easily move against him, believing that he has the gods on his side."[19]

Similar to America, the North Korean government uses a self-styled commixture of political/religious Exceptionalism, known as the Juche (self-reliance) to induce acceptance of its policies and practices. North Korea as well prides itself for its military might and instills war-based nationalism in its citizenry just like America. Up to 2 million people are said to have died from malnutrition-related ailments in the 1990s, but the people still believe nonetheless that North Korea is the embodiment of strength and prosperity.[20]

According to a documentary, *Welcome to North Korea*, the Juche teaches society to believe that their leader, Kim Jong Il, and his late father, Kim Il Sung, are mythical-like superior deities capable of performing miracles.[21] Juche precepts require absolute loyalty of citizens to the party, and Kim Il Sung, (known as the "Great Leader" and "President for Eternity") is "exalted and revered as a god" to be followed with "unswerving obedience."[22]

Americans are not under the strict political or religious controls of a "personality cult" of a single individual or tyrant. But contrary to "Separation of Church and State," there's a symbiotic relationship where religious influences are deeply entrenched within the state and vice versa, which make Americans "less apprehensive of illegal treatment, and they less easily move against the government, believing that it has God on its side," as Aristotle alluded.

In a court case involving the government's "unconstitutional endorsement of religion," the Supreme Court reversed a prior federal ruling affecting schoolchildren that removed the phrase "under God," from the Pledge of Allegiance.[23] In an 8-0 decision confirming the "Non-Separation of Church and State," the Supreme Court ruled to leave the words "under God" intact just as Congress had approved in 1954 as a means to "distinguish America's Christian values from those of communism."[24]

While it has become acceptable and even popular for preachers and politicians alike to invoke God's name for political purposes, as well as to bless America and curse enemies, conversely, it is religiously and politically unforgivable to associate God with retribution against America, as did New Orleans Mayor Ray Nagin.

Nagin was pegged in the media as a crazed misfit of society because, Exceptionalism makes it *unthinkable* that God would ever *punish* America. Public pressure eventually bent him to apologize for saying that: "God is mad at America. He sent us hurricane after hurricane after hurricane, and it's destroyed and put stress on this country. . . . Surely he doesn't approve of us being in Iraq under false pretenses. But surely he is upset at black America also. We're not taking care of ourselves."[25]

An *Associated Press* article titled "More Americans Want Religion, Politics to Mix," stated that "When politicians in this country try to blend religion and politics, they find a comparatively receptive climate."[26] However, by "religion," the article is not referring to just any religion, but strictly to Protestant Euro-Christianity. A politician who tries to blend Buddhism or Islam or anything else can forget about finding the same receptivity.

A study conducted by the Baylor Institute for Studies of Religion determined that 1 of 5 Americans believes in a "God who favors the United States in worldly affairs."[27] The study concluded that "the idea of God, the belief in God, can be in a political sense exploited for nationalistic purposes."[28] An example of this is found in Bush's 2004 inaugural address, where a Black minister named Kirby Jon Caldwell (one of Bush's spiritual guides and the author of *Entrepreneurial Faith*, who also presided over the marriage of Bush's daughter Jenna) performed an over-the-top benediction that synthesized Euro-Christianity with politics, nationalism, and support for war.[29]

More evidence of "Non-Separation of Church and State" and the exploiting of religion for nationalistic purposes is seen in state constitutions, where scripture-like references to "God" are cited in every preamble of all 50 states.[30] Here are just a few (boldfaces are my own):

Preambles of State Constitutions

(Alabama 1901) We the people of the State of Alabama . . . invoking the favor and guidance of Almighty God, do ordain and establish the following Constitution . . .

(Alaska 1956) We, the people of Alaska, grateful to God and to those who founded our nation and pioneered this great land . . .

(Delaware 1897) Preamble. Through Divine Goodness all men have, by nature, the rights of worshipping and serving their Creator according to the dictates of their consciences . . .

(Louisiana 1921) We, the people of the State of Louisiana, grateful to Almighty God for the civil, political and religious liberties we enjoy . . .

(Maine 1820) We the People of Maine . . . acknowledging with grateful hearts the goodness of the Sovereign Ruler of the Universe in affording us an opportunity . . .

(Massachusetts 1780) We . . . the people of Massachusetts, acknowledging with grateful hearts, the goodness of the Great Legislator of the Universe . . .

> (Missouri 1945) We, the people of Missouri, with profound reverence for the Supreme Ruler of the Universe, and grateful for His goodness . . . establish this Constitution . . .
>
> (North Carolina 1868) We the people of the State of North Carolina, grateful to Almighty God, the Sovereign Ruler of Nations, for . . . our civil, political, and religious liberties, and acknowledging our dependence upon Him for the continuance . . .
>
> (Vermont 1777) Whereas all government ought to . . . enable the individuals who compose it to enjoy their natural rights, and other blessings which the Author of Existence has bestowed on man . . .[31]

Document 6. Preambles of State Constitutions

Based on all the religious fluff contained in America's political *Doctrine, Documents, and Declarations*, if you just arrived from another planet you would never have a clue that Euro-Americans could stoop morally low enough to be unrepentant slave traders. It's kind of Twilight Zone-ish how they have convinced themselves that God has a special love for this country, or as the *Joint Resolution* states, that America is a "distinctive and blessed nation and people" . . . As though when you die, all you have to do is show God your new digitized, counterfeit-proof passport and you'll automatically get escorted to the VIP lounge of heaven.

None of this is meant to disparage the *truth* of Christianity, but rather to accent the *use* of Euro-Christianity. I guess it's the money that has society fooled. People commonly associate America's great wealth and prosperity as a "sign of God." Not to get preachy, but the Bible is loaded with examples of wealthy nations and prosperous lands that were evil and subsequently got destroyed. Just because nations or individuals are affluent, does not necessarily mean they are Godly or that God is with them. Wealth is not always indicative of righteousness. Wealth can also denote thievery and wickedness.

Meantime, preachers and religious institutions have stolen, embezzled, and defrauded their way into an ever-rising multibillion-dollar swindling industry. According to the North American Securities Administrators Association, about $450 million was stolen in religion-related scams between 1984 and 1989.[32] Records from 1998 to 2001 show swindling figures totaling $2 billion, and since 2006 "the size and the scope of the fraud is getting larger."[33]

Recently a particularly disturbing trend is moving afoot. With the advent of "prosperity ministries" in the early 1990s, a capitalist transformation has occurred where more and more churches are developing "corporate natures."[34] Emphasis has shifted away from educational, social, and community concerns, while "many of the most prominent black churches now focus mainly on building wealth."[35]

Some churches have political umbilical cords tied directly to the cupboards of the government's Faith-Based Initiative. In the process, some preachers who reap the harvest of this funding become politically and spiritually compromised, as evidenced by those who publicly coddled Bush when they should have rebuked him for Katrina and the Iraqi war debacle.

According to political scientist Fredrick Harris of the University of Rochester, participation in the Faith-Based Initiative may have had the effect of "silencing some black activist pastors who accepted money and now cannot be vocal in criticizing or praising the president."[36] The same "Golden Calf" of old that Moses contended with in Exodus, has reincarnated in modernized form, providing financial milk from the political udders of government.

Instead of coming together to collectively condemn America's war belligerence according to the nonviolent principles of Dr. King (which they presumably espouse), these paid-off preachers see-no-evil, hear-no-evil. My question to Black ministers is – Where exactly do Dr. King's principles of nonviolence begin and end? Because it seems today's preachers are only adamant about nonviolence when it comes to our relationship with Euro-Americans. When it comes to America's habitual violence against others (of which we ourselves are casualties) many waste no time preaching pulpit sermons of support for war.

At the time of Dr. King's assassination, he was preaching against America's unjust war in Vietnam. Today as I write, America is engaged in an unjust war in Iraq. America ceremoniously observes Dr. King's national holiday every January 15th, but the establishment chuckles in private because nonviolence to them is a figment of our imagination that they have no intentions to ever practice any day of the year.

This brings me to Dr. Jeremiah Wright, who was lambasted during the 2008 presidential campaign and denounced by Barack Obama for his searing critiques and sermons. Though he's a renowned Biblical scholar with a PhD, his misstep was in the "presentation" of his defense. I say this because, contrary to being "hate speech," Black Liberation Theology is just as bona fide as any other "Protestant" doctrine, be it Calvinism, Methodism, Lutheranism or the rest. All of them comprise precepts and dogmas containing elements of "protest" – hence "Protestantism." The only difference is that the "protest" of Black Liberation Theology is directed at this establishment, as opposed to Catholicism or the British Crown.

I'm not aware of a Biblical verse designating Europeans as the sole authors and validators of Protestant theology. But I am aware of a verse, ironically written in Jeremiah 22:12, that states: "Woe unto him who buildeth his house by unrighteousness, and his chambers by wrong; who useth his neighbor's service without wages, and giveth him not for his work." I wonder, according to Exceptionalist criteria, if this Jeremiah is being divisive and spewing "hate speech" too?

The act of worship is a telling barometer of the yearnings and spiritual essence of a people. Protestant theology as we know it emanates from tribulations that cause yearnings within people to relate and appeal to God to address their hardship circumstances. There has always been a strange irony however, between our Protestant worship of God and our political embrace of Americanization, since we face the spiritual paradox of praying to be integrated into a nation whose treacheries are not secret.

Blacks and Whites alike may be Protestants, but 11 A.M. every Sunday is the most segregated hour in America. Even the most conservative of Blacks will split off from White society to rejuvenate their essence by worshiping at the "Black Church." A 2008 ABC report segment titled "Two Nations Under God," determined that only 7 percent of all US churches are integrated.[37]

As much as government and society "looks" integrated Monday through Saturday, the segregation on Sundays offers incontrovertible evidence of a different essence and yearnings within us, rooted in our need to appeal to God to address our specific hardships and tribulations, of which the government has been part of the cause. Exceptionalism however, makes it difficult for Euro-Americans to fathom that they could be on the wrong side of God.

So of course Dr. Wright has to be denounced. Of course Black Liberation Theology has to be discredited. This establishment is not going to sit back and watch us, moreover watch a Black president, relate or appeal to God in ways that differ from them . . . And especially in ways that deem them the transgressors. It riles this establishment to no end to know that some Black people "condemn" their conduct to a "God-condemning" level. TV networks even bleep-out the words "God damn" at the point where Rev. Wright says, "God damn America" in his contentious sermon.

After becoming a focal point in the campaign, Rev. Wright had the entire nation's attention and the highest stage available to articulate the exegesis of Black Liberation Theology. With all due respect to him otherwise, it seems that the lights and cameras caused him to veer off course into areas that allowed today's Scribes, Pharisees, and Sadducees to do exactly what they wanted – Scrap-pile him into a mockery and reduce Black Liberation Theology to the likes of a passing sideshow of amusement that White society could watch on TV while enjoying popcorn.

Although Dr. Wright happened to be the subject, the underlying issues are still outstanding and much larger than him alone. The circumstances presented an opportune moment in historical time for Black ministers, (as an institution) to collectively align themselves and take a

"Biblical Stand" to call to accountability, America's spiritual and political duplicities that we all know exists. But through their raging silence they metaphorically chose to "Free Barabbas," the Biblical robber and thief, instead.

Authentic "Men of God" in the Bible invariably stood up to correct misguided powers and rulers. They weren't "friends" with governments. A running theme throughout the Bible involves their rebuking of governments. But Black ministers today are more concerned with "photo ops" and "getting in good with" the federal government. They want to be seen and recognized by the Ahabs and Herods and Pharaohs of these times. In fact, the prominence of some is largely tied to their political conformity.

Since the demarcations to separate "Church and State" are unclear, if not nonexistent, Black America should be circumspect whenever society attempts to merge God with government, nationalism, and war. If you strive to separate anything, it would be wise to separate your *soul* from your US *citizenship*.

<><><><><><><>

Military/Religious Exceptionalism

Considering that "Separation of Church and State" is a presumed cornerstone of this nation, it's interesting to hear the take of Supreme Court Justice Antonin Scalia on this subject. His opinion certainly counts, since he is 1 of 9 select individuals whose "interpretation" of the Constitution affects 300 million people. After speaking at an interfaith conference on "Religious Freedom" at a Jewish synagogue in New York in 2004, a newspaper headline read: "Scalia Rejects Religious 'Neutrality' in Government."

Scalia told them that while the church-and-state battle rages, the official examples of the presence of faith go back to America's

135

Founding Fathers: the word "God" on US currency; chaplains of various faiths in the military and the legislature; real estate tax exemption for houses of worship – and the phrase "under God" in the Pledge of Allegiance. . . . A religious-neutral government does not fit with an America that reflects belief in God in everything from its money to its military.[38]

Never has America been religious-neutral in war. Over the centuries its "holier than thou" military attitude has increased, especially when and where natural resources are involved. From its inception the government has consistently merged religious zeal with military incursions, under the guise of "fighting for freedom." Whenever such mergers occur, you'll see Exceptionalism functioning at its height.

The idea that God endorses the US military is reinforced in the "Oath of Enlistment" that all soldiers must "swear" in a cult-like rite. Aside from committing to "obey the orders of the President of the United States" the oath speaks of "faith" and eerily concludes with the words, "So help me God."

I, _____, do solemnly swear (or affirm) that I will support and defend the Constitution of the United States against all enemies, foreign and domestic; that I will bear true faith and allegiance to the same; and that I will obey the orders of the President of the United States and the orders of the officers appointed over me, according to regulations and the Uniform Code of Military Justice. So help me God.[39]

From George Washington until today, US presidents as Commander-in-Chiefs have been militarily motivated by religious-based Exceptionalism. Bush even said that he learned from "Bible Studies" that the US government has "Power of the Sword."[40] . . . What do you think about that? A *CounterPunch* article titled "American Exceptionalism: A Disease of Conceit" put it this way:

> This belief in American superiority finds its foundation in some of our culture's basic religious and cultural constructs. It's there in the first settlers' belief that they were conducting a special errand into the wilderness to construct a "city on a hill" in the name of their heavenly father and every single president and wannabe always implores this same heavenly father to "bless America" at the end of every one of his speeches. This is no accident.
>
> It is this belief that gave the Pilgrims their heavenly go-ahead to murder Pequot women and children and it was this belief that gave General Custer his approval to kill as many Sioux as he could. It made the mass murder of Korean and Vietnamese civilians acceptable to the soldiers at No Gun Ri and My Lai and exonerated the officers who tried to hide those and many other war crimes from the world.[41]

Running alongside in parallel to the "war against terrorism" has been a direct rise in the vim and fanaticism of the Evangelical Movement. A simplified definition as given by Jon Meacham, managing editor of *Newsweek*, is that an "Evangelical" is a person who believes: That the Bible is infallible; that they have a personal relationship with Jesus; and that the resurrection of Jesus will be a literal real-time event.[42] According to Webster's, "Evangelicals" are Protestants "marked by militant or crusading zeal" that emphasize: "Salvation by faith in the atoning death of Jesus Christ through personal conversion; Authority of Scripture; and Importance of preaching as contrasted with ritual."[43]

Links between Evangelicalism and the US military have never been secret. The US Air Force held a 4-day "Spiritual Fitness Conference" for military chaplains and their families at a cost of $300,000 in 2005.[44]

The *New York Times* published an article about the conference titled "Evangelicals are Growing Force in the Military Chaplain Corps."

> There were personal testimonies about Jesus from the stage, a comedian quoting Scripture and a five-piece band performing contemporary Christian praise songs. Then hundreds of Air Force chaplains stood and sang, many with palms upturned, in a service with a distinctively evangelical tone.
>
> The event was just one indication of the extent to which evangelical Christians have become a growing force in the Air Force chaplain corps, a trend documented by military records and interviews with more than two dozen chaplains and other military officials.
>
> Figures provided by the Air Force show that from 1994 to 2005 the number of chaplains from many evangelical and Pentecostal churches rose, some doubling.[45]

President Bush has unabashedly merged his Evangelicalism with governance. On countless occasions with crusader-like gusto, he's used encrypted Evangelical terminologies, like calling the 9/11 attackers "*evildoers.*"[46] And in alluding to a Evangelical "calling" of the government he said: "Freedom is the Almighty's gift to every man and woman in this world. And as the greatest power on the face of the earth we have an obligation to help the spread of freedom. . . . This is what we have been *called* to do."[47]

In line with the "Bush Doctrine," he has repeatedly warned nations that "If you harbor terrorists, you are just as guilty as the terrorists, you are an enemy of the United States, and you will be held to account."[48] Translation: If you harbor terrorists, you will face the Evangelical wrath of the government. Other Evangelicals with militant and crusading zeal have shot similar verbal cannonballs across the bow.

Pat Robertson, an "Evangelical leader," called for the outright assassination of Venezuelan President Hugo Chavez, yet it wasn't considered by the US government to be a "terroristic threat."[49] You can believe though that it would be altogether different if a Muslim religious leader called for the assassination of any American official. That would undoubtedly be considered an un-retractable "terroristic threat," which according to America's "homemade laws" for other nations would instantly land the person on the "most wanted," list with a hefty bounty on their head.

This same religious zeal for war motivated Lt. General William G. Boykin when he spoke at the Good Shepherd Community Church in Oregon. As he flicked through an overhead slideshow of pictures of Osama bin Laden, Saddam Hussein, and Kim Jung Il he asked rhetorically: "Why do they hate us? . . . The answer to that is because we're a *Christian* nation." Such enemies, he declared, "will only be defeated if we come against them in the name of Jesus."[50]

In return fire from Muslims, you'll find Islamic beliefs and perspectives that spiritually challenge the hypocrisies and immoralities of US government and society. Muslim cleric Massoud el Fassed, for instance, is quoted in Bruce Fieler's book *Abraham* as saying:

Look at the Muslim nation, look around the whole world. We worship God around the clock, five times a day, then do extra prayers. . . . God gives you [America] the opportunity to submit yourselves to him, and follow the rule of God. But you ignore Him because you have become strong. You can deliver your message around the world, you can switch the mind of the people. You do the opposite of what God wants. You open banks, sexual places, gambling. Evil things . . . And look at what happened . . . He sent people very strong, who killed themselves, in order to kill you. This is something unbelievable [September 11] what happened in America, but it came from God.[51]

The 9/11 Commission Report found that even though rejection of Western cultural and political dominance is common to Muslim populations in general, the number of so-called "Islamist terrorists" is significantly small; but widespread sympathy exists for "terrorists" and millions share some degree of approval for "terrorists acts."[52] These millions of sympathizers are believed to comprise "a ready audience to call for Muslims to purify their society, reject unwelcome modernization, and adhere strictly to the Sharia."[53]

You would think these findings would slow down America's use of military violence as a primary answer to what it defines as "Islamic terrorism." Military actions have not deterred terrorism, but have escalated tit-for-tat retaliatory violence, which has resulted in what I call an "Age of Reciprocated Terrorism." Nevertheless, Euro-Americans are clinging steadfast to their Exceptionalist "My God is mightier than your God" philosophy.

The solutions to the world's problems do not entail implementing a US style and system of government upon every nation that America dislikes. Muslim nations do not want America to set up an Islamic equivalent of a colonial "Williamsburg" anywhere in their region of the world. Despite the Exceptionalist notion that "God is *with* America to spread freedom," all the mayhem and mishaps in Iraq and Afghanistan are blaring signals of what happens when "God is *not* with you."

Military Exceptionalism

The original theological thrust behind the "Manifest Destiny" of early settlers still thrives no less in modern military aggression for wealth and resources. To use Thomas Paine's words against the government and society he helped to fashion, "From such beginnings of government, what could be expected, but a continual system of war and extortion?"[54] This corresponds with an interview of Princeton professor, Dr. Cornel West, where he said:

There are American soldiers based in 132 countries, a ship in every major ocean, and the disproportionate influence, after 1947, in shaping the regimes of South Korea, Turkey, Greece and other countries that were on the front line with the old Soviet Empire. It is different from the old Roman or British empires, but it is still an imperial presence.

There is an evangelical nihilism, where "might makes right" and unregulated coercion is the means by which one pursues his policies.

In terms of behavior, he [George Bush] acts so that justifications and rationalizations are ad hoc, and can change at any moment: "We've got the power, we'll follow through and I will not engage in any critical dialogue with the dissidents or critics."[55]

Without saying "Exceptionalism," West is essentially describing Exceptionalism. But let me clarify that although I've repeatedly cited Bush as a source of Exceptionalism, I am not promoting the politics or policies of the Democratic Party versus that of the Republican Party, or so-called liberalism versus conservatism. These terms signify the two wings of the same ideological bird. Be it Republicans, Democrats, or even Independents, they all represent a single political "System of Thought" that is by no means disconnected in any sense.

Equally so, America has flexed its Exceptionalist muscles under Republican and Democratic administrations. War, greed, and aggression are endemic to both parties. Both parties are intoxicated with Americanization. Both seek to export its influences globally. And neither has had sincere regard for non-Europeans who get harmed in the process. Take your choice of a Republican like George Bush or a Democrat like Harry Truman who ordered the nuclear attack of Japan and then went to church the morning after.[56]

Though America nuked Japan twice, killing hundreds of thousands of children and civilians, the US government now wants to "morally" monitor and select which government can or can't have nuclear weapons. Big commotion erupted when North Korea tested a dud underground nuclear weapon in 2006. Sure, this and any other nuclear test should raise concern in the world community. But, compared to North Korea's single test, America launched 1,030 nuclear weapons tests from 1945 to 1992.[57] Plus, the National Nuclear Security Administration has an estimated 189 metric tons of weapons-grade uranium stored at their "Y-12 Facility" in Tennessee.[58] What will become of this material, and when?

What we do know is that since 1945 the US military under both parties has serial-bombed country after country of non-Europeans in the "Name of Democracy." The list includes: Japan, 1945; China, 1945, 1950; Korea, 1950; Guatemala, 1954, 1960; Indonesia, 1958; Cuba, 1959; Vietnam, 1961; the Congo, 1964; Laos, 1964; Peru, 1965; Cambodia, 1969; Lebanon, 1983; Grenada, 1983; Libya, 1986; El Salvador, 1980s; Nicaragua, 1980s; Panama, 1989; Iraq, 1991 and 1993; Somalia, 1993; Sudan, 1998; and Afghanistan, 2001.[59]

There's no better example of Military Exceptionalism than the bombing and occupation of Iraq, which drove Iraqi President Jalal Talabani to scorn the report of the *US Study Group on Iraq* as "An insult to the people of Iraq. . . . One would think that it is written for a young, small colony that they are imposing these conditions on."[60] Or as Iraqi Prime Minister Nouri al-Maliki said, "There are American officials who consider Iraq as if it were one of their villages."[61]

Aside from the US military not being "met in Baghdad with flowers as liberators," as intelligence reports wrongly projected, 3 facts remain regardless of how the government attempts to validate the invasion. 1) The premise of "weapons of mass destruction" (WMD) was unfounded. 2) Neither the Iraqi government nor Iraqi people had ever committed a prewar "terrorist act" on US soil or against American people, so no "terrorism" originally existed inside Iraqi borders to "fight." 3) Billions of dollars have been drained from both economies, and unnecessary thousands of innocent Iraqis have been slaughtered. In sum: Baghdad won't be a vacation destination in your lifetime.

All of the once-alarming prewar accusations turned out to be (take your choice) false, misleading, and/or inaccurate. Reports of things like "mobile nuclear labs" were untrue and contrary to Colin Powell's presentation with tricked-out satellite imagery at the United Nations. None of the estimated 29,984 chemical weapons as claimed by the Pentagon existed.[62] After nearly 2 years of intense search operations, the US terminated its hunt for WMD in January 2005.[63] In the end, Iraq barely had the firepower to breakup a campsite or jamboree of Boy Scouts.

Speaking of Powell, his reputation has since been shredded, and he's gotten far more than he bargained for while "serving at the pleasure of the president" (as he would say). Although he won't publicly admit it, I surmise that he vehemently resents being *used*, which probably led to his refusal to "serve" a second term. He did however say on *Meet the Press*, "I'm very concerned. . . . It turned out that the sourcing was inaccurate and wrong and, in some cases, *deliberately* misleading. And for that, I am disappointed, and I regret it."[64]

Powell is still totally vested in Americanization, so chances are he won't join the Black Panthers anytime soon. But he now knows more than ever that, as a Black man, there is no true honor to gain from being politically elevated by this establishment. And he also knows that it is dangerous to "Dance with the Devil."

Exceptionalism makes the US government quick to allege war crimes against others, but yet it claimed "sovereign immunity" to keep itself blameless for the 3 million Vietnamese who now suffer chemical effects from Agent Orange that the US military sprayed during the 1970s war.[65] Every year the US leverages its weight on the UN Security Council for "blanket exemption" to shield US solders from the International Criminal Court (ICC).[66]

Concerns worry the US that the Hague-based ICC "could be used for frivolous or politically motivated prosecutions of American troops. The 94 countries that established the court, maintain that the ICC contains enough safeguards to prevent frivolous prosecutions."[67] Ample reasons exist for the US to fret about the ICC; especially since the sexual abuse at Abu Ghraib prison, along with all the confirmed rapes and murders of Iraqi civilians by US soldiers, aren't "frivolous" at all.

For this reason, the US lashed out to economically punish 12 Latin American and Caribbean countries for becoming ICC signatories.[68] Sanctions were passed against each country to halt military support and cut funding for counternarcotics and counterterrorism assistance.[69] "Countries that wish to join the ICC and evade sanctions have the option of signing immunity agreements with the United States that shield Americans from ICC jurisdiction."[70]

War by nature is unmerciful. Torture, rape, and other immoralities occur regardless of the nations involved. And there are enough reports, eyewitness accounts, and courtroom confessions to confirm that US troops have not been angels in Iraq. Army investigators even testified at one hearing that US soldiers calmly grilled chicken wings after taking turns raping a 14-year-old Iraqi girl then shooting her in the head.[71]

No one knows the precise number of Iraqi civilians killed since the start of the war, but the estimates from studies reported by the *Guardian* of the United Kingdom put the toll at between one hundred thousand and one million, as of the end of 2008.[72] Little is seldom mentioned of the estimated 3 million Iraqi children who've been orphaned by war.[73] Thousands of children who you never hear about have also been injured. But based on their trauma and steady-growing dislike of America, some are already psychologically primed to become the next generation of ardent enemies of America.[74]

Oh, by the way, according to the US Army Medical Command, "the number of attempted suicides or self-inflicted injuries in the Army jumped sixfold since the Iraq war began. . . . About 2,100 soldiers injured themselves or attempted suicide in 2007, compared with about 350 in 2002."[75] In total 121 soldiers took their own lives in 2007 and by early 2008 at least 5 soldiers per day were attempting suicide.[76] By August 2008 at least 93 soldiers killed themselves.[77] The number of US Army deserters has also progressively increased, with 4,698 desertions in 2007, compared to 2,357 in 2005.[78] These figures do not include Marine, Air Force, or Navy deserters.

By any measure the Iraqi invasion ended up being a disgrace and human rights catastrophe, unmatched in contemporary times. Iraqis have a saying: "Today is worse than yesterday and tomorrow will be worse than today."[79] If any other nation destroyed the sociopolitical composition of another country in like manner, the US would be the first to seek "war crime" prosecutions.

Did you notice how Pentagon and top military officials acted concerned about the mistreated prisoners at Abu Ghraib? Yet blame passed down to the bottom-most possible scapegoat guards.[80] The real "problem" with Abu Ghraib was not that torturing occurred, but the fact that photographs slipped into the wrong hands and circulated worldwide. Joseph Darby, the US soldier who reported the pictures, received so many death threats that, according to *60 Minutes*, he and his family were forced to live undercover and on the run, unable to return to his own hometown.[81] Absent him turning in the photos, US soldiers would probably still be fulfilling their sexual fantasies at Abu Ghraib.

The *action* at Abu Ghraib was like the *action* at any strip club joint in America where people pay for entertainment. Abu Ghraib simply mirrored American society, where soft-porn and pervertedness seep into nearly every aspect of life, encompassing everybody from priests to prisoners to politicians. Sexual influences and deviances are everywhere. Whether a television commercial is for prescription medication for seniors or back-to-school supplies for kids, a half-naked woman that has nothing to do with the product's performance is bound to appear in the advertisement. Even the Mormons recently broke longstanding taboos to get in on the *action* by selling "sexy" calendars of "shirtless" Mormon men.[82]

Contrasted with Islamic societies, Americanized Christian values come with sexual beliefs and conduct that are forbidden outright in Islam. So don't think for a moment that the orgy atmosphere at Abu Ghraib had no explainable context. US interrogators knew exactly what they were doing.

Prisons worldwide are breeding grounds for sexual perverts anyway. Furthermore, in this society, having a person restrained or cuffed also has known overtones of sexual domination. Handcuffs, blindfolds, and leashes for canines that are standard security and military items, can easily double for common "sex toys" that are popularly sold at sex shops all across America. So when soldiers with a socio-sexual mindset of this nature encounter Muslim POWs whose religion shuns such things – the freaky-deakiness of Abu Ghraib results.

Rather than using conventional methods, the intent was to demean and mentally break prisoners by using sexual warfare as the weapon of choice.[83] To make full sense of this, you must remember that a primary objective during the war's earliest stages was to gather all possible intelligence. Military officials therefore *needed* cooperation from POWs. Initial speculation was that some prisoners were withholding knowledge of classified materials, weapons programs, and the whereabouts of Saddam Hussein and others who were featured on the juvenile-devised "deck of cards."

Not only was this information considered vital to saving the lives of US soldiers, but also vital to defending the justification of the invasion itself. America's integrity hinged heavily on acquiring the very information that some prisoners were thought to know. So what better way to gather this info and simultaneously provide soldiers with home-style X-rated entertainment, than to make Islamic foes engage in sexual acts that their religion abhors?

Considering the magnitude of the war, nothing was left to chance. It is therefore implausible that the Pentagon and military brass were unquestionably commanding the entire war strategy, yet they would allow POW dealings to be indiscriminately left in the hands of low-ranking 19-year-old servicemen.

Remember too that the military was on an "eye-for-an-eye" mission to avenge September 11th. The Pentagon, which is hyped as one of the most sacred and protected facilities in the country, took a tremendously embarrassing hit that day. No military force on earth, let alone an Islamic "faction," is supposed to have the smarts or precision wherewithal to strike the almighty Pentagon. The fact that Al Qaeda was clever enough and efficient enough to pull it off, has to privately count among this establishment's greatest humiliations.

With all these variables at work, along with unilaterally proceeding without Security Council approval, it's naive to think that America would suddenly pause to meticulously follow the Geneva Conventions' checklist of "dos and don'ts." Colin Powell's then-chief of staff, Lawrence Wilkerson, said that White House and Pentagon officials believed that "The president of the United States is all-powerful and the Geneva Conventions are irrelevant [for foreign detainees in US custody]. . . . That as commander in chief the president can do anything he damn well pleases."[84]

Illustrations 2. "Geneva Conventions" - Cartoon

To show you another level of Exceptionalism, – If you recall, the Iraqis also captured US soldiers early in the war, with Jessica Lynch and Shoshana Johnson (a Black woman) included. After the Iraqis mockingly ran televised footage of the spooky-eyed US POWs trembling with fear,

US government officials immediately hollered foul play, saying the Iraqis were "violating the Geneva Conventions."[85]

Based on prewar reports, the American public had preconceptions that Saddam Hussein's government was notorious for persecuting its own people for trivial reasons. Speculations therefore swirled that American POWs would undergo vile and ruthless torturing. Highly paid analysts, retired generals, and so-called military experts appeared on every television channel with stone faces, postulating how females would be sexually abused and that Hussein would personally give orders for beheadings.

But in anticlimactic fashion – None of this happened. None of the initial POWs were tortured, raped, or killed while in Iraqi custody. Everyone returned in relative good shape, although some got roughed up. But all were basically treated humanely, even to the extent of receiving medical attention that included life-saving surgery for Lynch.

By her own accounts Lynch was well cared for by sympathetic doctors who even tried to return her, but were turned back when their ambulance came under US fire.[86] She was assigned the only special bed in the hospital and attended to by 1 of only 2 nurses on the floor, who later said, "I was like a mother to her and she was like a daughter."[87] At an April 2007 congressional hearing on "Misleading War Information," Lynch criticized the Pentagon, saying: "I'm still confused why they lied and tried to make me into a legend."[88]

Exceptionalism or not, the Iraqis objectively scored higher on their treatment of POWs than did the US. Unlike America's treatment of Iraqi POWs, there were no hooded prisoners connected to electrodes or handcuffed in bizarre stress positions. No waterboarding. No sexual pyramids or forced masturbation or smearing of menstruation blood. No dog leashes, dog bites, or dog attacks.

It's little wonder why the United Nations disapproves of America's "blanket exemption" from war crimes, or why even Colin Powell himself said: "The world is beginning to doubt the moral basis of our fight against terrorism.[89]

Naturally though, because of Exceptionalism the US government doesn't care what the United Nations thinks. Euro-American officials are not open to the idea of having other nations meddling around in America's sovereign affairs. This is especially true considering that future acquisitions of energy resources are at stake in both Iraq and Afghanistan. . . . Herein is situated a strategic point of intersection where Military Exceptionalism converges with Economic Exceptionalism.

Economic Exceptionalism

A false notion has fostered through Exceptionalism that the world would be more secure with the "democratization" of all nations. Since the World Wars and the Cold War, America has energetically sought to promote and export its democratic ideals abroad. According to the *US Foreign Policy Encyclopedia*, adherents to Exceptionalism who advocate US expansion and intervention in the affairs of other nations believe that:

> Unlike other nations, the United States is incapable of seeking dominion over other peoples in its self-interest. The American government will project its power abroad not to subjugate other nations but to help them become like the United States, to become free and democratic. These Americans seem to believe that inside every foreigner there is the potential, even the desire, to be an American. This assumption has led Americans to find it very difficult to understand that other peoples may place different values on things and have different perceptions from Americans of how the world should be.[90]

In an international sense, Exceptionalism is geared towards expanding both Americanization and capitalism. Tactics change and increase in sophistication over time, but the objective remains constant.

Although "freedom and democracy" are accepted catchphrases used to conceal underlying capitalist motives, wealth and resources always factor heavily in military decisions. Before the last bombs are dropped in any war, America wants to politically ensure its share of resource distributions.

This craving is not limited to energy and mineral resources alone. Human resources (enslaved or cheap laborers) have been just as crucial to capitalist expansion, which is why America never sent troops to Africa to "fight for freedom and democracy" against European colonialism. The US government was in fact a silent partner and beneficiary of Africa's occupation. Colonialism served as a reliable vehicle to acquire strategic resources, so the US government never felt an Evangelical *calling* to end terrorism in Africa, especially since it would have involved drawing blood from their European cousins. When it comes to relations between Euro-Americans and Africans, "Blood is thicker than democracy."

None of the near-40 million Blacks who now comfortably call America "home" are here because of freedom or democracy. Our presence is tied to capitalistic greed. Keep in mind that as *captive* laborers, we were the first substantial form of *capital* in America's formative years of *capitalism*, from which eventuated America's entire System of Capitalism. There's a cyclical and tightly intertwined correlation whereby direct lines can be drawn from point to point, linking the historical dots that connect captives, capital, and capitalism.

Extreme measures are no longer overtly used for capitalist expansion. Yet, as a high-tech industrialized nation, America is so resource-addicted that the international availability of certain resources impacts the economy's health. So even though slave-trading is a retired policy, contemporary history shows a troubling and aggressive trend in military and foreign policies whenever America's international access to strategic resources (e.g., oil, cobalt, coltan, chromium, uranium) becomes limited or threatened.

Wealth, resources, and productivity in America are tied to a long ongoing history of depravity and indifference towards non-Western nations and people. Even though this is clearly the case, Exceptionalism

150

has a way of steering Americans to think that America is efficient and prosperous because of the intellect and ingenuity of Americans. But to quote journalist Ron Jacobs:

America is not a better country than any other. . . . The only thing that sets us apart is our wealth. The only reason we have that wealth is because we stole it. God didn't give it to us, nor did any greater American intelligence or know-how. Robbery is what our foreign policy is based on, just like our racial policies. It's not the policies that need to change, but the foundation upon which those policies flourish. Until US activists accept this and give up their conscious and unconscious acceptance of the myth of American exceptionalism, any movement against war, racism, and other ills of our world is bound to fail.

Capitalism is an economic and political system that has no morals. It is not immoral, nor is it moral. It is amoral. In order to survive, it must expand, either by moving its operations into new regions or by taking over other capitalist ventures and their markets. Usually, the most successful capitalists employ both means. In recent history, the most successful capitalists have been mostly American. The fact that the US spends more money on weaponry and war is directly related to that phenomenon.[91]

The relationship Jacob describes between expansion and war spending, has become somewhat of an "unspoken law" that governs economic development in today's dog-eat-dog political world. You've probably heard the war adage: "To the victors go the spoils." Well, chief among the spoils in this age are strategic natural resources and degrees of political/economic hegemony over weaker governments. For this reason, there's little that America and other strong nations won't do to acquire and safeguard these modern spoils.

The growing military budgets of governments worldwide are not only testaments to this "unspoken law" but also testaments to increasing aggressions and distrust among nations. Along with a host of other factors, these variables are responsible for mountains of money being funneled into a "Global War Economy" where investors reap exponential profits.

Global military spending topped the $1 trillion mark in 2004 for the first time since the Cold War.[92] The increase is due in large part to "the US war against terror and the growing defense budgets of India and China."[93] Details from the Stockholm International Peace Research Institute's (SPIRI) *2008 Year Book on Armaments, Disarmament and International Security* cite:

- World military expenditure is estimated to have reached $1.339 trillion in 2007.

- This corresponds to 2.5 per cent of World Gross Domestic Product, or $202 for every person in the world.

- World military expenditure presents a real terms increase of 6 per cent since 2006, and 45 per cent since 1998.

- The USA is responsible for 48 per cent of the world total, distantly followed by the UK, China, France and Japan with 4 - 5 per cent each.[94]

Speculations and improprieties have long surrounded the billions in military contracts received by Halliburton, the company formerly headed by Vice President Cheney. Controversy however is not just limited to Halliburton alone. Some corporations are profiting from the production of weaponry and war technology that have little if anything to do with the so-called war against terrorism or curtailing the reasons behind events of 9/11.

Columbia professor Richard K. Betts pointed out in *Foreign Affairs* magazine: "With rare exceptions, the war against terrorists cannot be fought with army tank battalions, air force wings, or naval fleets – the large conventional forces that drive the defense budget. The main challenge is not killing the terrorists but finding them, and the capabilities most applicable to this task are intelligence and special operations forces. . . . It does not require half a trillion dollars worth of conventional and nuclear forces."[95]

Excesses in military productions and expenditures are no accident. It's all part of a stratagem involving interlocking corporations that have cozy relationships with the military, Defense Department, State Department, and the Pentagon. Together they comprise an elaborate and sometimes covert network that has been called the US Military Industrial Complex (MIC). This term gained popularity after a 1961 speech of President Dwight Eisenhower, wherein he cautioned of its dangers and "spiritual influences," as follows:

> A vital element in keeping the peace is our military establishment. Our arms must be mighty, ready for instant action, so that no potential aggressor may be tempted to risk his own destruction...
>
> This conjunction of an immense military establishment and a large arms industry is new in the American experience. The total influence – economic, political, even spiritual – is felt in every city, every statehouse, every office of the federal government. We recognize the imperative need for this development. Yet we must not fail to comprehend its grave implications. Our toil, resources and livelihood are all involved; so is the very structure of our society.
>
> In the councils of government, we must guard against the acquisition of unwarranted influence, whether sought or unsought, by the *Military-Industrial Complex*. The potential for the disastrous rise of misplaced power exists and will persist.
>
> We must never let the weight of this combination endanger our liberties or democratic processes. We should take nothing for granted. Only an alert and knowledgeable citizenry can compel the proper meshing of the huge industrial and

military machinery of defense with our peaceful methods and goals so that security and liberty may prosper together.[96]

This same MIC that Eisenhower said was "new in the American experience," has since become a well-oiled machine that has enlarged in scale and sophistication, generating billions in "war profit" for handfuls of select members. The profits and chief interest of these companies revolve around service contracts to manufacture military necessities like bombs, bullets, tanks, helicopters and other depreciable/exhaustible military hardware and equipment that requires constant repair, resupply, and/or replacement. A news article titled "Combat Keeps Arms Factories at Full Capacity" stated:

Fighting in Iraq and increased training back home are straining the military's supplies – and giving manufacturers in the United States a surge in business.

"There's no question that on many of the items that are being consumed rapidly in Iraq, like tank treads, like body armor, like small-caliber ammunition, the Army is beginning to run out, and the Army is becoming worried about its stockpile," said Loren Thompson, a defense analyst with the Lexington Institute.

. . . Tread usage is 5 to 10 times as high as in peacetime. Small-caliber bullet usage has more than doubled since 2001. Finding enough batteries for equipment like night-vision gear and radios has been tough.

Alliant Techsystems is churning out 1.2 billion bullets a year at the Army-owned plant it runs in Independence, Mo. – but it's already working 24 hours a day. So the Army has given contracts for 70 million rounds each to Israel Military Industries Ltd. and the Winchester unit of Olin Corp., said Lt. Col. Matthew Butler. . . .

Butler said he's trying to line up other bulletmakers for a total of 2 billion rounds a year of capacity, in case demand surges even more.[97]

Since 9/11 the MIC has added a new branch for revenues that thrives partially through use of shifty scare tactics. Some corporations and individuals parade themselves as security and terrorist "experts" who *self-generate* the source of their profits by "crying terrorist wolf." This intensifies public apprehensions and keeps false shockwaves of anxieties rippling throughout society. By keeping people edgy with terrorist jitters, they in turn profit from security and consultant contracts to "protect America" from an array of "theoretical dangers" that have yet to prove credible.

Anytime there's smoke or an unknown loud noise or a power outage in a city, news flashes appear on television, followed by some so-called terrorist expert who immediately begins hypothesizing about what "might" be occurring. Yet in advance of 9/11 when expertise was needed, none of these experts were anywhere to be found. Hijacked airliners were choreographed to fly into building after building for almost an hour before any "expert" ever knew what happened.

Judging from the military's own comedy of errors, these experts may need to protect the public from "F-Troop" blunders of the US military. In a mix-up in March 2008, instead of sending batteries for helicopters to Taiwan, nuclear fuses for intercontinental ballistic missiles were mistakenly delivered.[98] Earlier in August 2007 the Air Force flew 6 nuclear-tipped cruise missiles from a base in North Dakota to a base in Louisiana, without the pilots even knowing nuclear arms were aboard.[99]

Profits are nevertheless mounting sky-high for terrorist experts and security companies. Consulting firms specializing in terrorist-related businesses neared the $3 billion mark in 2006.[100] Many hire former US government spies and ex-military officers as executives and board members to make their pitch more plausible.[101] Men like former New York mayor and presidential candidate Rudy Giuliani have raked in wheelbarrows of money acting as experts of this burgeoning branch of the MIC.

Giuliani made almost $11 million dollars in 2006 by capitalizing on 9/11-related security speeches.[102] His multifaceted multimillion-dollar consulting firm, Giuliani Partners, "advises security companies and promotes their products, many of which have been marketed to federal agencies."[103] In March 2007 he profited undisclosed millions from selling the investment banking arm of Giuliani Partners that he originally acquired for $9.8 million in 2004.[104]

In his twin role as a presidential candidate and beneficiary of the "Global War Economy," he attempted to spook voters to his side and simultaneously boost profits for the war industry through his "cry wolf" campaign, by propping himself up as some sort of rare "security specialist" who knows how to "protect the country from terrorism." But in all actuality, the World Trade Center was destroyed on his watch while he was mayor, while he was just as oblivious to the attacks and attackers as you and I. He did nothing to prevent anything or protect anybody. His subsequent reactions were the equivalent of "closing the barn door after the horse had gone." All the damage had already been done and the attacks were already over. If he's an "expert" based on 9/11, then anyone who has ever given cough medicine to a child is a pediatric surgeon.

Another person of this ilk with a wheelbarrow for his money is Tom Ridge, who was the first Secretary of Homeland Security and former governor of Pennsylvania. He and close friend David Girard-diCarlo (chairman of the Blank Rome lobbying firm) raised $400,000 for Bush's 2000 campaign, and Girard-diCarlo raised significant funds for Ridge's campaign as governor.[105] On the day after Homeland Security was created in 2002, Ridge flew to Girard-diCarlo's home in Arizona for two nights, and then visited him at least twice shortly after his Secretary appointment.[106]

Despite their deep history of financial relations, Ridge's office maintained that the two *never* discussed money, clients, or business during these visits; yet a month after his initial visit, the first of two of Ridge's aides left Homeland Security to work for Girard-diCarlo, "focusing on homeland security issues."[107] Reports filed with Congress shortly thereafter verify that Blank Rome lobbied Homeland Security on behalf of at least 33 clients – One client, Raytheon, was awarded a $10 billion border protection contract and another client, BearingPoint, got a $229 million contract.[108]

According to the Institute for Policy Studies, since September 11th, 2003, the top 34 CEOs of the defense industry earned a combined 1 billion dollars in salaries by 2006.[109] Multimillionaire John Negroponte, who Bush appointed as the first intelligence chief, held substantial stock (referred to as "War Stock") in several major corporations involved in the reconstruction of Iraq, including Citigroup, General Electric, and GE Capital.[110] The following article from *Parade* magazine, titled "Making Money Off Iraq," lists other officials who are cashing in on the War Economy:"

Being an Iraq war planner has paid off for some US officials. Former CIA Director George Tenet negotiated a $4 million book deal. Paul Wolfowitz – [former] No. 2 at the Pentagon – had a $300,000 tax-free annual salary, a mortgage allowance and a golf-club membership. Retired Gen. Tommy Franks, who led the invasion, reportedly collected $5 million for his memoirs; he now serves on the board of Outback steakhouses; and Camden County, NJ, paid him $75,000 for a speech. Paul Bremer reportedly gets as much as $40,000 to speak and received more than $100,000 for a book about his year as US administrator in Iraq. By contrast, what do the folks fighting the war make? A private earns $3,104 a month; a corporal, $3,637; a captain, $6,373, and a one-star general, $12,809.[111]

Not only has the MIC expanded in production, but likewise in questionable activities and outright corruption. Randy "Duke" Cunningham, a Vietnam fighter pilot and former eight-term Congressman from California, cried crocodile tears after pleading guilty to bribery, fraud, and tax evasion.[112] This was after he had wheelbarrowed $2.4 million from

157

defense contractors in "exchange for government business and other favors. . . . Investigators said Cunningham, a member of a House Appropriations subcommittee that controls defense dollars, secured contracts worth tens of millions of dollars for those who paid him off."[113]

Perpetual cycles of MIC-related monies have been defrauded, misappropriated, and just plain old-fashioned stolen. In 2004 the Coalition Provisional Authority (CPA), which is a civilian oversight body set up by the US in Iraq, uncovered $1 billion in unaccounted funds that were supposedly spent on reconstruction projects.[114]

> The [CPA] investigators reviewed 43 contracts and found 29 had incomplete or missing documentation. For each of the 29, "we were unable to determine if the goods specified in the contract were ever received, the total amount of payments made to the contractor or if the contractor fully complied with the terms of the contracts," investigators wrote.[115]

Also, according to the *Associated Press* at least 10 US companies with billions in Iraqi reconstruction contracts were penalized over $300 million in fines from 2000 to 2004.[116] Charges range from fraud, to bid rigging, to environmental damages, to delivering faulty military parts. Some of the companies and their fines included: Northrop Grumman Corporation, $191.7 million; Lockheed Martin, $85.5 million; Fluor Corporation, $8.5 million; Computer Sciences Corporation, $6.4 million; and American International Contractors Inc., $4.7 million.[117]

> The contracts are legal because the Bush administration repealed regulations put in place by the Clinton administration that would have allowed officials to bar new government work for companies convicted or penalized during the previous three years. . . . The Bush administration suspended the new rules during its first three months in office, and revoked them in December 2001.[118]

As a side hustle to subsidize the MIC, the US military also dabbles its hands in the gambling business. To offer what it describes as "touches of home," overseas military bases come complete with thousands of slot machines that scraped $130 million in loot from soldiers in 2006.[119] "Critics say it is an outrage that the military, which has a budget of more than $500 billion, takes money from the pockets of its troops and runs slot machines that generate revenues that equal a medium-sized Las Vegas casino operation."[120]

All of the billions in war profits and the trillions spent on munitions may seem exorbitant on the surface. But these dollars are logistically and strategically necessary for the US establishment to achieve its larger Exceptionalist objective to install "allied governments" in Iraq and Afghanistan that will be at the beck and call of Washington. This will guarantee the US greater secured-access to the multibillion barrels of fresh oil and gas deposits that are bubbling throughout the Gulf region.

So in bulldozering forward with its capitalist tradition of expansion through extirpation, America is betting that its massive short-term war investments will ultimately pay off worthwhile in long-term spoils of war in the form of political control and resource acquisitions. But growing numbers of Muslims in the Gulf are wagering counter-bets and practicing Exceptionalism of their own. One thing that is certain is that the military/political struggle for energy resources in the Gulf is bound to intensify before subsiding.

In all fairness to Euro-Americans let me conclude by saying that it is neither inherently good nor bad for a people to pursue or practice Exceptionalist ways. All nations should strive to play Exceptional roles in world affairs. However, these roles should be unfailingly just, always principled, and never accomplished or maintained via indifferences or inhumanities against others.

To this end, I am convinced that there exists a special segment amongst Africans in America who can stand politically perpendicular on our own feet, without leaning on any European crutches. We too can carve ourselves a destiny that is just as great, just as noble, and just as Exceptional as any other government or society.

"The Constitution, on this hypothesis, is a mere thing of wax in the hands of the Judiciary, which they may twist and shape into any form they please."

Thomas Jefferson

"Americans will always do the right thing . . . after they've exhausted all the alternatives."

Winston Churchill

"It is not difficult to show for example, that the two great political parties in America represent only one English party . . ."

Seymour Martin Lipset, Author

"There isn't a dime's worth of difference between the Democratic and Republican Parties."

George Wallace, Alabama Governor and Presidential Candidate

5

Placebo Progress and Politics

<><><><><><><>

Majority "Whites-Only" Drinking Fountain

Within the current structure of American democracy, the Exceptional potential of Africans in America will always remain contained and underdeveloped. Perception may suggest otherwise, but there are strict limits to the level of political power that any minority group can amass in this country. The political predominance of Euro-Americans is fixed and unmatched in nature, and they indeed plan to keep it so.

There's a general "pecking order" of power in every ethnically diverse industrialized nation, starting with the group most able to leverage their capital into political might. One sure measurement of any peoples'

161

political power, or lack thereof, is found in the degree to which they control the government and economic activities of their nation. All other measures (i.e., constitutional rights, legislative reforms, voting acts) are more like political window dressings that may boost emotions, but lack in comparative substance to the power of those who hold the reigns of political and economic controls.

Similarly, people who've unknowingly taken sugar pills as medication have also experienced boosts in health. This "Placebo Effect" is due to what the FDA says is a person's "expectation" that the pill "will be helpful."[1] The *Dictionary of Behavioral Science* defines "Placebo" as: "A substance with no medicinal properties which causes a patient to improve because of his belief in its efficacy. It reinforces the patient's expectations, though it does not really act on the individual's condition."[2]

Behavioral scientists have found that, in addition to sugar pills, "conditioning agents" of Placebos can also be activated through "psychological associations." Patients are known to "enter a cure mode when something associated with a cure is present. It could be the setting – a doctor's office or a hospital – where one expects to get help."[3]

In much the same way, our association with Americanization has activated political Placebo Effects. Placebos (Civil Rights, Integration, Citizenship) have functioned as "conditioning agents" to give us expectations of power, when in reality these agents lack the necessary "political properties" for us to achieve the status (Sovereignty, Independence, Statehood) of Euro-Americans. When you add up the political scorecards, the total of all legislative reforms has not accrued enough power for us to equal the governmental authority or undo the political influence of Euro-Americans.

Much of what does or doesn't happen in the future to remedy our conditions hinges on what happens politically. Politics and policies will always affect our development. With the wide circulation of so much misinformation and misassumptions about voting, partisan platforms, and electing a Black president, these next two chapters fittingly probe Electoral

Politics and the Electoral Process, so as to evaluate where we as Black people rate on America's scale of political and governmental powers.

Being psychologically reared to accept "notions of equality," most Blacks may not think of themselves as being politically unequal or invisible, particularly since the ascension of President Barack Obama. During past eras of enslavement and segregation our inequality and invisibility was imposed through obvious legislation and force. Although things are not so obvious today, a more modern measure of our political inequality and invisibility can be gauged through the racial configuration of the highest levels of elected office – Governorships, the Senate, and the House of Representatives.

There is good news and bad news to this gauge. The good news is that at the time of this writing, Africans in America are proudly riding an all-time high of elected representatives in these offices. The bad news is that that there is a Placebo Effect to this progress since the "total number" of Blacks *ever* elected as governors and senators, to date, almost mirrors exactly the number at emancipation when there were 0 Black governors and 0 Black senators. . . . The more things seem to change, the more they really are the same.

To examine our Political Inequality, let's take a brief historical tour of the racial composition of these government offices. Keep in mind that political life for us did not begin with our introduction to America, since Africa had sovereign kingdoms and city-states prior to our enslavement. So, for us to have minimal representation in any European government is not something to stick out our chest and boast about.

Fact One: There are always 50 governors seated in office; 1 representing each state. But when you do the math, you'll see that there have only been 2* elected Black governors in history. Douglas Wilder, being the first, was governor of Virginia from 1990 to 1994. Duval Patrick, the second, was elected governor of Massachusetts in 2006. David Patterson, who became New York's governor in 2008, was not elected (hence the asterisk*), but as Lt. Governor he "assumed" the governorship after Eliot Spitzer was forced to resign for getting snagged in a prostitution sting where he was soliciting and paying for sex.

Factor into these numbers as well, the political declivity of Governor Wilder after his term. The office of governor is the best-known path to the White House these days. Bush Jr., Clinton, Reagan, and Carter were all former governors. When Wilder sought the presidency in 1992 he was met with one door after another slamming faster and harder. Instead of springboarding to the presidency, he nosedived over a 15-year period from the height of being "governor" of the state of Virginia in 1990 to "mayor" of the city of Richmond in 2005.[4]

Fact Two: There are always 100 members in the US Senate; 2 representatives for each state. Prior to Barack Obama's 2004 election, only 2 other Blacks had ever been elected to the traditionally all-White Senate since Reconstruction (1866 – 1877). Edward William Brook was Senator of Massachusetts from 1967 to 1979. Carol Moseley Braun was Senator of Illinois from 1993 to 1999. Excluding Obama, this means that since 1877 we have only had Senate representation for a total of 18 measly years. This is wholly unacceptable by any measure for a people who underwent 246 years of enslavement under the same government.

Fact Three: Of the 435 members in the House of Representatives of the 110th Congress, only 42 are Black, constituting less than 10 percent. Having a few Black faces mingled in the halls of Congress may seem like progress, but it is really nothing more than continued repression in modern disguise. I make this assertion because a core issue dating all the way back to slavery that remains unchanged and unaddressed, is that, our political relationship with Euro-Americans has historically been based on – them governing over us. Think about it. It is no exaggeration that since 1619, there has not been a single second in time that they have not governed over us.

Up until the mid-1960s, "Whites Only" signs were ubiquitously plastered from coast to coast. Suppose that "Whites Only" signs reappeared on water fountains today. Boy, talk about being outraged. Black leaders and civil rights groups would be huffin' and puffin' all over the news – As though the signs were "proof" that something has gone awry.

Although you won't see "Whites Only" signs today, you don't need actual signs to verify "proof" of inequality. Living under a White-dominated and controlled government with little or no Black representation is the political equivalent of 21st-century "proof" of a modern-day "Whites Only" water fountain of inequality. The only difference between signs and no signs, lie in perception and sophistication of the times.

Majority "Whites Only" Political Water Fountain

Governors
50 Total Members with Just 2 Blacks (Only 2* Elected Blacks in History)

Senators
100 Total Members (Only 3 Elected Blacks Since Reconstruction)

House of Representatives
435 Total Members with Just 42 Blacks (Less Than 10%)

Document 7. "Whites Only" Political Water Fountain document

After almost three and a half centuries of slavery and segregation, how can we regard ourselves as equal to Euro-Americans when they have overwhelmingly controlled all major political seats to this degree? There can never be such a thing as Political Equality as long as Euro-Americans reside at the top of the government foodchain as they do. Laws and constitutional amendments may profess equality on paper, but the Placebo realities of these numbers tell a much different and very disturbing story.

Albert Einstein, who was a close observer of social details, once spoke about "notions of equality" in the 1940s in a way that somewhat explains why and how such a racial imbalance can continue to persist uncontested in government today. He said:

There is, however, a somber point in the social outlook of Americans. Their sense of equality and human dignity is mainly limited to men of white skins. Even among these there are prejudices of which I as a Jew am clearly conscious; but they are unimportant in comparison with the attitude of the "Whites" toward their fellow-citizens of darker complexion, particularly toward Negroes. The more I feel an American, the more this situation pains me. I can escape the feeling of complicity in it only by speaking out.

Many a sincere person will answer: "Our attitude towards Negroes is the result of unfavorable experiences which we have had by living side by side with Negroes in this country. They are not our equals in intelligence, sense of responsibility, reliability."

I am firmly convinced that whoever believes this suffers from a fatal misconception. Your ancestors dragged these black people from their homes by force; and in the white man's quest for wealth and an easy life they have been ruthlessly suppressed and exploited, degraded into slavery. The modern prejudice against Negroes is the result of the desire to maintain this unworthy condition.[5]

Within democratic norms of settlement to conflicts and disputes, it is commonplace for opposition members and representatives of repressed people to receive key cabinet and political posts in ruling governments. Kenya, for example reveled-in the 2008 New Year with a bloody upheaval. Although America never implemented such a "power-sharing" policy with us, the US government made "explicit requests" to Kenyan President Mwai Kabaki to assign government posts to opposition party members.[6] Zimbabwe reached a power-sharing compromise where President Robert Mugabe agreed for Morgan Tsvangirai to become Prime Minister.[7]

Probably the majority of us know in our hearts that we too should do something about the political dominance of Euro-Americans. Yet our silence conveys capitulation. When do you remember a mass uproar or a national conference to address the racial imbalance of Congress? Though you don't hear a peep from Black leaders on this issue, nothing is unreasonable about a repressed people demanding voice and visibility in the government that governs them.

As great as it was, the Civil Rights Movement did not pursue any power-sharing or reconfiguration of the government, thereby leaving a gaping escape hatch for Euro-Americans to get away clean without any real transfers of authority. Because we've since been lured through Placebos to think that "we are already equal," we feel no present need to demand a minimum percentage of congressional seats or key political posts. We've become so accepting and so accustomed to being underrepresented, that it doesn't even vaguely compute within our political senses that we are being blatantly taken advantage of.

In comparing and contrasting the parallels, you'll find that it didn't take Euro-Americans 4 centuries to understand the value of having political and governmental control over their affairs. When they similarly faced circumstances of inequality and invisibility, they called it "Taxation without Representation" and then went to war in response. Yet they now ironically subject us to the exact conditions they've already condemned and deemed unacceptable for themselves. Regrettably, we accept the very political circumstances that they not only rejected, but warred against.

Let me cut through all the political fog of race and inequality to sum all this up in a single sentence: Euro-Americans expect and receive levels of political compliance from us that they in kind would never accord to us. Political Equality for us is therefore nonexistent and impossible as long as we allow them to politically "do unto us" what they would never allow us to politically "do unto them."

<><><><><><><><>

Seeking "Approvals" for Voting Rights

About 10,000 people marched across the Edmund Pettus Bridge in Selma, Alabama in March 2005 to mark the 40th anniversary of Dr. King's 1965 demonstration for voting rights.[8] "President Lyndon Johnson signed the Voting Rights Act (VRA) in August 1965, months after black civil rights protesters were savagely beaten in Selma, Alabama."[9]

Contrary to what is commonly believed however, the VRA does not constitutionally "guarantee" voting rights. It rather provides protection from "voting discriminations." According to Congressman Jesse Jackson Jr., "Technically, it is misnamed. It should have been called the 1965 *Non-Discrimination* in Voting Act."[10]

Certain provisions of the VRA are also subject to congressional "approval and renewal" every 25 years, and 2007 marked the last due-date for expiration.[11] At the 2005 march, Rev. Joseph Lowery of the Southern Christian Leadership Conference (SCLC), who also marched with Dr. King in Selma, "urged the nearly three dozen House and Senate members who participated to renew those portions of the law."[12] He went on to say: "Their presence here is a mockery unless they go home and do the right thing."[13]

Then in August 2005, thousands more participated in a "Keep the Vote Alive March" in Atlanta, chanting and singing songs like, "We Shall Overcome."[14] Congressman John Lewis (who got "savagely beaten" during the Selma march with Dr. King) told the crowd, "Forty years later, we're still marching for the right to vote. . . . Don't give up, don't give in. Keep the faith, keep your eyes on the prize"[15]

Lewis' words to me are more troubling than inspiring. The fact that we have to actually march in the 2000s for *anything*, especially voting, is a political affront as I see it. What do we owe Euro-Americans that justify our marching in the hot streets for political permission slips from them in the 21st century? You would think from the lopsidedness of the relationship that they are our political overseers or that we have some kind of a political deficiency that only they can administer to.

When Rev. Lowery's comment is respectfully analyzed from a sovereign context, the real "mockery" has nothing to do with whether White politicians "do the right thing." The real mockery is that we remain in an unprincipled political relationship with a European people who hold "parental authority" to conditionally approve what they feel is politically best for us. The real mockery is that Black soldiers militarily support and defend the very same constitution which does not adequately secure our voting rights.

Aside from expecting or relying on others to "do the right thing" for us, action should be taken beyond their approvals. Thus far Congressman Jackson Jr. has introduced *House Joint Resolution 38*, which according to him contains provisions to constitutionally secure voting rights in ways not addressed by the 15th, 19th, and 26th Amendments.[16] Four provisions are listed below; the second unfortunately is tied to war.

First it would give every American an individual right to vote. *Second* when Americans turn 18 (male and female) and are required to register with the Selective Service System they would *at the same time automatically* be registered to vote. The Selective Service System would send their voter registration to their local board of election and in the future the US Postal Service would automatically transfer any change of address from the old local board of election to the new board of election. *Third*, while this amendment does not eliminate the Electoral College it does require the Electoral College vote in every state to reflect the majority popular vote in that state. *Fourth* it would give Congress the power and authority to make laws that would provide a unitary voting system that is fair to all - that is, give every American citizen an equal access to vote, shield our voting system from fraud and abuse, insure that every vote is accurately counted, and review our voting system every four years to make sure it is the best and most secure voting system in the world.[17]

Although Congress did renew the VRA in 2007 for another 25 years, there are Placebo influences at work. The lesson here is not about how well American democracy works. To the contrary, this is a textbook illustration of what can happen to people who do not write their own constitution or participate in the actual writing of the constitution by which they are governed.

Trust me, Euro-Americans would never march from city to city, holding rallies in hopes that another people would approve legislation on their behalf. Before they would ever allow anybody to decide any portion of their political fate they would crank up the jetfighters for a spin, drop bunker-buster bombs, and never miss a wink of sleep worrying about the death toll. Bombs and freedom are flipsides to their coin of democracy. Fighting and dying in great numbers for their sovereignty is something they've never hesitated to do.

Since we as a people are obviously not fighting and dying for our sovereignty, then we should seriously ask and answer the question – How do we define "the prize" of freedom that John Lewis referred to?

It seems our prize has always centered on securing "rights." But there are definitive differences between "fighting for freedom" and "fighting for rights." This too is something that Euro-Americans understood early in their struggle. According to *Britannia*, "Before the Declaration [of Independence] the revolutionaries had seen their cause as mainly fighting for their *rights* as British subjects against a stubborn English Parliament; after the Declaration, they saw their fight as necessary to protect their *natural rights as free men* against a tyrannical and out-of-touch king. This indeed was a cause worth fighting for."[18] (Italics my own.)

Even though all roads of our political pursuits are routed through Euro-Americans who have the power to confirm or deny our interests, I'm not sure if the majority of Africans in America are prepared to become "free enough" to alter the unprincipled nature of this relationship. The weight of this rests squarely on us, because the records of history show that people do not fight and die to achieve sovereignty and then turn around voluntarily to equally and altruistically share the control panels with other races of people.

As obsessed as Euro-Americans are with amassing political and economic powers, we should know by now that they are among the last people on earth that would politically or economically empower others, especially if the process entails disempowering themselves in any way. History confirms that they are takers, not givers. They do not give without expectant returns in some form. They give to gain. They only *give* as much as expediently *necessary* in the short term, in order to *gain* as much as strategically *possible* in the long term.

This government will therefore gladly *give* us an Act in order to *gain* our continued loyalty, especially during a time when America's international reputation and ideological influence is on the hot-seat from being embroiled in an unjust, unwinnable war that has vexed far more Muslims than it has "freed."

For the sake of salvaging their image, Euro-Americans could not afford to have the whole world watch them tamper further with our voting rights, while they simultaneously blabber rhetoric about freedom and democracy in Iraq. Renewing the VRA was therefore an easy tradeoff that was more of a Placebo than a "significant breakthrough" as described by Congressman Jesse Jackson Jr.[19]

And just so you'll know for the years ahead, the fact that Euro-Americans are fast becoming a "demographic minority" in their own country is not unrelated to why the VRA must be reviewed in 25-year increments. Don't think for a moment that this establishment is democratically dumb enough to sit idle and watch themselves get outvoted by ex-enslaved Blacks and day-laborer Mexicans.

<><><><><><><>

Deja-Vu Defeats of Black Candidates

Voting is hyped up in America as an instrument that makes democracy superior to all other systems of government. Due to our long history of being forcibly denied the right to vote, we naturally take tremendous pride and have a particularly high reverence for voting since it marks a pivotal milestone in our still-emerging political experience.

Meanwhile, as we have understandably placed great energy and emphasis on honoring the people and events of history that made voting possible, our issue of being underrepresented in Congress remains untouched, even though it looms large as ever. It's not enough to laud the mere 40-something members of the Congressional Black Caucus as "progress," or to believe that "the Voting Rights Act has worked" as postulated in the pages of the *Covenant with Black America*.[20]

Generally speaking, having the "right to vote" is one thing, however having "true political representation" that supports your needs is quite another. Yes, voters do elect representatives. But as in our case, the racial imbalance of Congress verifies the fact that, just because an ethnic or minority group engages in the *act* of voting, doesn't necessarily translate into guaranteed representation for them.

Technically, an ethnic group can vote for a winning candidate and belong to a winning party, yet still lack true representation if the candidate or party is uncommitted and unresponsive to addressing their political specificities. So, it is quite possible for people who vote in democratic elections to face varying degrees of "political irrelevance."

Again, because of "notions of equality" most of us do not think of ourselves as being politically irrelevant, especially since America now has a Black president. Let's be honest, though – comparatively so, Euro-Americans have always maintained the upper hand in determining who and what is politically relevant or irrelevant.

A revealing but unintended testimony of our irrelevance came disguised as an honor when Bill Clinton eulogized Ossie Davis. To the rousing applause of the crowd, he remarked that Davis "would have been a very good President of the United States."[21] You may wonder how such an accolade relates to political irrelevance. Well, when you evaluate the competence of the Euro-American men who've become president, it is certainly plausible that Davis "would have been a very good president."

However, the real issue is not "would he," but rather "could he" have actually been president? Everybody with common sense knows that he and Black men and women of similar age and caliber couldn't even get elected governor or senator – So forget about "president."

Barack Obama (who is the exception, not the rule of American politics) needed Secret Service protection in May of 2007 due to credible threats against his life. With 18 months prior to the election, this was the earliest any presidential candidate had ever received the agency's protection.[22] Given the agency's recent racial discrimination law suits and hanging nooses found at its headquarters, legitimate question marks can be raised about how secure a Black man will be in the hands of agents.[23]

Interestingly, radio host Don Imus said in December of 2006 that it's "dangerous" for a Black man to run for the presidency, and that "they" [Whites] would have shot [Black] Congressman Harold Ford, Jr. (D-Tenn.) "if they had to" to prevent him from winning a Senate seat in Tennessee.[24] Imus later admitted that he himself "received death threats" for publicly supporting Ford.[25]

Ford was favored to win. He's young, popular, smart, squeaky clean with proven leadership skills, and he rose successfully through the knocks and ranks of the House of Representatives. He ran a very inclusive, centrist, colorblind campaign but he lost to a Euro-American who arguably paled comparatively in every major account and category. The problem was that, many Whites who gave Ford rah-rah-rah support in public, did not vote for him. On Chris Matthews' *Decision 2006: Battleground America*, an all-White panel called this "a hidden vote against African Americans."[26]

Other names like Lynn Swann, Kweisi Mfume, Ken Blackwell, and Michael Steele surface as a recent batch of Black candidates who experienced "Déja-Vu Defeats" and learned that White people don't and won't vote in numbers significant enough to elect Blacks to high offices. Rev. Jesse Jackson Sr. and Rev. Al Sharpton learned this lesson earlier as they too held hopes of elected office that could not materialize. Then you can go from state to state and compile a long list of qualified Blacks who've had unsuccessful runs for the House.

Whether you believe it or not, another more stealth factor that I surmise is that there appears to be unvoiced resentment related to the Civil Rights Generation that has pricked some lasting nerves of older Whites. Just as every White institution and individual didn't rejoice when slavery ended in past times, the same is true when segregation ended in our lifetime.

America doesn't like to be cited for its flaws, and certain elements within this establishment do not like looking at the faces of Black people who conjure bad memories related to the correcting of its civil rights flaws. Not to be crass, but if 50 of the most prominent Black men and women from the civil rights era were glued together, they wouldn't comprise a candidate worthy enough for these elements to support or fund to the White House.

Obama however is much different from the rank-and-file "old school" leaders. He is considered a "safe risk," which means he represents a more fully-Americanized ilk of Black politicians who are politically divorced from confronting systemic flaws of Americanization and the endemic nature of racial inequities. Once a Black person "crosses the line" to broach systemic/endemic issues of injustice, they are forever regarded as "damaged goods" because the establishment knows there's always a possibility they may revert back to the other side of the line, and perhaps "get too big for their britches" while holding a high elected office.

Unfortunately, some of the "Déja-Vu Defeated" and other Blacks who've witnessed these routine defeats aren't deterred from filling their pockets with money from the very corporate and political coffers that thwart our political rise. Knowing that they themselves can never be a governor or senator, they board the gravy-train as "party consultants" and "political strategists" whose job is to publicly endorse White candidates and assist in increasing Black voter turnouts, while lip-syncing party viewpoints.

174

If you've noticed, there's now a "political business club" of Blacks who fly First Class to political events and have the cell phone numbers of establishment people. Though they have no political power themselves, they always get to "hang around" people who do. The "political fad" for some is to be seen on television "grinning" at press conferences, standing behind rich White politicians who run for office or make announcements. Since in recent decades we couldn't even enter the same buildings where political press events occur, their presence is meant to convey the Placebo impression of African-American progress and power.

The issue of who and what is politically relevant has particularly interesting implications when Rev. Al Sharpton's unfulfilled political aspirations are contrasted with the fulfilled political aspirations of the late Senator Strom Thurmond – Especially since Thurmond's family is the former slaveholder of Sharpton's family. Records published in February 2007 confirm that Thurmond's ancestors "owned some of Sharpton's enslaved ancestors in South Carolina."[27]

Thurmond had a storied Senate career, whereas Sharpton is shutout from ever knowing the feel of being a senator. As polar opposites in life and on the political spectrum, the ironies of their inverted experiences transcend them both as individuals. Their divergent pathways have national and historic reaches that dig deep into undealt-with issues of racial and political inequalities that are camouflaged by all the perceptions of government and pageantry of electoral politics.

A snapshot paradox of their careers shows that, not counting his presidential run in 2004, Sharpton also lost races for State Senator of New York in 1978; US Senator of New York in 1992 and 1994; and Mayor of New York in 1997.[28] Despite his civil rights notoriety and connections to the "White world," he's been unable to win any public office, even though the media airs his political commentary and bills him as a top African American "leader" everywhere he goes.

Thurmond however, a confirmed racist and segregationist with the sexual proclivities of his slaveowning ancestors (he secretly fathered a child with a Black woman, even though he publicly despised Black people), served a remarkable 49 years in the US Senate.[29] Being elected in 1954, his tenure represented nearly a quarter of the Senate's 214-year history when he retired in 2003 at age 100. In 1997 he became the longest-serving senator in US history, only later surpassed by Senator Robert C. Byrd in 2006.[30]

For the record, Byrd is a Democrat and self-admitted former Ku Klux Klansman, (Exalted Cyclops in rank) who once vowed never to fight "with a Negro by my side," saying, "Rather, I should die a thousand times, and see Old Glory trampled in the dirt never to rise again, than to see this beloved land of ours become degraded by race mongrels, a throwback to the blackest specimen from the wilds."[31] As the President *pro tempore* of the Senate of the 110th Congress in 2008, he stood third in line to the presidency behind Vice President Dick Cheney and House Speaker Nancy Pelosi.

Thurmond set the Senate record in 1957 for filibustering for 24 hours and 18 minutes against civil rights.[32] He also helped author the *Southern Manifesto* in 1956, wherein southern legislators vowed resistance to school desegregation.[33] He said there weren't "enough troops in the army to force the southern people to break down segregation and admit the Negro race into our theatres, into our swimming pools, into our homes and into our churches."[34] Yet he could not resist the beauty of a Black woman.

My intent is not to pick on either Sharpton or Thurmond because as I said, this goes beyond their public and private lives as individuals. This shows that what began as "personal chattelism" during the days of Thurmond's ancestors has transmuted into what is now a form of "political chattelism" that impugns the very democratic fibers and electoral standards that supposedly set America apart from so-called "undemocratic nations."

So hold your applause, because as much as Clinton may have seemingly commended Ossie Davis, by saying Davis "would have been a very good president," he was really pointing a subliminal finger at the unfair degree to which competent Africans in America are politically irrelevant under this system of government, while Euro-Americans with questionable characters get to determine policies that shape the nation.

This should prompt us to question why we willingly impede ourselves governmentally, knowing that qualified and deserving Black people are unable to take their rightful place as the political architects they are qualified, and even born to be. It doesn't make 21st-century sense for a people with our sovereign potential to continue to defer our political greatness.

<>><>><>><>><>><>><>>

Color, Kind, and Class of Candidates

Some might contend that "we are all Americans," and therefore color, class, and ancestry of government representatives is secondary or perhaps insignificant. Others might even argue that just because a person is Black in color, doesn't necessarily mean they will represent "African-American" interests.

In any case or whatever your position, we are and have always been underrepresented as African people, even though we have an abundance of intelligent, capable men and women who could and should be senators, governors, and president. But that would contradict the purpose of why our ancestors were clunked over the back of their heads and brought here in the first place.

In a 2006 interview Rev. Al Sharpton said he planned to spend a lot of time in Ohio and Pennsylvania because they were "running Blacks as Republicans" so he wanted to let Black voters know that the candidates "were our color, but not our kind."[35]

From what I see, the only "kind" of people who run are mainly Democrats or Republicans; the large majority of whom mostly share characteristics of being White, male millionaires from privileged backgrounds, who collectively comprise a private culture and class of men with power and prestige. Maybe I'm wrong, but I would even venture that most grew up in un-integrated environments away from everyday Black people, and they probably had their first up-close contacts with Blacks *after* entering the public arena.

Assumptions of such men being "our kind," are extensions of the "Master, *we* sick?" syndrome. If we took objective looks, we'd see that those who occupy high government seats have Euro-commonalities that make them "a *kind* unto themselves." Be they Democrats or Republicans, they have a greater political and cultural mutuality among themselves through their European heritage, than with us as Africans through party affiliation.

By tradition most Blacks are card-carrying Democrats who believe that the Democratic Party is "our party," and that Democratic philosophies and applications represent the political vehicle for our progress. Whenever Democratic leaders take partisan stances on whatever the issue may be, Black party members follow suit to support whatever the belief or position of the day may be. The Democratic machinery runs nonstop to ensure Black allegiance to the party, even to the extent of sometimes using child-like psychology.

Take the words of Democratic Party chairman Howard Dean as an example of this psychology in action. He had the nerve to offend the common sense of Black leaders and journalists at a San Francisco political forum, saying:

> "You know, the Republicans are not very friendly to different *kinds* of people. They're a pretty monolithic party. Pretty much, they all behave the same, and they all look the same. . . . It's pretty much a white Christian party. . . . Republicans always divide people.
>
> It does make a difference that we [Democrats] now have senior management that is African American . . . which means we're not going to have the white boys club make all the decisions anymore."[36] (Italics my own.)

If Republicans are a "white Christian" party, then what are Democrats – a "non-white, non-Christian" party? From the outside looking in, there does appear to be partisan boundaries between the parties. But could it be that the greatest differences lie more in perception than actuality? Could the varied stances that supposedly distinguish them exist more in *theory* among constituents, than in *practice* among the hierarchs?

This is not to suggest that there are no philosophical differences amongst candidates, party platforms, and ordinary folks who engage in barbershop and water-cooler conversations. But as I said, Republicans and Democrats represent a *single* political/ideological System of Thought that is by no means unconnected. To quote Gary Allen and Larry Abraham in their book, *None Dare Call It Conspiracy*, America has "Two political parties but only a single ideology."[37]

> Although there are philosophical differences between the grass roots Democrats and the grass roots Republicans, yet as you move up the party ladders these differences become less and less distinguishable until finally the ladder disappears behind the Establishment's managed news curtain and come together at the apex.[38]

You've probably heard the rationale that, "All Black people shouldn't belong to one party . . . We should be Republicans too. This way, Democrats won't take our votes for granted." If this is supposed to be some sort of "political strategy" on our part, then we are really in trouble because Republicans have responded with tactics of their own to promote Black candidates. Let me differentiate here that, just because both parties now feature Black candidates, doesn't mean that either party is embracing our "kind" of interests. To the contrary, we are expected to further embrace the culture and thinking of Euro-politics.

Robert Taylor of the *National Black News Journal* wrote about the Republican chess move to front Black candidates. Though his following quote specifies Republicans, it equally pertains to Democrats and their liberal policies as well.

> In other words, this neo-conservative strategy appeals to white voters on the basis of substance (the Black candidate's support for neo-conservative ideology) while appealing to Black voters on the superficiality of the candidate's skin color. . . . The net result will be a little more color in the Republican party but no substantive change in the party's neo-conservative policies.[39]

The same applies to Barack Obama. His presidency is not a shift or an indicator that the Democratic Party is becoming more open to "African-American ideals." Let me say that again: His presidency is not a shift or indicator that the Democratic Party is becoming more open to "African-American ideals." It rather indicates his commitment to ideals of the Democratic Party – Including its "kind" of foreign policies and zest for war. What I mean by this is that, based on partisan expediency, the Democratic establishment is against "Bush's war" in Iraq but, they are not against starting a war of their own.

George Stephanopoulos mentioned in a May 2007 interview with Obama that his "rivals" were saying his "instincts were soft" on war.[40] In a gang initiation-like fashion to prove his political street-credibility, Obama had to pass the Verbal SAT Requirements of War to convince the Democratic headship that he is unafraid to dip his hands in blood as president. To uphold the war torch that was lit by the founders and passed to every president, he was coerced to say that he "would strike swiftly, promptly and vigorously," if there was an attack.[41]

This of course is precisely what the Democratic and Republican hierarchs want to hear from "their kind" of leaders – Not any of that weak, "soft instinct" Dr. King *stuff* (as they would define it) that's typical of civil rights-styled Black leaders.

Since there are only two major parties, Africans in America don't have the option to choose the "best" party for us. We are left rather to choose the one that will presumably do the "least" harm to us. In the process, the Democratic Party wins by default – Not because their candidates are "our kind" or because they represent our core interest. It's more a case of, "If you can't beat 'em, join 'em."

For this reason Democrats don't stay awake tossing and turning all night worrying about losing Black voters, because they know the majority of us will never jump ship to vote Republican. And Republicans generally don't waste a whole lot of time or money scrambling for a relatively small percentage of Black votes that they know they'll get anyway from committed Black constituents, along with protest votes from disgruntled Black Democrats who vote Republican "as a strategy."

It's no mystery why George Bush confidently snubbed annual invitations to speak at NAACP conventions from 2001 to 2005, or why he sidestepped meetings with other civil rights organizations.[42] According to Congressman Donald Payne of New Jersey, Bush met with the Congressional Black Caucus only twice; once at the beginning of each term.[43] Remarkably, as much as Black people were seemingly dissatisfied with Bush's first term, he still managed to increase his second-term percentage of Black votes from 9 percent to 11 percent.[44]

With Latinos being the largest minority group, both parties now court Latino voters more than ever. Republicans do heavy fishing to reel in immigrant blue-collar and professional-class Latinos. Bush even appointed Alberto Gonzales as Attorney General, and Carlos Gutierrez as Secretary of Commerce.

In 2007, for the first time in history, 3 Latinos were voted into the Senate: Mel Martinez who is a Republican, and Democrats Ken Salazar and Robert Menedez . . . something that we as Africans have never come close to doing. Latinos are parlaying their resources and banding together, circling their political wagons. In a comparatively short span of time they are steadily moving up the ladder with strides that are beginning to politically eclipse centuries of Black political milestones.

181

Placebos of a Black President

Barack Obama's 2004 Senate victory came with a sneaky insult to the intellect of Africans in America. Let me explain how so. The election pitted him against GOP candidate Alan Keyes, who is also Black. With the Senate being basically an exclusively White institution throughout history, all of a sudden two Black candidates ran for the same Senate seat – guaranteeing victory for one.

Understand however that Keyes entered the race as a last-gasp resort after the original GOP candidate, Jack Ryan, was forced to withdraw at the 11th hour because of embarrassing sexual indiscretions. After several high-profile Republicans declined to run (including former Governors Jim Edgar and James Thompson), Keyes was then "imported" from Maryland, where he'd been slaughtered in "Déja-Vu Defeats" in two previous Senate races, losing by 24 percent in 1988 and 42 percent in 1992.[45] In addition, he had two failed presidential bids on his political record at the time.

No disrespect meant towards Keyes, but for all intents and purposes he was already politically "washed up" before ever stepping into the ring against Obama. If former governors dared not answer the bell at the last moment, what in the world did Keyes think he could do? As bright and qualified for the Senate as he may otherwise be, he allowed the Republican machinery to push his image and common sense over a cliff.

The GOP knew then and knows now that he had no realistic elected future ahead of him. Moreover, polls clearly showed that Obama's solid base of supporters and widespread popularity made Keyes' candidacy laughable. And sure enough, he lost by a super landslide as Obama received 70 percent of votes, which was "a record blowout for a Senate election in Illinois."[46]

The insult came in the form of Placebo Progress as the establishment and mainstream media propagandized the race as "the first US Senate election with two black candidates representing the major parties."[47] This in turn led to nationwide Placebo talk about "how far society has advanced." But the entire race grew out of fluke circumstances that culminated as a Republican "concession in advance" because under ordinary conditions the Illinois GOP would have never, ever endorsed Keyes for a Senate seat.

Obama thereafter catapulted into the limelight on course for the White House. Aside from being a "safe risk" and staying away from issues of systemic/endemic injustices, the question we should ask ourselves is – Why Obama; and why now has a Black man ascended to his height? Before his keynote speech at the 2004 Democratic National Convention he was just a green newcomer and a lone Black man in the Senate. Afterwards, out of nowhere, he outpaced every contender in the Senate pack and suddenly became "presidential" in a league all to himself.

Early into his campaign, talk circulated about whether or not he was "Black enough." Obama clarified that he's "rooted in the Black community, but not *limited* by it."[48] But my question is – "What crime did we commit as a people where someone would have to make such a political defense for himself?"

The fact that he felt it necessary to even make this disclaimer (as though there's something less decent about being Black) is a tacit admission on his part that supports my premise that there's no such thing as "equality" between the races because, being Black has perceived and actual "limitations" that are not associated with being White . . . Which is why, even though he's also half-White, he did not conversely feel compelled to say that he "isn't *limited* by the White community." You get the point?

There's always been something about "being Black" that makes government and society uncomfortable. The term "Black," as we originally used and defined it during the Black Power Movement, related both to color and consciousness . . . Specifically, a "Black Nationalist" consciousness that emerged over the centuries as a direct result and response to institutional injustices. Since America is a European nation with a European form of nationalism, naturally Black Nationalism is an unwelcome concept.

To show you exactly what I mean, consider the following discrepancy in the definitions of "Nationalist" and "Black Nationalist." Technically, every political superlative ascribed to "Nationalist" should duly pertain to "Black Nationalist" in relation to our body politic. But not according to Webster's, and not according to this society. "Nationalist" is defined as: "An advocate of or believer in nationalism: A member of a political party or group advocating national independence or strong national government;" while "Black Nationalist" is defined as "A member of a group of militant blacks who advocate separatism from whites and the formation of self-governing black communities."[49]

For us, being a "Nationalist" is stigmatized with racial overtones that connote negativity and advocate militancy and "separatism." Whereas for others it connotes positive attributes that advocate "national independence" and "national government." This is another prime exemplifier of the control that comes with having the power to define words and concepts. Somebody somewhere is spewing political conflict between the conjoining of "being Black" with "being Nationalist" . . . As though affinity between the two is impermissible.

These days, however, "Black" is a more socially accepted term than during the Black Power Movement. It now signifies either color or consciousness, and there is no such thing as a Standard of Blackness by which Obama or anyone else can be measured. "Black" is now used interchangeably to encompass everything and everybody from the consciousness of the Black Panthers to the color of Bryant Gumbel.

If you want to become president of the US you can be "Black" in color, but definitely not "Black" in consciousness. No African-American candidate can receive White approval or votes if they are suspected of being "Black" in consciousness. This means you must have all the "Kunta Kinte tendencies" whipped out of you, and you must prepare to turn a blind eye to a lot of distorted versions of history and denounce a lot of people along the way. At the rate Obama had to reject Black people and organization, he would have only had his wife and kids behind him if the campaign lasted any longer.

He had to play cautious middle-line party politics and speak sterilized, politically-mushy language to make White people feel comfortable about things like guns, healthcare, housing, taxes and foreign policy. Fears of stirring "language controversy" caused him to cancel a mosque appearance scheduled by (African American-Muslim) Congressman Keith Ellison, who said he would "never forget the quote" of Obama's aide who said the cancellation was because Obama has a "very tightly wrapped message."[50]

If you noticed, no candidate during the 2008 campaign had a "loosely wrapped message" that ever mentioned that an "African-American Agenda" even existed. This is because there is no political capital and absolutely nothing for any candidate to gain by recognizing Black-related issues as a platform component. Hence, Black interests were effectively neutralized throughout the entire campaign and unmentioned during presidential debates, even though everyone knows the magnitude of need to address the plight of Black communities.

During a Florida campaign stop a member of the International People's Democratic Uhuru Movement (InPDUM) interrupted his speech and questioned Obama about "speaking to concerns and attacks on the 'Black community.'"[51] After thoughtfully searching for the right combination of words, Obama departed from his usual courteous tone, and ended up telling him that he could "vote for someone else or run for office himself" if he was dissatisfied.[52] Knowing that the questioner represented something "Black" in consciousness, there was no political risk at all for Obama to respond dismissively and devalue his vote.

Glen Ford, executive editor of the Black Agenda Report, interestingly critiqued race and the unfoldment of Obama's campaign as follows:

But the great tragedy of the current campaign season is the total failure of what passes for Black leadership to have any influence on the growing Obama phenomenon, a corporate manifestation that has never promised anything to Blacks, yet claims to be the

185

center of a "movement." . . . Having sold their votes for nothing, African Americans have for some time been irrelevant to the current campaign discourse.

He was packaged and presented by the Democratic National Convention in August, 2004 as the New Black Look and Attitude of the Party . . . while claiming: "there is no Hispanic America, there is no Black America, there is no white America; there is only the United States of America."

The effect of this strategy would be to marginalize Blacks as a group while focusing attention on Obama as an individual. But despite the clear contradictions, millions of Blacks began to vicariously feel powerful because of Obama's actual location in the bosom of real power. Of course, Obama didn't get his power from you (Black folks), but from Goldman Sachs and other rich whites.

For the rest of the campaign, Black opinion was irrelevant. Black Americans appeared to fear that if they asked for the slightest political assurances on traditional Black concerns over peace, the social safety net, and race-based public policy responses to race-based problems, Obama might go poof! . . . and disappear.

Once white males began voting in huge numbers for Obama, the last holdouts among Black voters came around. African American support for Obama became practically unanimous. And at what cost to Obama? Nothing. Better yet, Obama was now free to more brazenly woo Republicans and Reagan Democrats . . . .[53]

If the political goal of Africans in America is to remain under the jurisdiction of the US government, "Black" will more and more become a political non-factor anyway. So, in 21st century terms of our Evolution, it's not a matter of whether Obama or any other politician is "Black enough." The more definitive barometer is whether they are "sovereign-minded enough," since "Black" is in effect becoming politically devoid of value within the larger context of European politics. So, if we fail to become "sovereign-minded enough" as a people, future generations will still be Black in color, but clones in consciousness of Western political thinking.

Physically, Obama is Black in color and looks like any other Black man walking the streets. But all Black people in America and Africa are not the same, just as all White people in America and Europe aren't the same. Forget about him growing up in untypical places that most Black Americans have never even visited, because that's minor. What sets Obama definitively apart from the historical and political experience of most Africans in America, is that he is not a descendant of Africans who the US government disinherited and dispossessed of sovereignty.

This does not mean he's not "a Brother," because he is a Brother. He's just not a Brother who historically shares and politically represents the lineage of those of us whose ancestors arrived here from the trans-Atlantic slave trade. In fact, based on his mother's ancestry he is the 8th cousin of Dick Cheney.[54] Based on his father's ancestry he could "return" to Kenya and become the president there.

None of this means that I'm against Obama. I support him as a Black man and fellow African just as I would support an African president of France or Russia. But that doesn't mean I'll want to become French or Russian either. The primary reality that mustn't get lost is that Obama's political rise does not preclude our historical and ancestral obligation to reclaim sovereignty, any more than did Andrew Young's appointment as Ambassador to the United Nations or Clarence Thomas's appointment to the Supreme Court. These are all sworn positions of "job designations" for furtherance of Americanization. So even if Obama did happen to share our historical and ancestral lineage, his "job designation" and calls for change as president would still not void the urgency or need for our sovereign pursuits.

Obama was not the first, nor will he be the last person to run a campaign promoting "change." What exactly does change mean in real terms? Does it mean dismantling the majority block of White men in

Congress who've wielded unchallenged political power for centuries? What about changes in foreign policy that caters to Israel unconditionally and caters to Africa when convenient?

Obama is not an alternative to Americanization. He represents all that is Americanization. Unlike governments around the world in places like Cuba, Zimbabwe, and Saudi Arabia, the US government is a well-greased European system that is policy-driven, not personality-driven. No single individual, either Black or White, can therefore change, control, or interrupt Americanization. If one of the Little Rascals became president today, the country would neither change nor fall apart tomorrow.

Thinking that a Black president can change America is like believing the outcome would have been different if the ballroom was another color on the Titanic. A Black president epitomizes all "Political Placebos," since the color of the president is really no more relevant than if he or she is left-handed or right-handed, because as I said, America is policy-driven, not personality-driven. Professor and scholar Na'im Akbar metaphorically said of the White House: "It's not who's in the fashion show, but who makes the fashion."[55]

So why the overnight urge to elect a Black president? Well, Euro-Americans did not build a superpower nation by being politically un-crafty. Remember, they are not amateurs. We are dealing with a people who've been involved in tactical operations of governance since the latter 16th century. They are government specialists who know how to politically "eat fire" and devour whole carcasses of political prey with ease.

At this moment in history however, the repercussions of centuries of greed and immoralities are coming home to roost. Not only is America experiencing an internal crisis of leadership and financial collapse, its superpower image is jeopardized like never before. Confidence in its political integrity is eroding internationally as the world community frowns upon the obvious ignorance and inhumanities of America's war escapades.

As a consequence, America as a nation and Euro-Americans as a people are in dire need of an image and character makeover, as people worldwide are beginning to see that the "The Emperor Has No Clothes."

In response, it has become strategically expedient for Euro-American males to urgently deflect the war-pressures and terrorist-focus of the government away from themselves (perception-wise) as wealthy plutocrats who have historically exerted hegemony over lesser-developed nations.

Obama's combination of Ivy League education, mixed racial identity, and articulate idealisms make him a perfect proxy and decoy to divert attention away from the all-White male establishment that really sits in the cockpit of controls of Americanization. As Pat Buchanan put it, Obama is a "great political athlete."[56] He puts a fresh non-threatening face of "change" on what otherwise is a wounded government and crippled economy.

Similar to the Lone Ranger suddenly designating Tonto "the leader" after being surrounded by Indians, the establishment in the same way hopes Obama can put society and the world community more at ease by giving the appearance that the US government is no longer a big, bad, all-White wolf with the blood of Black and Brown people dripping from its fangs. So, at this critical phase of Americanization, it greatly benefits establishment interests to promote Placebo impressions of racial and political equality by letting Obama's persona do all the work.

Let me make clear however that Barack Obama is not an anomaly. . . . His rise and White-acceptance is an anomaly, but not his competence, charisma, or speechmaking ability. Emanuel Cleaver, a Black congressman from Missouri, said during a radio interview that Obama is "articulate," which is why he's supported by White voters, but "in the Black tradition, he would probably be mediocre. . . . If you put him on a level with a lot of other African-American public speakers, he may not even measure up."[57]

Although I contend that he is just one among a number of Black would-be standouts on the worldstage, my intent is not to reduce his significance or accomplishments in any way. My point is to make known

189

some lesser-known factors that explain why "Obama-caliber" Black men and women *seem* to be in short supply. I say "seem" simply because we have a plethora of "undiscovered" political talent.

One of the main reasons we don't see more "Obamas" is that, since we are an un-sovereign people who live in an absolute sovereign nation, government and politics have not historically been family career pursuits. Unlike Euro-Americans, we don't have the resources or luxury of being part of dynasties where our grandfathers, fathers, and uncles in government have made way for succeeding generations to be escorted through political doors of power, even if we haven't "earned our stripes."

More controversially, a lot of otherwise qualified Black (in consciousness) men and women have no interest or patriotic allegiance to represent the US government, any more than they would want to represent the Romanian government or any other European government. This is not something historically new or bizarre, because I don't think men like Nat Turner and Gabriel Prosser would have wanted to represent this government either.

Additionally, US government and society aren't structurally formulated to accommodate the political prominence of hundreds of Black people. Only one or two, if any, "Obamas" or "MLKs" or "Fredrick Douglasses" are allotted space on this political stage at any given time. For every one of us who did gain notoriety, countless qualified others have been stifled. Many among the comparative few who did manage to slip onto the stage, like Tunis Campbell, Ralph Bunche, Shirley Chissom, Thurgood Marshall, and Adam Clayton Powell have made indelible marks in history.

A main mark of Obama is that he is making it possible for Africans in America to see politics in ways unlike heretofore, which is consequently enlarging the scope of how we view the institution of government. Many Black Democrats for instance who once loved the Clintons, now see them as any other falsehearted power-hungry politicians that smile in your face. If we looked a tad further, we'll see that it really makes no more sense for us to continue to accept the sovereign jurisdiction of Euro-Americans, than for Obama to have accepted Hilary Clinton's twisted psychology that "*he* should become *her* vice president."

Using this same psychology, the establishment wants us to think that Obama's story is possible because "there's something special about America," when the truth of the matter is that, "there's something special about who we are as a people."

He proved that there is a general thirst for the very substances found, not in America, but in the untapped political and intellectual reservoir that we can offer America, ourselves, and the world. From a standpoint of *Sovereign Evolution*, Obama provides a glimpse into the world of excitement and sovereign potentialities of "what could be."

When Obama spoke in cryptic terms, saying he's "rooted in the Black community, but not *limited* by it," we as Black people understood where he was coming from, since the rationale was that he was running to be president of "all Americans." Fine, but what should concern us most is the unseen, unchallenged "source" that compelled him to make this disclaimer; because it has the proven wherewithal to reduce us to a state far less than our true political worth.

Knowing that this is a dangerous source that cannot be trusted, we need to garner a counter-source to defend our worth and to make space on the worldstage for a new caliber and new generation of Black men and women to emerge as the sovereign people and leaders that our "Sovereign Manifest Destiny" requires us to be. This will send a cryptic message of our own for the establishment to decipher, as we respond in return to notify them that we are "rooted in American democracy, but not *limited* by it."

"Bush verses Gore undermined people's trust in democracy. And confidence in the system is a prerequisite for participation. This is an especially crucial moment for our democracy because people feel so passionately about it and so many new voters are entering the process."
Heather Gerken, Professor, Harvard Law School (2004)

"We have incredibly high involvement, an incredibly divided electorate, and issues that are seen as more important than has been the case in any election in recent memory. The fact is that a close election exposes all the vulnerabilities and incompetence of the democracy. Our electoral system is simply not prepared to deal with these types of close elections."
Nathaniel Persily, Election Law Expert, University of Pennsylvania (2004)

"Any people anywhere, being inclined and having the power, have the right to rise up, and shake off the existing government, and form a new one that suits them better. This is a most valuable - a most sacred right - a right, which we hope and believe, is to liberate the world."
Abraham Lincoln

6
Relativities of Voting and Deal-Makings for Presidents

Modern Segregated Sub-Standards

The voting controversies of the 2000 presidential election became topics of conversation and curiosity that ignited a growing interest in electoral politics which carried over into 2004 and 2008. Young Africans in America, especially, are probably more concerned and enthused about voting than ever before in history. While this is great, we should also be cognizant of certain sociopolitical relativities that impact voting and influence the outcome of elections.

In our particular case as Africans in America, these factors are far too consequential to ignore in favor of our wholesale embrace of the "act and ideal" of voting. Americanization has convincingly swayed us to focus primarily on all the perceived grandeur associated with voting. However, I am more convinced that our inability to properly discern and surmount certain relativities is among our greatest political failings.

This chapter details a few of the more challenging sociopolitical factors that impinge on us as a minority. Examined also are some financial features and political deal-makings that have turned electoral politics into a virtual "Political Economy" with massive spending and revenue streams, where exorbitant price tags hang on every seat of high elected office.

To better understand the basis of how sociopolitical relativities affect voting, consider first how like-factors have affected segregation. Everyone knows that segregation is over; Right? Well, let's pry a little to see if this is true.

Educationally, the much-hailed 1954 Supreme Court ruling *Brown vs. Board of Education of Topeka* legally struck down school segregation. Today this decision is an acclaimed precursor to the future success of the Civil Rights Movement. Interestingly though, the headline of a 2004 newspaper read: "Black Leaders Decry a Backslide Toward School Segregation."[1]

A panel of NAACP leaders at their convention assessed that: "The nation's civil rights movement must work harder to fight trends that are making schools increasingly separate and unequal once again for black students. Panel speakers warned that while the ruling [*Brown vs. Board*] sparked decades of progress in efforts to close the educational gap between white and minority students, those gaps are growing once again."[2]

According to Rev. Jesse Jackson Sr., "While it [*Brown vs. Board*] outlawed segregation, it left such issues as school funding up to individual states, creating wide differences in the quality of schools in rich and poor areas. He called for a constitutional amendment that would guarantee the right of an equal education to all Americans."[3] His son, Congressman Jesse Jackson Jr., sponsored legislation in attempt to do just this.

As the gulf of segregated-related disparities continues to enlarge, so has the debate and actions toward solutions. In April 2006 the Nebraska Legislature boldly planned to divide the Omaha school system into three districts: one mostly black, one predominantly white, and one largely Hispanic.[4] Opponents say the new system is state-enforced segregation. Supporters say "the plan gives minorities control over their own school board and ensure that their children are not 'shortchanged' in favor of white youngsters."[5]

Omaha Senator Ernie Chambers, the bill's sponsor, who is also the only Black person in the Legislature, said, "There is no intent to create segregation."[6] He argues that "the district is already segregated, because it no longer buses students and instead requires them to attend their neighborhood school. . . . The schools attended largely by minorities lack the resources and quality teachers provided others in the district."[7]

Race-based disparities have never been a secret in education, neither is it a secret that many schools nationwide are segregated by virtue of racial demographics and economic strata. Schools that are located in low-income Black communities generally lack comparable human and material resources. In spite of this and the fact that *Brown vs. Board* supposedly desegregated schools, the Supreme Court nevertheless rendered a controversial 5-4 ruling in 2007 that "sharply limits the power of local governments to achieve diversity using race-based criteria."[8] Chief Justice John Roberts wrote that "Other means besides race considerations should be used to achieve diversity in schools."[9]

A recent study on educational disparities conducted by the Civil Rights Project of Harvard University "traced much of the problems to white flight from metropolitan areas and recent court decisions that have accelerated a return to neighborhood schools. It also faulted the system used by many states of funding schools through property taxes, which creates inequities between rich and poor districts."[10]

Without knowledge of these sociopolitical factors (state funding disparities, school board controls, resource shortages, quality of teachers, white flight, and school funding through property taxes), perception makes segregation *seem* like a thing of the distant past. But now we know. Now we know that even though segregation is illegal by law, "segregated conditions" have reemerged in sophisticated and unsuspected forms that have resulted in educational substandards among Black youths in low-income areas. So, despite perception and despite de-segregation rulings from the highest court in the land, academic inequities stemming from sociopolitical relativities have produced a modern-day "Educational System of Re-Segregation."

The "Three-Fifths" Relativity

Just as this is true of *Brown vs. Board*, certain sociopolitical factors have similar bearings on the Voting Rights Act of 1965. These factors severely limit the perceived power that Africans in America attribute to the *act* of voting.

One of history's greatest confirmations that attest to relativities of voting is found written within the pages of the US Constitution in the "Three-Fifths Clause." This stipulation is like a signed confession from Euro-Americans that debunks the popular theory that the "act" of voting alone equates to power. The need and inclusion of this clause verify that the real power of voting lies not only in having the "constitutional right," but also the "numerically right" percentage of voters who can elect candidates to serve their best interests.

What I'm saying is that the act of voting alone is not power to an ethnic group that votes for winning candidates who in turn are unaccountable and uncommitted to their interests. This unfortunately has routinely been the case with Democratic candidates that African Americans have helped elect. Proof is seen everywhere throughout lower-income communities where Black people have religiously voted for Democrats who have done little or nothing to turn the tides of unchecked poverty, crime, and deficient school systems. If the mere act of voting alone was power, our communities would not be slum eyesores and hot zones of violent danger.

Why was the Three-Fifths Clause significant and necessary? Well, for census purposes it mandated that every 5 slaves would be counted among the general population as 3 free persons. Article I, Section 2, Paragraph 3 states:

> Representatives and direct Taxes shall be apportioned among the several States which may be included in this Union, according to their respective Numbers, which shall be determined by adding to the whole Number of free persons including those bound to Service for a Term of Years and excluding Indians not taxed, three-fifths of all other persons."[11]

It was during the Federal Conventions of 1783 and 1787 that the clause was formulated. The all-White, all-male conventioneers of the North and South had opposing views about whether slaves should be counted as part of the general population because congressional representation was at stake. Just like today with all the gerrymandering and redistricting, the greater the population of a state, the greater the number of representatives it qualifies to have in Congress. So the outcome of the dispute was crucial to the "balance of power" between the states, since it would directly determine the number of congressional votes per slave state. As I wrote in *Pawned Sovereignty*:

> In the end, the "Three-Fifths Clause" became the agreeing compromise. Despite what is commonly believed today, the clause had nothing to do with classifying Black men as "less than a man." It was wholly political and enacted to accommodate Southern slave owners with increased congressional representation. Ultimately, every 5 slaves were counted among the population as 3 people. . . . Hence, "three-fifths of all other persons."

In essence, it was a mathematical formula designed to politically recognize the value of slave-capital. By no means did this 1787 decision give slaves the right to vote. (Remember, we had to fight and die until 1965 to secure that right). To the contrary, the clause literally rewarded slave owners by strengthening and expanding the base of their political power.

This deliberate *padding* of the population so that slave states could have more congressmen, clearly confirms that the true value of voting is relative to the number of voters. It this were not true, there would have been no need for the "three-fifths clause."[12]

Of course Euro-Americans want us to think that the act of voting alone is power, because according to the prime Law of Democracy – the "Majority Rules." We therefore do not pose any serious threat to their "rule" since they comprise the majority of the nation's 300 million population.[13] As a 13-percent minority in a race-based government and society, we lack numerical capacity and therefore do not nearly stand the chances of probability to win elections as do Whites. The records of election history clearly show that we are playing a racial numbers game that makes it politically and mathematically impossible to prevail much further than our current standing.

This goes back to why portions of the Voting Rights Act must be renewed every 25 years. Projections forecast that due to rising birthrates of non-Whites and rising immigrant numbers, Euro-Americans will ultimately become outnumbered in their own country. When this numerical shift occurs, changes will also undoubtedly occur to the electoral system and the way democracy is practiced. Anyone who thinks that today's minorities will rule as tomorrow's majority don't understand the extremes that Euro-Americans will employ to safeguard the European-ness of their sovereignty.

Dialing-for-Dollars, Pay-to-Play Democracy

Probably the most decisive sociopolitical factor that makes voting relative is the sources and massive financial resources that back candidates. A private political/corporate culture exists between the government, corporations, and wealthy Whites, wherein hundreds of millions of dollars change hands annually that impact candidates, campaigns, and election outcomes. Blue-chip corporations and Blue-blooded plutocrats have major controlling influence with politics and politicians via campaign financing, party contributions, Political Action Committees, and lobbying.

Corporate America and clusters of elite Whites are known to use their wealth to leverage political benefits that further consolidate their economic power. However, the extent to which this occurs is often underestimated and certainly not challenged enough by the overwhelming majority of Blacks and Whites who lack such wealth, privileges, and political access.

Corporate dollars greatly determine who is and isn't a viable candidate, and who ultimately sits in the highest seats of government. Once you can trace the major funding sources of a viable presidential, gubernatorial, or senatorial candidate you can then largely identify the issues and causes that he or she is *pre-obligated* to represent and support.

Long before ballots are cast and long before campaigning begins, there's a pre-commitment of finances that predetermines the viability of contenders. The act of voting is at the tail end of a multiphased electoral process. Since Africans in America basically have no involvement in the phases where big money is dispensed to campaigns, we are not politically vested in candidates, who in turn feel little obligation to serve us. While we focus on the final phase when ballots are cast and counted, those who seek real power know the political value that comes with participating in the financial phase where commitments are made.

Individuals enter concealed booths to cast their votes in private, behind closed curtains. Unless you tell, no one is supposed to know who you voted for. This shroud of secrecy afforded to constituents extends in like manner to secretly shroud the political influence afforded to major donors within the private culture. By the time you close the curtain of your voting booth, the financial machinery behind American democracy has performed layers and levels of "curtain closing" of its own.

Candidates nowadays are practically bought and sold by the pound to the highest contributors. So our main concerns should be less about what candidates *say* they stand for, and more about the corporate and institutional sources of a candidate's funding. During these hard times of unnecessary wars, economic tumult, and rancid decay within our communities, it's not politicians that need changing per se; it's the modes of operation that financially fuel the political system that need changing.

Though he said he wanted to change the culture of Washington and the way lobbyists and special interest groups splatter money all around to influence policymaking, President Barack Obama has not escaped the financial gravity of Wall Street. During his brief Senate tenure he received the second most in history in campaign contributions from Fannie Mae and Freddie Mac, the very institutions at the epicenter of the government's $700 billion bailout of Wall Street's credit crisis.[14] According to *Open Secrets* from the Center for Responsive Politics:

The securities and investment industry is Obama's second-largest source of bundlers, after lawyers, and at least 56 individuals have raised at least $8.9 million for his campaign. (Bundlers are those wealthy individuals who hit up their coworkers, family and friends to raise hundreds of thousands of dollars, in addition to any contributions from their own pockets). Bundlers in the larger finance, insurance and real estate sector have collected at least $13.4 million for Obama, making it his most generous sector.

Overall, the securities and investment industry contributed about $10 million to Obama and $7 million to McCain. ... Contributions from the commercial banking industry

[were] roughly split between Obama and McCain – $2 million for the Democrat, $1.9 million for the Republican.[15]

To all federal candidates for president and Congress, and to political parties, the [securities and investment] industry has contributed more than $101 million in the 2008 election cycle, 56 percent of it to Democrats. The Democrats' edge is a relatively recent development, however; Republicans had the advantage for most of the last 10 years. . . . The banking industry has contributed about $25 million in this election cycle to federal candidates and parties, giving 52 percent to Republicans.[16]

Aside from pointing to the acute lacks of oversight and regulations, combined with greed, ignorance, and corruption within government and corporate America, I have only two brief comments about the $700 billion socialist infusion to Wall Street. First of all, for any multibillion dollar financial institution to crumble overnight without prior warnings, while executives pocket tens and hundreds of millions in the process, automatically spells criminality; and somebody from that firm and possibly the government needs to crumble in prison just as fast. Second, if any business becomes "too large to fail" (as was said of some companies), that alone should stipulate it as a "monopoly," which should therefore qualify it under Antitrust Laws to be broken up long before its failure could devastate the economy.

It is impossible to run a successful presidential campaign without Wall Street funding or influences from policy and political opinion-shaping apparatuses like the Council on Foreign Relations, Trilateral Commission, Center for Strategic and International Studies, Heritage Foundation, Brookings Institution, RAND Corporation and Hoover Institution. No US president can avoid being politically indebted to the policy and financial institutions of his times.

Chief donors do not make large campaign contributions because of patriotism or the goodness in their hearts. They do so in exchange for privileged posts and/or the passing of favorable policies and legislation to protect and progress their interests. Members of this private culture are also known to hedge their odds by making hefty campaign contributions to both parties and both presidential nominees. They automatically win regardless of who wins the White House.

More and more, America is becoming a full-fledged "Pay-to-Play Democracy," where corporations and wealthy individuals buy their way into political favoritism and political offices. Larry Noble, the executive director of the Center for Responsive Politics said of this, that "just because it is done often, does not make it right."[17] To peep quickly behind the closed curtains of this culture, consider the following from a news article titled "Bush Rewarded 246 Top Fund-Raisers with Posts:"

A third of President Bush's top 2000 fundraisers or their spouses were appointed to positions in his first administration, from ambassadorships in Europe to seats on policy-setting boards, an Associated Press review found.

The perks for 246 "pioneers" who raised at least $100,000 also included overnight stays at the White House and Camp David and overseas travel with US delegations to the Olympics and other events.

At least two dozen of the 2000 pioneers or their spouses became ambassadors, mostly to Europe. At least 57 contributors or their spouses were named to agency positions, advisory or decision-making committees and boards, or US delegations.

Three top Bush fund-raisers became Cabinet secretaries: Bush 2000 finance chairman Don Evans at Commerce, Elaine Chao at Labor and Tom Ridge at Homeland Security.

The practice is ingrained in Washington. Bill Clinton, in his first year in office, picked five $100,000-plus Democratic donors to be ambassadors.[18]

Additionally, some of the more notable and important boards to which Bush appointed his donors were: the Advisory Committee for Trade Policy and Negotiation; the Internal Revenue Service Oversight Board; the Kennedy Center, Overseas Private Investment Corp. (OPIC); the President's Export Council; the President's Foreign Intelligence Advisory Board; and the US Advisory Commission on Public Diplomacy.[19]

Although Pay-to-Play has just started to grab national headlines, especially since the arrest of Illinois Governor Rod Blagojevich, there's nothing new about wealthy individuals and corporate representatives being politically and economically rewarded for contributions. In fact, all the aggregated capital generated over the years and all the resulting favoritism and privileges are part of a flourishing multibillion dollar "Political Economy" that has its own "Presidential Industry." *Open Secrets* reported that:

> Fundraising is not just a way that candidates demonstrate their viability; it's a necessary task given the tremendous costs of running a campaign. Running for president is a bit like running a medium-sized business for two years, and the overall race amounts to a decent-sized *industry*. How candidates spend the money entrusted to them by donors can say as much about the campaign as where the money came from.[20]

Regardless of how many democratic creeds you can recite by memory or how much you believe in the American Dream, unless you can put your hands on the right amount of resources (multimillions) from the right sources (corporate and White elites) you can forget about ever becoming president, governor, or senator. And unless you contribute "X Amount" to campaigns and receive acceptance into this private culture, you can forget about having political access and influence. An article from *Capital Eye* titled "Spending Money to Make Money," stated:

> Money begets money in politics, and candidates who develop a reputation for being superior fund-raisers are often rewarded

with even more cash from impressed donors. But raising money isn't just about image. From buying television airtime to paying an army of staff, the reality is that running a successful campaign is an expensive endeavor.[21]

There's a dollar figure associated with every level of political office, with an accompanying amount for corporations and individuals who wish to gain political access and influence. With each election these figures skyrocket along with the value of the overall Political Economy. According to the National Institute on Money in State Politics, senate elections in 36 states in 2002 raised $861 million.[22] Gubernatorial races in 36 states in 2006 spent $2.4 billion.[23] The Center for Responsive Politics ran a November 5, 2008 article, titled "Money Wins Presidency and 9 of 10 Congressional Races in Priciest U.S. Election Ever," stating that:

In 93 percent of House of Representatives races and 94 percent of Senate races that had been decided by mid-day Nov. 4, the candidate who spent the most money ended up winning. . . . Continuing a trend seen election cycle after election cycle, the biggest spender was victorious in 397 of 426 decided House races and 30 of 32 settled Senate races. . . . The average cost of winning a House race in 2008 was nearly $1.1 million, and almost $6.5 million for a Senate seat. As of Oct. 15, congressional candidates spent almost $1.4 billion in the last two years, and the estimated 2008 total cost for Congress and the White House is $5.3 billion.

Advertising is a major campaigning expenditure of the Presidential Industry. But over the decades only drops in the bucket have been spent with Black advertisers or on ads targeting Black-related issues. John Kerry raised $266 million in 2004 but he only budgeted $2 million towards Black ads, yet this was by far "the largest of its kind in presidential campaign history."[24]

Speaking of Kerry for a moment, I can't resist commenting on how Black people had so much hope in him. After he lost, folks were moping in disappointment as though he was going to stop the war and improve America on our behalf. If you don't know already let me tell you that there is nothing politically special or remarkable about John Kerry or his views. If anything he is excruciatingly ordinary. In fact, you can literally spin a bottle and run whoever it points to among Senate-wannabes for president because each is just as average-minded as the next.

With all the talk that circulated about Sarah Palin's lack of qualifications and preparedness to be vice president, I hasten to add that being prepared or highly educated is not necessarily a criterion to be president. Woodrow Wilson was the only president to date with a PhD, and 9 presidents didn't even attend college.[25] So it's really more of a political illusion that presidents are so smart and qualified.

It's not the *mind* it's the *money* that makes a president or governor or senator today. Having money or access to raise money is a foremost determinant of a candidate's viability. Having credentials and experience to hold office is somewhat secondary, if not almost meaningless, compared to a person's fundraising abilities to pick up the telephone and "Dial-for-Dollars."

Even though Africans in America have the right to vote and the right to run for offices, we have been comparatively unable to Dial-for-Dollars within the existing Political Economy with the same ease and efficiency as Whites, and we certainly have no means to establish rival sources of funding.

Bush and Cheney had it both ways. Not only were they already multimillionaires when they took office, but Dialing-for-Dollars has never been a problem for them, which largely explains why they are two-time winners.[26] Both of them are so drenched in oil money that they probably left smudges all over the Bible used to swear them in.

When Kerry/Edwards battled Bush/Cheney, it was a head-to-head lineup of multimillionaires, spending multimillions of other people's money. Counting his wife's wealth, Kerry would have been among the wealthiest of all people "to ever occupy the White House."[27] Commenting on the unfair advantages of multimillionaire candidates, Charles Lewis, executive director of the Center for Public Integrity said, "It's a sad commentary on our system."[28]

New Jersey's former acting governor, Richard Codey (who took office when James McGreevey resigned after getting snared in a homosexual scandal with his Israeli aide/lover), said that the US Senate is a "Club of Multimillionaires."[29] Oh, but don't worry about McGreevey's future, because he's far from being ruined or disgraced. He'll make millions aside from his *Confessions* book where he talks about having "anonymous sex" with men at rest stops along New Jersey highways.[30]

The "money game" of politics is not endemic to America alone. Modern institutions of governments in general seem to be increasingly becoming more corrupt and immoral worldwide. It's become visibly obvious that many top government officials in the world, live lavish lifestyles compared to average citizens of the world's 6-plus billion population. And in America, the trait of being "filthy-rich" is not exclusive to Republicans. "Who's the Richest in Congress?" was the title of a *Parade* magazine article that revealed:

The GOP may be richer overall, but the Democrats have the *really* big bucks. Though 32 of the 50 wealthiest members of Congress are Republicans, the top four are all Democrats, according to the Capitol Hill newspaper *Roll Call*. Leading the wealth brigade: Sen. John Kerry (D., Mass.), with $750 million, mostly from his wife, Teresa Heinz Kerry. Next is Sen. Jay Rockefeller (D., W.Va.) heir to the Standard Oil fortune and worth $200 million. Sen. Herb Kohl (D., Wis.) a former department-store owner, has $136 million. And Rep. Jane Harman (D., Calf.) has a net worth of $128 million, thanks in part to her husband, an electronics magnate. Rounding out the top five is Rep. Darrell Issa (R., Calf.), with $121 million. By the way, Senate Majority Leader Bill Frist (R., Tenn.) is No. 13, with $14.2 million.[31]

Members of the congressional fraternity who aren't multimillionaires upon arrival, have business options to make millions upon departure. While in Washington they sit on key committees and enact policies that allow them to develop corporate relationships (domestic and foreign) that ultimately serve as sources for personal enrichment when they leave. Some eventually make financial fortunes that the average American (Black or White) couldn't earn in ten lifetimes. Providing they play their "congressional cards" right, they'll get cushy jobs and sit on corporate boards once they leave Washington, guaranteeing them millions in return for the political favoritism rendered while in office.

Just so you'll know, since 1995 at least 272 former members of Congress have become lobbyists.[32] This, according to watchdog agencies, has "led to a system in which members of Congress could be making policy decisions not on what they see as the public good, but on self-interest."[33]

Since Congress as an institution is beholden to the corporate interests that back it, the needs of the Black underclass are relegated as secondary to the symbiotic sustainment of this political/corporate culture. Each exists and thrives by virtue of interdependence of the other, so there's no way the strength and benefits of this culture and economy will be watered-down to accommodate Black needs.

<><><><><><><><>

Electoral College & Office of the Presidency

The year 2000 marked the advent of not only a new century but also a new era in American politics and leadership. Bush's tenures harbingered "an America" that will never politically be the same either domestically or abroad. Based on his electoral controversies and unnecessary fomenting of war in Iraq, he has triggered a domino effect that has no foreseeable end.

I concur with Russian President Dmitry Medvedev and others that Bush's presidency is a historical point of reference where America has

206

changed politically, economically, and militarily for the worst. Medvedev said, in an article titled "US Supremacy Eternally Over," that "The time of domination by one economy and one currency has been consigned to the past once and for all."[34] John Gray wrote in the UK *Observer* that America's market and financial upheaval signals "a historic geopolitical shift, in which the balance of power in the world is being altered irrevocably. The era of American global leadership, reaching back to the Second World War, is over."[35]

I am not singling out Bush as an aberration who headed an incompetent administration. He represents the continuity and culmination of the Office of the Presidency and all Democratic and Republican administrations before him. I use this term "Office of the Presidency" because presidents come and go, while the *office* remains occupied. From a sovereign standpoint of government, it is the *office* moreso than the *individual* that is considered sacred . . . Which explains how it's possible that even though 4 US presidents were assassinated, most people know only Kennedy and Lincoln, not Garfield or McKinley who you seldom hear about.[36]

As much as there may have appeared to be partisan divisions surrounding Bush's elections, evidence shows that there was far more collusion than discrepancies. Amid the tumult in 2000, Democrats alleged that Bush stole the election, claiming that he was "selected" not "elected." Grievances from Black America centered on voting irregularities in predominately Black communities in Florida, including reports of ballots being thrown away, machines malfunctioning, and police intimidation at and near the polls.

In response, Black organizations and civil rights groups launched nationwide awareness campaigns in effort to avert reoccurrences in 2004. Everyone from elders of civil rights to youngsters of hip hop culture participated to increase voter registration and urge people to the polls. Hip hop trendsetters even went so far as to promote a "Vote or Die" slogan, which starkly contrasts with Euro-America's erstwhile "Give Me Liberty (Sovereignty) or Give Me Death" slogan.

The election irregularities in 2000 were real and the subsequent responses were necessary. However, the one issue that should have drawn the most attention hardly made headlines. And that issue concerns the relativities of the Electoral College and its power to directly determine the outcome of presidential elections. Due to its enigmas, Bush became "The first candidate to assume the presidency after being defeated in the popular vote in more than a century, since Benjamin Harrison defeated Grover Cleveland in 1888."[37]

> Bush's victory came by virtue of the US Supreme Court decision which shut down the recount of disputed ballots in Florida, allowing him to carry the state by only 537 votes out of 6 million cast, and capture all 25 of the state's electoral votes. The Republican electors met in the state capital, Tallahassee, and cast their ballots at a session of the state legislature chaired by the Republican candidate's brother, Governor Jeb Bush. . . . Completing the anti-democratic travesty of the 2000 US presidential election, the 538 members of the Electoral College met December 18 in 50 states and the District of Columbia, handing the presidency to the candidate who lost the November 7 popular vote."[38]

As the 2000 controversies unfolded, the astonished public found itself instantly enrolled in an overnight crash-course on the functions of the Electoral College. Now the general public knows that the "voice of the people" can be supplanted by the "voice of the Electoral College." It is not the voting power of the people, but the voting discretion of the Electoral College system that determines who will be president. House Majority Leader, Nancy Pelosi, aptly summed up presidential elections by saying to the effect that "delegates choose the final presidential candidates, and the Electoral College ultimately chooses the president."[39]

The powers of the Electoral College are constitutional and date back to 1787. According to Article II, Section I of the Constitution:

The executive Power shall be vested in a President of the United States of America. He shall hold his Office during the Term of four Years, and, together with the Vice President, chosen for the same Term, be elected as follows

Each State shall appoint, in such Manner as the Legislature thereof may direct, a Number of Electors, equal to the whole Number of Senators and Representatives to which the State may be entitled in the Congress: [40]

Although it may have been well-suited for its time in the 1700s, the Electoral College is problematic because "Electors are typically party loyalists and donors."[41] These "donors" represent yet another level of Pay-to-Play democracy since "Each elector, although pledged to a candidate, is free to vote for someone else – especially if he deems his party's nominee unfit, for whatever reason."[42] Even if the presidential candidate of an elector's party wins the popular vote in the state, the designated elector is still not obligated to vote for his own party's candidate.

The freedom of the electors to cast their votes for a candidate other than the one chosen by the people of their state is only one of the many peculiar features of the reactionary and archaic Electoral College structure. Only 27 of the 50 states require electors by law or by oath to cast their ballots for the candidate to whom they are pledged, but only five states impose any penalty on faithless electors. The remaining 23 states and the District of Columbia have no restrictions at all. As a result, [in the 2000 election] 140 of the 271 electors for Bush were not bound to vote for him.[43]

Seldom is it mentioned that the Civil Rights Act of 1964 (signed by Democratic President Lyndon Johnson) is unintendedly linked to the Electoral College in a way that unfavorably affects the Democratic Party.

Given that racism and segregation was more concentrated in the South among Republicans, the Act left a vengeful taste in the mouths of White southerners that resulted in fixed numbers of predictable electoral votes for Republicans.

Contrary to the portrayal of Bush's former senior advisor Karl Rove as a genius campaign strategist, the simple truth is that, up until the 2008 election, heavy partisan populations in key Southern states gave Republicans an automatic and overwhelming electoral advantage. Mathematically and geographically so, it doesn't require brilliance to calculate that Republican candidates needed "only a few major states in the North, perhaps only one or two, to reach 270 electoral votes and win the White House."[44]

> President Lyndon Johnson called it the "Electoral Lock." He helped create it, with Civil Rights and Great Society social legislation that spurred the rise of the GOP across the Old Confederacy.
>
> Johnson ruefully predicted the changes he abetted would lead to a string of GOP presidential victories. And mostly, he has been proved right. Republicans have won six of the past nine presidential contests, beginning in 1968, and might have won more but for the Watergate scandal.
>
> Democrats who managed to break the lock were Jimmy Carter and Bill Clinton – both Southerners who shed the liberal label and broke the solid GOP grip on the South. Even winning the popular balloting by more than 500,000 votes couldn't gain Gore an Electoral College majority.[45]

The ambiguities of the Electoral College have placed a spotlight on the electoral system that has not escaped notice of other nations, including those that America views as lacking in democratic principles, like Russia. During a European visit in 2005, Bush attempted to lecture and scold President Vladimir Putin about Russia's undemocratic tendencies. Putin responded by calling the Electoral College a "secret ballot" and then sarcastically retorted, "It is not considered undemocratic, is it?"[46]

In terms of amending the Electoral College, the controversies of 2000 prompted "No fewer than six reform proposals in Congress. . . . [But] nothing came of them. In the 111 years before that, 587 constitutional amendments on the subject met the same fate."[47] Remember as well that a provision of *House Joint Resolution 28*, proposed by Congressman Jackson Jr., (Chapter 5) requires Electors to cast their vote to "reflect the majority popular vote" in their state."[48] But you can bet this provision is bound to meet the same fate. It seems that Euro-Americans are resistant to making alterations because, as Ron Jacobs wrote, "It's as if our electoral system is beyond reproach, fair beyond criticism and impossible to taint."[49]

The "Selecting" of a President

If you objectively analyze the history of electoral politics, you'll also find that a higher sovereign Bond and Commitment exists among the Euro-American power structure . . . A Bond and Commitment that transcends partisan tenants and party loyalties. Although this may seem far-fetched on the surface, there is a clear factual and logical basis to substantiate it.

Bear in mind first of all the nature of American government and politics from 1776 to 1965, where institutional practices and shared attitudes of racism were norms among those who governed. It's just been within the last few decades that Black people have been allowed in the Capitol Building without mops and dust pans. Only in recent times have non-Anglo Europeans become cabinet members and congressmen. So in order to really understand the true nature of US government, you have to thoroughly erase from your mind all the political falsities that go on and on about stuff like "Land of the Free" and "Justice for All."

Illustrations 3. "Equal Justice"

An often overlooked reality is that, for almost 200 years of government, Euro-American officials have only dealt domestically with other Euro-American officials. There were no significant minority influences in government that they had to work with or be politically mindful of. For the overwhelming majority of their sovereign days, Euro-Americans have been solely driven by political self-concerns – not multiculturalism or concerns for other ethnicities. The concept of "political correctness" is relatively new.

Over this duration Euro-Americans had countless political squabbles and disagreements, even a bloody civil war where they slaughtered themselves to the tune of over 600,000.[50]   However, *their* differences were *their* differences alone . . . left exclusively unto themselves to resolve.   Naturally, based on America's current level of political and economic development, you know that at certain points in time they had to make internal agreements and arrangements amongst themselves for the greater good of the whole.   You cannot fault them for sticking together to make *their* government succeed.

With this in mind, let's zoom forward to contemporary times. Throughout his presidency there's been lots of anti-Bush, anti-Republican rhetoric from Blacks and Democrats alike. Many find it hard to believe that he could become president since he's so "un-presidential." His nitwit quotes and stumblebum behaviors are punch lines of comedy worldwide. But being a member of the Bush Family Dynasty as well as a former governor of Texas, he was no stranger to the establishment before he became president.

He's the same George Bush today that he was yesterday. So it shouldn't be surprising that he distortedly envisaged himself as a modern-day Emperor Charlemagne, ordained to Euro-Christianize the world. His theo-political outlooks and fondness for "playing cowboy" by spilling the blood of 152 death-row inmates while governor, were all well known prior to him "playing army" by spilling blood in Iraq.

Knowing all of this, it seemingly defies logic that after all the partisan mudslinging and the multimillions spent on campaigning, that Al Gore and the entire Democratic hierarchy would lay down and surrender to Bush's so-called *selection* in 2000 without exhausting all protests and proceedings. So, the real questions aren't about his incompetence or voting foul-play. The real questions should center on what the Democrats did and didn't do to aid and abet his victory. The real questions should center on the "Presidential Deal-Makings" that transpired between both parties.

Deal-makings however, are not unprecedented in US history. But before citing other examples, it's interesting to note that many presidents and vice presidents were blood relatives anyway. So when it comes to electing a president, it's not like Euro-Americans are foreigners to each other, or that there's an ominous internal threat to overthrow their Republic. For them it's always been "All In The Family."

George W. Bush is a cousin to 40 other presidents and vice presidents.[51] I've already mentioned that Obama and Cheney are distant cousins. Additional research shows that Obama is also a distant cousin to 6 presidents that interestingly includes G. W. Bush and G. H. W. Bush, along with Gerald Ford, Lyndon Johnson, Harry Truman, and James Madison.[52]

The following reference is a partial list of Bush's presidential relatives that includes Washington, Jefferson, and Lincoln.[53]

Presidential Relatives of President George W. Bush

President John Quincy Adams .... 5th cousin 6 times removed

President Chester A. Arthur...................... 6th cousin 5 times removed

President James Buchanan ....11th cousin 7 times removed

President George Herbert Bush.. Father

President Jimmy Carter .... 14th cousin 6 times removed

Vice President Dick Cheney.. Half 10th cousin

President Grover Cleveland .... 7th cousin 3 times removed

President Calvin Coolidge......................... 6th cousin 3 times removed

President Gerald Ford................................... 7th cousin once removed

President James A. Garfield .... 4th cousin 4 times removed

President Ulysses S. Grant .... 6th cousin 6 times removed

President Warren G. Harding .... 19th cousin 4 times removed

President Benjamin Harrison .... 12th cousin 6 times removed

President Rutherford B. Hayes................... 6th cousin 3 times removed

President Herbert Hoover.......................... 7th cousin 5 times removed

President Thomas Jefferson...................... 12th cousin 7 times removed

President Abraham Lincoln....................... 7th cousin 5 times removed

President James Madison .... 8th cousin 8 times removed

President James Monroe........................... 12th cousin 7 times removed

President Richard Nixon .... 9th cousin twice removed

President Franklin Pierce .... 5th cousin 5 times removed

Vice President James Danforth Quayle........ 10th cousin once removed

President Franklin D. Roosevelt................. 6th cousin 4 times removed

President Theodore Roosevelt................... 7th cousin 4 times removed

President William Howard Taft.................. 5th cousin 4 times removed

President Zachary Taylor....................... 10th cousin 10 times removed

President George Washington ....11th cousin 8 times removed

Document 8. Presidential Relatives of George W. Bush

Their European heritage has historically withstood the test of time to forge a reliable Bond and Commitment among themselves that can and does outweigh partisanship, especially when critical matters of sovereignty are concerned. Flowery partisan speeches have been delivered on the floor of Congress for centuries, yet closed-door dealings have taken place where political agreements have been reached which the general public have never known or suspected.

Election history shows that it's not new for one party to roll out the red carpet and throw confetti to welcome the *rival* party to the White House after major controversy. Aside from Bush's 2000 election, evidence of Presidential Deal-Making appears in 3 previous contentious elections (involving cousins of Bush), where their Bond and Commitment took precedence over the dispute. If this were not the case, it's very possible that America would have had more than one civil war.

The first dispute occurred back in 1800 when Thomas Jefferson and Aaron Burr ended up tied in electoral votes. Militias in Virginia and Pennsylvania stood ready for war if Burr had been named president.[54] Before they got to the point of dusting off the cannonballs, the parties convened in the backrooms, and for the first time in election history their sovereign Bond and Commitment proved strong enough to supercede an election dispute. In the end, they crafted a deal where Jefferson was *selected* president; Burr was named vice president; and the militias were called off in compliance with the compromise.[55]

Yale University political scientist Stephen Skowronek said that "The 1800 election resulted in the first peaceful transfer of power from one political party to another – from the Federalists to Jeffersonian Republicans – and helped cement the democratic system."[56] This transfer stood as a template for solidarity to avert future election-based military conflicts.

Two additional facts are important for Africans in America to keep in perspective. First, America was not a melting pot at that time. Second, democracy was being used as an instrument to enslave and politically restrict Africans. Obviously then, none of the terms or provisions of this

215

deal to select Jefferson involved us or any other minority group. This controversy and subsequent resolution was "family business" exclusive to and for Euro-Americans. So my point here is to establish proof showing that Euro-Americans have a veritable track record of political collusion amongst themselves when it comes to potential presidents.

The second case of Presidential Deal-Making occurred in the 1824 election when John Quincy Adams was *selected* into office. This election involved Andrew Jackson, Henry Clay, and William H. Crawford. "In the four-way 1824 race, no one had a majority of the electoral votes but the House chose second-place finisher Adams as part of a deal engineered by House Speaker Henry Clay, who later became secretary of state. The deal widely known as the 'corrupt bargain,' left lingering bitterness and helped make Adams a one-term president."[57]

Again, I reiterate that America at that time was not a melting pot; democracy was still being used as an instrument to enslave and restrict Africans; and the terms and provisions of the deal concerned Euro-Americans alone. This substantiates further historical and factual evidence of their colluding in a presidential election.

The third case occurred 52 years later when Rutherford B. Hayes was *selected*. After what was called a "Constitutional Crisis," he was dubbed with the nickname "His Fraudulency" by Democrats.[58] *AllPolitics. com* wrote: "The most questionable of presidential elections, in 1876, settled with deals and favors for the Republicans after their man lost the popular vote and probably a fairly counted electoral vote to Democrat Samuel J. Tilden. . . . Republicans, supported by the federal troops of Reconstruction, made sure Hayes got the contested electoral votes in the South."[59] According to *Grolier Encyclopedia*:

On election night it seemed that Hayes had lost to his Democratic rival, Samuel J. Tilden. Tilden had a popular majority and 184 of the 185 electoral votes needed to win. Hayes had 165 electoral votes. A total of 20 in Oregon, South Carolina, Florida, and Louisiana were disputed. If Hayes had won all of these, as the Republicans claimed, he would have won. With competing returns from the contested states, Congress created an electoral commission, which decided that Hayes should receive all 20 disputed ballots and thus ensured his inauguration in March 1877.

A series of sectional bargains, which have been called the "Compromise of 1877," brought about this peaceful result. Southerners in Congress accepted Hayes because of Republican assurances that Reconstruction would end with the withdrawal of federal troops. Republicans also made less definite commitments about appropriations for internal improvements in the South, while the South's representatives said that the political rights of black Americans would be safeguarded. None of these informal deals survived the early months of Hayes's term.[60]

In this instance, the rights of Black people were included as a bargaining chip to the deal, of which the terms of course were breached. Although slavery had been abolished and we were used as pawns in the deal, America was still not a melting pot and democracy was still used just as blatantly as an instrument to restrict us.

Government and society has since become integrated with a host of ethnicities. Non-Anglo Americans who now populate the country have growing stakes and interests in presidential procedures and outcomes. A lot of *other* eyes closely watch election dealings. So nowadays, Euro-Americans must use extra discretion when the political need arises for them to collude. But in keeping with tradition as the next segment details, Bush's election shows that their sovereign Bond and Commitment exists nonetheless, and Presidential Deal-Making can still occur if necessary.

Political Lynching of the CBC

Although the exact terms and provisions are unknown and open to speculation, initial hints of the deal-making to put Bush in the Office of the Presidency surfaced with a rare sequence of events beginning in December 2000, which culminated in January 2001 with all Euro-Americans senators from both parties, ganging-up to "Politically Lynch" the Congressional Black Caucus (CBC) for attempting to *interrupt* his selection.

It was on December 12 that a strange reversal of stance and attitude occurred, as White congressional Democrats posed no challenge to the Supreme Court ruling that ultimately handed Bush the White House keys. This was the first suspicious sign that Euro-American Democrats and Republicans were visibly demonstrating a Bond and Commitment beyond partisan norms.

From that point onward, an intricate pattern of bed-fellows and cooperation could be detected between the Electoral College, the Supreme Court, the Senate and Democratic nominee Al Gore himself. At the joint session of Congress on January 12, 2001 when the electoral votes were officially tallied, the consolidated unity of Euro-Americans from both parties hit an all-time height, while the functional weakness of the CBC hit an all-time low.

Here's a brief overview of what happened. Due to all of the reported voting controversies and discrepancies in Florida, the CBC wanted to wage a formal "Objection" to Bush being awarded all 25 of Florida's electoral votes.[61] The snag was that the entire CBC were members of the House, and according to an "1887 law governing the counting of the electoral vote," the signature of at least one senator is required to "sustain an objection."[62] Remember, this was the "Pre-Obama Age," so the Senate was operating with its usual number of Blacks – Zero.

With the CBC having no standalone powers, they needed what in essence was "White-signature authorization" from their political superiors. Since America is supposed to be the world's greatest example of a "two-party democracy," it seemed routine enough that at least one

218

White Democratic senator would feel duty-bound to sign the Objection on behalf of Florida's disenfranchised voters . . . Especially considering that Gore did win the popular vote and these very senators represented the 51-plus million constituents who had cast the majority ballots for Gore.[63]

Every election you always hear the common refrain that, "This is the most important election in your lifetime," and the same had been said in 2000. You would therefore think that the criticality of the issues and outcome of the election would have been serious enough for deep partisan lines to be drawn between the two parties.

Instead, the senators collectively displayed unanimous consensus for Bush. Not one of the 50 Democratic senators even blinked in the direction of signing the CBC's Objection. "If even a single Democratic senator had signed an objection, the joint session would have adjourned and the House and Senate would have convened separately to vote, with the majority of both Houses required to sustain the objection. . . . But Senate Democrats refused to back any objection."[64]

It was pitiful and painful to watch the proceedings. As a steady stream of politically agonized CBC members stepped to the podium to voice protest, every Democratic senator sat speechless and motionless, consenting by their silence to 4 years of Bush – The man who they supposedly loathe so much. Even White Democrats of the House were unified in silence. "Only one white Democrat, [Congressman] Peter Deutsch, whose district includes much of Palm Beach County, Florida," supported the CBC objection.[65]

For those who think that "we are all equal" or that sovereignty "doesn't matter," here was a case where the sovereign ability of Euro-Americans to control this government was uncontestedly exercised against African American subjects. Through their non-actions, they single-handedly voided the very democratic principles of voting that they sold to us, that we hold so dear. Despite any semblance of perceived power that the CBC may have, this event revealed a stark and enduring dichotomy of race and politics that often gets overlooked because of the presumption that Black faces in Congress equate to power sharing.

Now mind you, the CBC is not some sort of radical opposition party that you might see in *other* countries. Like all other House Reps, they too are elected officials. But based on the raggedy way they were treated, you would have thought they were some kind of fringe or splinter group.

CBC member Jesse Jackson Jr. made a tear-jerking emotional plea that fell on deaf ears. Lamenting for "just one" White senator to cooperate, he said: "It is a sad day in America when we can't find a senator to sign the objection."[66] Yes, it is a "sad day in America," but not because White folks didn't sign another "permission slip" to validate our civil interests. It's a "sad day" because after nearly 400 years, Euro-Americans hold such undeserved, unchallenged political authority over us, while we for some strange reason remain submissive.

The finishing blows to the CBC and final evidence of deal-making came directly from Gore. At the time the Senate was split 50-50 between Democrats and Republicans. Gore, being vice president, was therefore President of the Senate, which constitutionally assigns him the voting obligation to settle all ties in the Senate.[67]

Had the Objection been sustained, it would have moved to the Senate, where if senators had then voted along party lines as they generally do, Gore would have held tiebreaking control in the palms of his hands. But being part of the deal, he too joined the lynching party even though he stood to gain most, since his last chance to become president hinged on the Objection's outcome.

When CBC member Maxine Waters of California stood on the floor and defiantly said, "I don't care that it [the Objection] is not signed by a senator," Gore slammed down his gavel in peremptory fashion and sarcastically responded: "The chair would advise that the rules do care."[68] At that point, the chamber erupted with ridicule-like snickerings from White members of both parties, as Gore and his European compatriots left the CBC stranded and defenseless without recourse.

This wasn't the first time White senators made public spectacles of Blacks. If you recall, Clarence Thomas got lampooned during his

Supreme Court confirmation. Despite knowing his lifelong loyalty to Americanization, White senators still felt comfortable enough to humiliate him anyway. Up until that point he was colorblind and race-neutral in his public life. Surprisingly though, once the senators started deriding and gouging-out his dignity to make him look like a "cat-daddy" pervert on the prowl, he suddenly became Black and responded like a grad-student from the School of Malcolm X, saying he was being subjected to a "high-tech lynching."[69] His exact words were:

> From my standpoint as a black American, as far as I'm concerned, it is a high-tech lynching for uppity blacks who in any way deign to think for themselves, to do for themselves, to have different ideas, and it is a message that unless you kowtow to an old order, this is what will happen to you. You will be lynched, destroyed, caricatured by a committee of the US Senate rather than hung from a tree.[70]

Since his confirmation however, he's been voicing legal opinions as though he'd never been "lynched" . . . As though the racism he spoke of vanished once he zipped into his robe. Although CBC members weren't "hanged from a tree" either, they too were "politically lynched" in broad daylight. Here's what Dr. Lani Guinier of Harvard University wrote about the proceedings in an article titled, *What We Must Overcome*:

> The anger over what happened in Florida has only been reinforced by the failure of the Democratic Party leadership to move quickly and seriously to engage with this legitimacy issue. Right after November 7, when the perception first emerged that the election was literally being hijacked, the Gore campaign actively discouraged mass protest. On January 12, when Gore presided over the counting of the Electoral College votes, it was only members of the Congressional Black Caucus who rose, one by one, to protest the filing of Florida's votes. They could not

get a single Democratic Senator (from a body that includes not a single black representative) to join their objection. The silence of white Democrats in Congress turned the CBC demonstration into an emphatic recapitulation of the election drama. As the presiding officer, Al Gore overruled the protests.

"It was the Black Caucus, and the Black Caucus alone," James Carroll wrote in the Boston Globe "that showed itself sensitive to . . . what is clearly true about the recent presidential election in Florida." That truth is the gap between what the rules permit and what democracy requires.

The CBC protest shows that outrage over the election continues. But the CBC protest also speaks to the fact that the conversation about the true meaning of democracy is not happening yet, at least not at the highest levels of government. There is talk of course about fixing the mechanics of election balloting; but it is the rules themselves, and not just the voting process, that are broken. Which is all the more reason that this conversation, which needs to address issues of justice, not just compassion, also needs to rise up from communities and a citizens movement.[71]

Guinier's point that "Right after November 7, when the perception first emerged that the election was literally being hijacked, the Gore campaign actively discouraged mass protest," is another indicator of collusion that a deal was in the works. Since no "citizens' movement" occurred as she suggested, the government has not had to officially address what happened on that fateful January day. And you can bet the CBC will not revisit this nightmare again.

Like with Justice Thomas, they too now act as though a "lynching" never occurred. Even though CBC members of the 110th Congress received key committee and sub-committee chairs, they must remain circumspect about addressing political/institutional racism in government or they risk alienating voters and self-destructing their political careers.

When it comes to Electoral Politics and the Political Process, it's clear that Euro-Americans hold all aces and high cards. Voting rights may have placated the demands of the 1960s, but the act of voting has not produced anything remotely close to parity of political powers between the races. I don't know about you, but I didn't signup my life to be ruled by rich, privileged Europeans who now have Black proxies to camouflage the voracity of their political and electoral powers.

None of this means that we hate White people or that we are anti-American. It means that we love ourselves as we rightfully should and that we have full political confidence in ourselves as we rightfully should. Yes, there's a "gap between what the rules permit and what democracy requires," as Dr. Guinier wrote; but this gives too much credit to a faulty voting system which, by design, is inherently unequipped to provide us with the "change" we need and the "power" that its philosophy promotes. So it's not simply the "rules" or the "voting process" that needs to be fixed, as she alludes.

To sum this up metaphorically – We must fix the political axis of our thinking and expectations to align properly with the hardcore realities we face, because the change and power we need cannot be actuated through the current electoral process of Democratic/Republican party politics. Our belief that "Democrats will and Republicans won't" redress our plight is a misaligned political notion because, in terms of our most outstanding quandaries, the "Republican Party" is no more the cause than the "Democratic Party" is the solution.

"If you will not fight for right when you can easily win without bloodshed; if you will not fight when your victory will be sure and not too costly; you may come to the moment when you will have to fight with all odds against you and only a precarious chance of survival."
Winston Churchill, British Prime Minister

"Those who make peaceful revolution impossible will make violent revolution inevitable."
President John F. Kennedy

"The time has come for the Negro to forget and cast behind him his hero worship and adoration of other races, and start out immediately, to create and emulate heroes of his own. . . . We must canonize our own saints, create our own martyrs, and elevate to positions of fame and honor black men and women who have made their distinct contributions to our racial history."
Marcus Garvey

"Those who can make you believe absurdities can make you commit atrocities."
Voltaire, Philosopher (1694-1778)

7
No Substitute for Sovereignty

<><><><><><><>

The Un-Birth of a Nation

America loves to boast of its government and democracy as being prototypical for the world to follow. But for Africans in America who are born with the sovereign bloodstreams of our forefathers, we are compelled by nature and ancestry to reestablish a sovereign prototype of our own. Hence, history and circumstances dictate that a proverbial fork in the political road will become both inevitable and necessary at some point.

Many complicated impasses certainly lie before us, since sovereignty doesn't happen overnight or without travail and opposition. But foremost at this time, it is essential for us to know and understand that ideologies and applications of sovereignty vary in forms and frameworks that span in range from limited to absolute. This final chapter delineates this range, citing examples that cover the diminished sovereignty of Native Americans as well as the unique brand of sovereignty exercised by the Vatican.

Up until now, Africans in America have basically related to Euro-Americans strictly on their terms, in accordance with their form and framework of sovereignty. But in this chapter I stress the need and outline the possibilities for us to have nothing less than a form and framework that is set to our own sovereign terms and desires. And as such, it's imperative that we begin to uniquely see ourselves as a true body-politic of an evolving nation in the throes of natural birth pangs.

Oftentimes we refer to ourselves as residing in *neighborhoods* when we really are stratified *nationhoods*. No, we are not an independent nation-state. However, with a near 40 million in population, we numerically encompass what could easily amount to several nations within a nation. Economically, according to the University of Georgia's *Selig Center for Economic Growth*, we will top over $965 billion in collective purchasing power by 2009. This exceeds the Gross National Product of all but 9 (the US, Japan, Germany, China, Great Britain, France, Italy, Span and Canada) of the near-200 nations in the world.[1]

Except for engaging the actual process to independently govern ourselves, we've already proven as political and military proxies for Euro-Americans that we can operate on the scale of a nation-state. But due to contrived chaos and circumstances of history, we have yet to make the transition from an integrated nation within a nation into a fully functional nation-state. This segues to remarks made by former Secretary of State Henry Kissinger, regarding the chaos and circumstances of Iraq's history.

After saying that "Iraq is not a *nation* in the historic sense" and commenting on what he called "the *evolution* of democracy," Kissinger said that democracy usually has to go "through a phase in which a nation is born." . . . Attempting to "skip that process" can produce "instabilities."[2] Accordingly, he said the Bush administration assumed that democracy would be fostered by affording Iraqis the "right to vote," but it was a mistake "to think that you can gain legitimacy primarily through the electoral process."[3]

Though the historical details are completely unalike, if you didn't know he was speaking of Iraq, you could presume Kissinger was critiquing the African plight in America since we certainly "skipped the process" of being born as a nation, plus we face chronic "instabilities." Violence and turmoil in our communities are definitely not political or religious-based like in Iraq. Yet our kids are gunned down in the streets and imprisoned just the same, while voting and electoral politics ironically occur simultaneously – as though one has no connection whatsoever to the other – just like in Iraq.

Much can therefore be commonly applied and extrapolated from Kissinger's appraisal. Why hasn't the "evolution of democracy" brought African Americans to the phase where we were "born as a nation?" What are the current and historic factors that caused us to "skip this process?" Has the "electoral process" established legitimacy for Euro-Americans to govern us?

Questions of this nature are sure to rattle mainstream nerves since the answers require long, hard looks underneath political rocks that have previously been left untouched and unturned. It's much easier and convenient to close our eyes to truth and pretend that we didn't "skip the process" and that we were "born as a nation" somewhere between 1776 and 1964. But based on Kissinger's assessment of the "evolution of democracy," I summate the political experience of Africans in America as "The Un-Birth of a Nation."

Numerous factors account for why we are "not a nation in the historic sense," however two immediate factors stand out. First, no other people in contemporary history have been as willingly loyal to a foreign people as we Africans have been to Euro-Americans. Considering our loyalty and all the centuries we've lived here, it is highly abnormal and politically unacceptable by any standard (democratic, communist, fascist or any other) that we must still fend daily to protect our human rights.

Secondly, no other people in contemporary history have fought and died in comparable numbers to us, without achieving sovereignty. We have fought and died in military combat (foreign and domestic) to secure and defend the freedoms of this democracy, and we've fought and died in the streets of America to secure and defend our freedoms from this democracy. Not to mention the countless, nameless, faceless millions who fought and died facing the savagery of slavery. Nevertheless, we still find ourselves fighting and dying.

At this stage of our "Un-Birth of a Nation," considering the distrustful nature of this establishment and its uncalled-for injustices, we could do ourselves a big favor by intelligently assessing the specifics of what we are fighting and dying for. Seriously, ask yourself: What exactly are we fighting and dying for? This question is now more relevant than ever before, since we can now contemplate answers and implement solutions that are more possible than ever before.

Former French President, Jacques Chirac, frequently spoke about the "Multi-Polar" nature of the world in ways that make this question even more relevant. In a BBC interview he postulated about the future, saying that "there will be a great American pole, a great European pole, a Chinese one, an Indian one, eventually a South American pole, with the United Nations mediating."[4] Yet notice, nowhere did he mention an "African pole" or an "African American pole."

The National Intelligence Council wrote a report titled *Project 2020*, which forecasted probable world scenarios and international sociopolitical changes that could occur between now and 2020. Likewise, it too dismisses any mention of Africans rising as world powers or playing leading roles in the world during this period.

It's not expected however, for Europeans to consider us "contenders for world power," since doing so would conflict with plans that expand their interests. Europeans don't regard Africans as competitors . . . They count on us to be cooperative. They expect us to play complementary roles that support and supplement "Globalization" as they envision it. From slavery and colonialism of yesterday, to so-called free-market capitalism of today, the European goal of hegemony over Africa and Africans remains intact.

Marcus Garvey rightly said in the early 1900s that "The world does not count races and nations that have nothing. Point me to a weak nation and I will show you a people oppressed, abused, taken advantage of by others. Show me a weak race and I will show you a people reduced to serfdom, peonage and slavery. Show me a well organized nation, and I will show you a people and a nation respected by the world."[5]

In the final analysis, the real issue for some Africans in America boils down to whether it's important that we become an independent power in the future. Sure, this is a non-issue to those who love and are willing to continue to die for Americanization. But let me assure you that there is "No Substitute for Sovereignty." So for those of us who desire to be "Sovereign Equals" among the other "Powers of the Earth," we must *Manifest the Destiny* for a "Re-Birth of our Nation."

<><><><><><><>

Where Have All the Black Men Gone?

Allow me to be direct and set the tone for the remaining segments of this work. If you want to reach the root of why we have not evolved beyond a stage of "Un-Birth," then look no further than the political complacency and sovereign limitations of our own minds. Among many other downfalls, our mindset has aided the pandemic street crisis that we helplessly watch like a horror movie as it particularly devours young Black men in record numbers.

I'll begin by putting a Biblical frame around the death and dearth of Black men because somewhere along the way, one of the Bible's most unforgettable themes – "Kill the Male Child" – has been forgotten or misapplied by the millions who attend church every Sunday. Pharaoh sought to "Kill the Male Child" in Exodus. Herod sought to "Kill the Male Child" in Matthew. "Kill the Male Child" is an age-old sociopolitical tactic used by one people to control or prevent the rise of another.

Maybe we think we need to guard our "Male Child" from people like the Viet Cong or the Taliban. Ask yourself though, who fits this Biblical script. Who in our history sought to control our rise and "Kill our Males?" For answers we don't need CSI investigators and we don't have to venture beyond America's borders. We just need to open our eyes to see and accept the obvious.

Tides have turned and young Black males have become "do-it-yourself" practitioners of the same destruction that once stemmed from forces beyond our control. Nowadays it is not slave traders or the KKK or lynch mobs or corrupt cops or government medical experiments being used to "Kill the Male Child." Black men have become so dangerous to each other that the need for systemic mechanisms has become secondary.

A 2005 Justice Department study determined that 93 percent of Black homicides of teens and kids in their early 20s were committed by other Blacks.[6] Joseph McMillan of the National Organization of Black Law Enforcement Executives (NOBLE) said that we now face violence from the new KKK – "Kids Killing Kids."[7]

"Taxes and Death" no longer stand alone as two unavoidable certainties of life as Benjamin Franklin once quipped. Now you can officially add a third: "Increasing homicides and imprisonment of Black males." This immutable rise has become so much of a fixed fact of American life that murders and lengthy prison sentences of Black men now casually render an indifferent, "Oh well, what's new?" response.

It's not even considered alarming or a State of Emergency, and wasn't even a major point of discussion during 2008 presidential debates that over 1 million Black men are incarcerated.[8] Or that 37.7% of Black men are unemployed.[9] The National Urban League issued a 2007 report on incarcerations, joblessness, and AIDS among Black men that found:

African-American men are more than twice as likely to be unemployed as white males while earning 74 percent as much per year. They are nearly seven times more likely to be incarcerated, with average jail sentences about 10 months longer than those of white men. . . . Black males between 15 and 34 are nine times more likely to be killed by firearms and nearly eight times as likely to suffer from AIDS.[10]

You can expect the establishment to remain lax in finding solutions as long as these "Black trends" do not spillover to engulf larger society. Conventional analyses seem to always conclude with the presumed panacea that "we need more jobs." Advocates keep strumming and politicians keep campaigning on the assertion that "jobs" are the missing ingredient. But if you don't know already, let me be the first to tell you that we were brought here to "work" for Euro-Americans. "Working for them" is our defined function for being here. Heck, everybody had a job during slavery, even 5-year-olds and great-grandmothers too. Employment was 100 percent, 100 percent of the time.

These days you don't necessarily have to pick cotton without wages to be enslaved. Conversely, just because you do receive a wage doesn't necessarily mean that you are free. Besides, America is going broke anyway. Places like China, the European Union, and Arab nations have become formidable economic contenders that are making America's products and services seem second-rate.

America is over $9 trillion in debt, and 44 cents of every US dollar is owed to foreign creditors like the governments of Kuwait and China.[11] Sovereign Wealth Funds (financial institutions of foreign governments that invest in the economies of other nations) are pouring into America faster than immigrants. From November 11th of 2007 to January 15th of 2008 alone, the foreign governments of Kuwait, China, Singapore, United Arab Emirates, and Korea invested over $40 billion in US banks.[12]

The US government was not only born in debt from war-costs of its revolution, it has recorded annual debts in all but two years of its existence.[13] Since 2001, the dollar's value has tail-spun in decline to the point where it is no longer the world's strongest currency.[14] Look closely in big cities like New York and you'll see that some businesses now accept Euros in place of dollars.

Jobs are really a secondary issue. Unemployment and rising prison populations are nasty coughs, runny nose symptoms of greater ills ... Ills that plague the minds of Black people. Ills that cannot and will not be resolved by anyone other than ourselves, because the remedies we need are contingent upon "sovereign self-realizations."

Gangs, guns, drugs, dropouts, and drive-bys are *externalities* that have less to do with a lack of jobs than with the *internalities* of misguided thoughts. Kids, as a consequence, shoot and kill each other over the most-pettiest things imaginable, undeterred by thoughts of prison. Some youngsters even seem encouraged by the future prospect of prison-life. To them, prison is the place to "get strong." Recidivism occurs like clockwork because – many incarcerated Black males are not just "*in* prison," but "prison is *in* them." Prison resides in their hearts and minds just as much as religion resides in the hearts and minds of congregants.

Men of this nature, who are unable to outrun urban avalanches, get conditioned in prison to not even want a "job." Even worse, prisons themselves are designed to corrupt more than to reform, especially since some operate as "for-profit" private enterprises, like hotel chains, where revenues depend on new and repeat business from "guests" groomed for perpetual delinquency. Just as it should be illegal for healthcare corporations to prey on and profit from the sick, it should likewise be illegal for private corporations to prey on and profit from prisoners. But this is capitalism, American-style.

Cycles of incarceration have reached a point of what I call "double occupancy" where fathers and sons are imprisoned at the same time and even at the same prison. Sons sometimes get released, only to return home to a father who just got out the joint himself . . . "like father, like son," and "the blind leading the blind."

But it doesn't stop there. From what I'm hearing, we've reached instances of "triple occupancy" of father, son, and grandson. Statistics also show a rise in violence and incarcerations among young girls. As early as 1999, *US News and World Report* reported a story of a young Black girl being incarcerated in the same prison with her mother and grandmother.[15]

It's not just poor and uneducated Blacks. Gil Scott-Heron and Huey P. Newton are two notably brilliant Black men that I randomly select, who like so many others got sucked into this bottomless street vortex. Huey was shot dead in drug-related pettiness on the same California streets where he was formerly hailed as a leader and genius of the Black Power Movement. Gil, who was a premier thought-revolutionary and musician in the 1970s, prophesied his drug difficulties in his lyrics from *The Bottle*, saying: "I'll tell you a little secret. If you ever come lookin' for me, you know where I'm bound to be, in 'The Bottle.' Turn around. Look around on any corner, if you see some Brother looking like a goner, it's gonna be me."

Other Black entertainers and athletes also attain great fame and fortunes from their "jobs," yet they still face charges or get jailed for a variety of nonsensical things. Naming names is unnecessary because we all know who's who and what's what. But what we don't seem to realize is that we do not suffer from the need for "jobs" per se, as much as from political complacency and misguided thoughts that are directly linked to the sovereign limitations of our minds and desires.

What lies ahead in the next 25 years if murders increase and cycles of imprisonment continue to overflow with young, fatherless, undereducated Black men who have no one to guide them but older fatherless, undereducated men who are caught up even deeper in the same dead-end cycles? One nightmare forecast was given in a newspaper article titled: "Where Have All the **Black Men** Gone?"[16] And that's right, "**Black Men**" was written in boldface type. In answering this question the article states that "Most are dead. Many others are locked up." It went on to say:

232

There are nearly two million more black adult women than men in America, a stark testimony to how often black men die before their time. With nearly another million black men in prison or the military, the real imbalance is even greater – a gap of 2.8 million, according to US Census data for 2002. On average, then, there are 26 percent more black women than black men; among whites, women outnumber men by just 8 percent.

Perhaps no single statistic so precisely measures the fateful, often fatal, price of being a black man in America, or so powerfully conveys how beset black communities are by the violence and disease that leaves them bereft of brothers, fathers, husbands and sons, and leaves whole communities reeling.

Exponentially higher homicide and AIDS rates play their part, especially among younger black men. Even more deadly through middle age and beyond are higher rates of cardiovascular disease and cancer.

In Harlem and Chicago's South Side, two-thirds of black boys and one-third of black girls who reach their 15th birthday would not make 65.

Chilling stuff. But says [Dr. David] Satcher, "The real question is, does the nation really care to solve this problem?"[17]

Just so you'll know, Dr. Satcher is far from being inexperienced or a loudmouthed radical. He was the Surgeon General during President Bill Clinton's administration and thereafter became the Director of The Satcher Health Leadership Institute at Morehouse University School of Medicine.[18] So for him to question if this "nation really cares to solve this problem" is not just jarring, but jarring with weight and credibility. Most likely, it wasn't his intention, yet his suspicion has a context that borders on sovereign reckoning.

Anyone who similarly questions America's will, should know that there are crucial points in the historical experience of every repressed people where "self-remedies" are the only remedy. In *God the Black Man and Truth,* Ben Ammi wrote the following account of America's lack of will to solve our problems and our consequent need for self-remedies:

> The problems of Black America are defined as the most complex in the world; so complex that after 400 years, not one of the major problems touching the lives of the captives has been solved. Today we still see the social problem, economic problem, educational problem, political problem, and race problem as acute as they ever were. Therefore either America *cannot* solve these problems, or America *will not* solve these problems. Either way, it leaves us no choice. We must take our destiny into our own hands and solve the problems ourselves.[19] (original italics).

Social deterioration in nations does not generally exist in isolation without political and/or economic tributaries that flow into some source of profits that benefit an establishment. Governments do not allow societal decay to accrue to the point where it becomes a net drain on needed national resources. And America is no different.

Believe me, it serves an interest of Americanization for a certain percentage of Black men to crumble into non-traceable dust. If not, the government would have long interceded to stop our bleeding – for its own benefit. Slavery and segregation have already fulfilled their purpose as engines that accelerated America to super-power status. Those of us who choke on the exhaust fumes are regarded as disposable and replaceable, especially in this age where immigrant laborers eagerly wait in long lines to mow lawns and mix concrete for minimum wage.

Until we politically take full command of ourselves, the worst is sure to come, because American democracy is not intrinsically structured to "justly undo what it has unjustly done."

If it weren't for the success of gentrification to uproot whole Black communities throughout the country, as with ongoing processes in places like Newark, NJ and Harlem, NY, this establishment would probably want to use force elements like the National Guard or perhaps private security/mercenary groups like Blackwater to storm in and *purify* the ethnic blight of America's "hoods." Dress rehearsals for this may have even taken place, as I already outlined in the "Controlled Chaos Drill" segment regarding New Orleans. But drastic means are unnecessary for the moment, due to the effectiveness and revenue streams connected to things like gentrification, the prison industrial complex, and the New KKK (Kids Killing Kids).

This brings to mind comments of the rapper Cam'ron who on *60 Minutes* gave a rundown on "snitching."[20] First of all, it was clear from the interview that he is poised and sharp-minded enough to easily represent the voice of young people in a sovereign movement. Based on what he called a street "Code of Ethics" in the hood, it's a violation to cooperate or give information to the police.[21] A group of teenagers who were also interviewed echoed sentiments of the same.

Even if he knew of a serial killer living next door, Cam'ron claimed he would either move or keep quiet before he told police. Later on he issued an apology, saying "I'm not saying it's [snitching] right, but it's reality."[22] He said he spoke out of frustration from being shot and carjacked himself in 2005, and he could see how his comments "could be viewed as offensive."[23]

Nothing is new about Black people not trusting or cooperating with the cops. This is not something that started with hip hop. Warnings about "the authorities" have passed down throughout our generations. The notion of "police being our friends" is new. "Police" and "Policy" have worked together like anvils and hammers. Inasmuch as US policies have historically imposed unjust restrictions, the police have been a dependable arm of policy enforcement.

Since law enforcement agencies in general have been Gestapo-like, it's understandable how and why youngsters would disassociate themselves from the cops, the FBI, ATF, ICE etc. But youngsters of late are taking practical caution to irrational extremes, which cause more harm than help. There's nothing intelligent about apathy or lawlessness that corrodes your living environment and destroys you and your own people. Animals even have instinctive senses to not defecate where they sleep.

Young men must realize that a primary responsibility of being a man is to love and protect women and children. For all the gangsta Brothers who like to emulate fictional gangsters from movies, this principle was stressed throughout *The Godfather*. We can also learn from real-life Hasidic Jews who have their own security patrols in some of their New York neighborhoods. They don't outwardly carry themselves as ganstas at all, but they'll do more than snitch if you even look like you might do something sideways to their women and children.

If Black men allow serial killers, drug dealers, and petty thieves to run around loose in our neighborhoods, who then is responsible for protecting our women and children? "No Snitchin" equates to "No Protection," which partially accounts for all the accidental bystander deaths we constantly hear about.

"No Snitchin" is clearly a self-defeating "Street Code" that perhaps millions of our youth live by, and the reality is that they are not going anywhere by tomorrow. They possess a mindset that must be reached and reckoned with since our future progression as a people cannot be detached from the ultimate rise or continued decline of our youths who live in various "hoods" around the country.

<><><><><><><>

A "Girl and Government" that Look Like Us

Thoughts produce substance. The substance (or lack thereof) of Black America is a byproduct of our thinking. Our accomplishments as well as our infestations can be traced directly without detour to the thoughts of our sociopolitical mindset. Given that our near-400 years of collective intellect has yet to produce the substances or quality of life we desire, something must therefore be wrong or a least inadequate with our thinking.

One thing for sure is that we have not controlled the *end-use* or *end-users* of our education or intellect. Ask yourself – To what end-use is our collective education and intellect currently being applied, and who are the ultimate beneficiaries or end-users? With the current end-use and end-users, we have not found answers to stop our children from shooting and killing each other in America, or to stop 3,000 children from dying everyday from malaria in Africa. We can't even stop our youngsters from cussing and using vulgarities in front of elders, much less rescue entire Black communities from being held hostage to poverty, crime, and drugs.

But as 102-year-old Prince Jervey Thomas once told me, "Any condition created by human thought can be altered or recreated through human thought. . . . The mind is the Great Determinator of who and what man becomes in life." Albert Einstein similarly reasoned that you "cannot alter a condition with the same mindset that created it in the first place."[24] Solutions, in other words, require an approach from an alternate or expanded scope of thought that traverses the bounds of preexisting thoughts from which a condition emanates.

Gleaning from both these insights, I have correspondingly deduced that our most complex conditions exist because we think and act like a people who are content with being "governed by others," rather than thinking and acting like a people who strive to "govern for self." To alter our conditions we must alter our approach by adopting a traversing mindset that can arrive at sovereign-minded conclusions and solutions.

Today's lasting implications of the notable "Doll Test" that was conducted and documented in the 1940s, typify Einstein's point and corroborate my approach. Psychologists Kenneth Clark and his wife, Mamie Phipps Clark, designed this test using Black and White dolls (identical except in color) to study and determine racial perceptions and preferences of Black children, ages 3 to 7.[25] Kenneth Clark even wrote a subsequent summary paper for the White House Mid-Century Conference on Children and Youth in 1950, which the Supreme Court cited as a supportive reference in its *Brown vs. Board* ruling to desegregate schools.[26] Here's what they discovered:

Almost all of the children readily identified the race of the dolls. However, when asked which they preferred, the majority selected the white doll and attributed positive characteristics to it. The Clarks also gave the children outline drawings of a boy and girl and asked them to color the figures the same color as themselves. Many of the children with dark complexions colored the figures with a white or yellow crayon. The Clarks concluded that "prejudice, discrimination, and segregation" caused black children to develop a sense of inferiority and self-hatred.[27]

Six decades removed, the same test was re-conducted in 2005 by a young film student, Kiri Davis, in documentary short titled "A Girl Like Me," for the expressed purpose to "shed new light on how society affects black children today and how little has actually changed."[28] Her 2005 findings were eerily identical to the 1940s . . . Black children racially profiled and negatively stigmatized the Black dolls as "bad" and "ugly," while the White dolls were preferred; positively related to; and perceived as "nice" and "pretty."[29]

As adults we gasp, realizing the psychological urgency to correct these confounded inclinations. But this mal-habituation to overvalue White images does not dissipate automatically with age or time. Instead, it advances into a full-blown sociopolitical mindset with fixed affinities to further idolize "that which is European" at the expense of "that which is African." As such, these children exhibit the early stages and servilities of a graduated continuum and pathology, wherein the very psychological inducements that trap them to embrace and prefer a White doll, correspondingly induce and trap Black adults during advanced stages to equally embrace and prefer a White government.

The true gasping should therefore be reserved for our urgent need to recognize that this psychological plague upon our children to covet European images, not only stems from our mental and political shortfalls as adults, but it also foretells of future predilections to covet European ideals and institutions just the same.

Since we do not prefer "A Government that Looks Like Us," it shouldn't be shocking that this mindset trickles down so that our children do not prefer "A Doll that Looks Like Them." The "Doll Test" can be expected to repeatedly render the same inescapable results for uninterrupted decades or perhaps even centuries to come because, as Einstein affirmed, you "cannot alter a condition with the same mindset that created it in the first place."

Cyclical adversities and complications of this sort are unfortunate aftereffects that are prone to occur over the long term when a people allow others to vicariously become the psychological source and sovereign deciders of their fate. Until we recognize and unshackle the European yokes that have colonized our thoughts, we will be defenseless to alter the confused mindsets of our children and the sordid conditions of our communities.

From birth, our children are bombarded with positive European images, beginning with the White "Gerber Baby" on food labels that they learn to psychologically associate with satisfying their hunger. Kindergarten is the doorway to formally ensconce them into a "system of educational thought," wherein "White" is the officially recognized paradigm of beauty, intellect, and power. At this point, they are well on their way to being just as spellbound to the perceived beauty of White dolls, as adults are spellbound to the perceived greatness of White governments.

"Acting White" is a tagline that Black kids have used even before my childhood to deride Black kids who are academically smart. Naturally the adult response is that "there's nothing White about being smart." As much as this is true, it also misses the point and fails to address the psychology of what drives young minds to associate "education" with Whiteness.

Yes, the world is factually round and $1 + 1 = 2$. These are universal facts of education that are neither Black nor White, America or African. The problem however, goes back to the end-use of education and intellect . . . because the end-use for which nations use information to educate kids about this "round world" is not always neutral. Education in

America is based on processes and purposes of Euro-centrism that place European images, ideals, and institutions as the center frame of reference and relevance.

Hence, the designation of "Acting White" is an attempt by our youths to convey something that we already know but have not marshaled the wherewithal to correct – Which is that America's "system of educational thought" defines the totalities of this "round world" through the filtered lenses of White perspectives and interpretations.

A "White dominance" prevails over Black children in classrooms and textbooks just as much as it does with Black adults in workplaces and society at large. Our mistake is that we consider it sufficient to simply take portions of what has become popularly accepted as "Black History" and then stick tidbits of it to the larger body of American history. This fosters a misbelief that "Black History" is being taught to our kids in schools. Yet the process, purpose, and end-uses of education are still as Europeanized as ever. Students in Russia may also learn tidbits about Benjamin Banneker or George Washington Carver, but you better believe that Russia's "system of educational thought" will still have the same end-use and will still be conveyed no less through the process and purpose of Russian eyes.

It doesn't make sense for a people to pay taxes to have their children educated through the filtered interests and viewpoints of another people's sense of greatness. A portion of the sovereign strength of any people can be weighed and measured by the extent to which their children are educated to see themselves as the source and center of their own world experience. Wherever you find a strong contemporary nation, it's assured that you'll also find a "system of educational thought" where children have a strong sovereign-sense of themselves.

Being pasted onto the periphery as appendages and footnotes to an already-existing "system of educational thought" of another people, falls short in magnitude to rectify our quagmire where 58 percent of Black males don't even graduate high school.[30]

The *Civil Rights Project* at Harvard University and the Urban Institute produced a report titled, "Losing Our Future: How Minority

Youth Are Being Left Behind by the Graduation Rate Crisis." It found that half or more of Black youths are getting left behind before high school graduation in a "hidden crisis" that is ironically obscured by regulations of the *No Child Left Behind Act* which "allow schools, districts, and states to all but eliminate graduation rate accountability for minority subgroups. Graduation rates tell only half of this story. The other half is just how much did the students learn? Black students that do graduate score far lower on standardized tests of knowledge on average than white students that also graduate. So the picture is even grimmer than it first appears."[31] A *New York Times* article reached similar conclusions:

> Black men in the United States face a far more dire situation than is portrayed by common employment and education statistics, a flurry of new scholarly studies warn, and it has worsened in recent years.
>
> Focusing more closely than ever on the life patterns of young black men, the new studies, by experts at Columbia, Princeton, Harvard and other institutions, show that the huge pool of poorly educated black men are becoming ever more disconnected from the mainstream society, and to a far greater degree than comparable white or Hispanic men.
>
> By their mid-30s, 30 percent of black men with no more than a high school education have served time in prison, and 60 percent of dropouts have . . . Among black dropouts in their late 20s, more are in prison on a given day (34 percent) than are working (30 percent).[32]

One of the most common reasons kids give for dropping out is that "they don't find classes interesting."[33] Research was conducted to this end with students from Maine and Texas, who were given two different stories to read to determine if "culturally relevant" material would prove more interesting and inspirational.[34] Here's what occurred:

One story was read by all kids in the study. The other story was culturally relevant to their individual lives or geographic location. The study found that children better understood the culturally relevant story – which may imply that "relevance can make a difference in kids' achievement."

Although few educators would blame the lack of African American-themed reading material for the achievement gap separating black and white students . . . anecdotal evidence suggests these books [authored by African Americans] may be inspiring more black children to read, which may help to redress the divide.[35]

Unless we self-correct this educational disaster you can be sure it will persist, because no one is going to rush to our rescue. As John Henrik Clarke wrote, "If you expect the present day school system to give history to you, you are dreaming. This, we have to do ourselves. The Chinese didn't go out in the world and beg people to teach Chinese studies or let them teach Chinese studies. The Japanese didn't do that either. People don't beg other people to restore their history; they do it themselves.[36]

Jews can also be added to Clarke's reference. They are known for their Yeshivas to teach and keep their people grounded in a Jewish "system of educational thought." Then they have their *Daf Yomi* (Page a Day) studies, where "tens of thousands" of Jews worldwide, collectively study a Page a Day for an hour, for 7½ years to complete the reading of the 2,711-page Babylonian Talmud (Biblical commentary of rabbis from different eras).[37]

Jews examine groups of commentaries that delve into Jewish laws and interpretations on everything from holiday celebrations, candlelighting and agriculture to business, ethics and sexual relations between spouses. Secular Americans might equate it to reading discourses by Abraham Lincoln, Thomas Jefferson and

Franklin D. Roosevelt on the same subject, interspersed with speculation on what George Washington might have thought.[38]

At completion in 2005, 46,000 Jews gathered in New York at Madison Square Garden and in New Jersey at the Continental Airlines Arena to celebrate via satellite with compeers from Chicago, LA, Moscow, Buenos Aires, Montreal and elsewhere.[39] Learning discipline and commitment are among the main lessons of this program, so shortly following every 7½-year cycle, a brand new 7½-year cycle begins to further instill the Jewish psyche and system of thought into their culture.

In this same vein, we have little reason to trust the educational oversight of any people more than we trust the same of ourselves. We need to teach and guide upcoming generations to become the kind of leaders we need to specifically answer the challenges we face. To quote Dr. Clarke again: "Our children should be picked out and trained for leadership from birth. You can watch how that child handles a fork; watch that child's ability to share with the group; watch that child's ability to protect the group and to accept the training that will make that child improve. We should spot leaders early and begin to train them. We should make a priesthood of this effort."[40]

For the sake of our children who are not only being "left behind," but "thrown away," we need an academic "system of educational thought" that reflects our unvarnished history, that can rectify their distorted perceptions of themselves and the world. Only then can our children gain a sovereign-sense of who we are and stand a chance to psychologically become self-assured enough to embrace and prefer both "A Girl and Government that Look Like Us."

<><><><><><><>

243

Evolutionary Body Politic

Over the years, the so-called best and brightest Black leaders, intellectuals, and urbanologists have convened nationwide to debate and decipher "what's wrong" and "how to solve" our ills. Gang truces, after-school programs, and anti-drug campaigns have all been attempted to no measurable avail. So far "all the king's horses and all the king's men" haven't been able to reassemble our fractured pieces.

I've observed that conference participants tend to primarily deliberate the effects, symptoms, and surface of issues, while skimming over the origin, cause, and source of problems. Many also seem to be psychological captives of disbelief of what is possible to accomplish without Euro-American consent and involvement.

Noticeably absent and alien at these conventions is discourse with "sovereign reasoning." Panelists in fact, never even utter the word "sovereignty" in typical forums . . . It's as though the concept doesn't even exist. Without sovereign reasoning it is fairly certain that Americanization will automatically get undeservedly pardoned from critique of both its culpabilities and its abuse of sovereign powers. In addition, it becomes difficult for us to see ourselves as the source, center, and self-deciders of our own political fate.

Sovereign reasoning immediately informs us that we are dealing with two very distinct but interrelated set of factors – The human flaws of Americanization and our human failings as a people. Sovereign reasoning provides the keenness of mind to first identify, and then separate, the flaws of Americanization from our failings as a people. Without doing so, we remain saddled to faulty mental approaches that venerate Americanization as a paradigm that we need to follow as opposed to a flawed system that needs to be fixed. → over Thrown

Take for instance the annual *State of the Black Union* forum, organized by the Tavis Smiley Group (TSG). Jamestown, Virginia was selected as the 2007 venue in order to honor its founding as the first English colonial settlement 400 years prior in 1607. Though Jamestown is ornately billed by Euro-Americans as the birthplace of "representative government," I'm sure our once-sovereign forefathers who experienced "imposed government" would take umbrage at such a claim.

In an article titled, "From Jamestown to Virginia Tech: Colonization and Massacres," Roxanne Dunbar-Ortiz describes the settling of Jamestown as the arrival of "ragged mercenaries" and the "beginning of British overseas colonialism."[41] The TSG however promoted Jamestown and the forum as a gathering that would "Commemorate America's 400th anniversary with . . . Black thought leaders, educators, public policy makers, religious leaders and community organizers."[42]

This type of "marketing" bodes well to attract corporate sponsors, but there's an ever-abiding creepiness to Jamestown, and even more creepiness with Black people attempting to embrace Jamestown as some sort of "democratic success story" of our own. Not to be crass, but our embrace of Jamestown is like the political equivalent and self-indignity of us smashing a pie in our own face. This is another resounding example of the mistaken belief that we share a "common history" rather than a "related history" with the founding people and events of this nation.

Furthermore, other than sponsorship funding, what do we gain by memorializing a place like Jamestown? Jamestown is no ancient Timbuktu or Mecca or Jerusalem that has sacred significance. Though it may bolster pride for Euro-Americans, there is no historic honor or glory in Jamestown for us. Plus, I can guarantee you that the broad majority of Africans in America are not emotionally tied to Jamestown. And since the focus of TSG forums partly concerns ridding the havoc from our communities, I can further guarantee you that youngsters in the "hoods" are even more distant from Jamestown.

Leutisha Stills succinctly summed up the *State of the Black Union* forums in an article in *The Black Agenda Report* titled, "Black Leaders . . . or Leading Blacks."

The forum has evolved into an annual substitute for genuine politics in a Black polity that is bereft of institutions of accountability. By default, Tavis fills the void with his road shows and media exhibitions. But Mr. Smiley is not the problem: he is simply a businessman, who sees a hole in the market where a *movement* used to be.

However, the most important lesson learned from the totality of conversation, was the awesome absence of coherence in current Black politics - much less a plan to revive a movement as an engine for progress.

Smiley's self-assignment, for which he is hugely competent, is to assemble luminaries offering a variety of viewpoints, allowing African Americans to pick and choose among divergent opinions. Yet the mechanisms to implement any of the items on the eclectic menu through mass or elective action, are either missing (the absence of a movement) or broken (incoherence within Black electoral political formations such as the Congressional Black Caucus). Tavis, the impresario, can't fix that, but he does put on a good show - which, at present, is all we've got.[43]

I wouldn't venture as far to say that it's "all we've got," but to my knowledge it is the largest annually televised forum "that we've got." Let me stress that I do support the efforts of this and other forums that bring real issues to the fore. However, I do not subscribe to the thinking that American democracy merely needs a bit of tweaking here and there for it to function on our behalf.

Yes, as citizens we do reap *some* benefits of this democracy but as I've pointedly stated, our worth to this nation was, is, and always will be predicated on our labor, loyalty, and consumption. Black president or no Black president, Euro-Americans will never politically, economically, or socially "tweak" this nation into something other than what it is – A European nation that is majority-owned, fully controlled, and absolutely governed by Anglo-European principles and policies.

My hope and recommendation is that Black forums in general will broaden in capacity to include panels and panelists that can offer sovereign dimensions to topics, so as to enrich and expand discourse into areas that otherwise would be unlikely. Based on empirical observations and interactions, I sense that growing percentages of Africans in America are historically ready to open their minds to sovereign possibilities.

They comprise what I define as an "Evolutionary Body Politic," who I believe can become exponents of the mindset and outcome alluded to by Einstein that can "alter the conditions created by our existing mindset." By "Body Politic" I am, by definition, simply referring to a "collective unit." Although this unit undoubtedly exists, it is not functionally organized into an official entity of any sort. Even so, it is the potential, not the performance of this unit that is currently important.

Interestingly, the fact that this Body Politic exists is secondary to the rare cross-sector of its makeup. There is no typical profile that's outwardly noticeable or identifiable. Members do not support any militant school of thought or even one particular organization. They occupy different strata in economics and education, and contrary to what may be presumed, not all are of the ilk of Garveyites, Black Nationalists, or reparations activists. Many are faithful church-goers who unfailingly vote Democratic, while others span the gamut from high school dropouts to Phi Beta Kappas; gang-bangers to Baptist preachers; ex-cons to corporate execs; the gainfully unemployed to the gainfully accomplished.

Despite this array of differences, members of this Body Politic share a common mindset of sociopolitical disgust and have overlapping dislikes and distrusts of government and society. They also take deep exception to the unchecked ways of White privilege and White favoritism that are normalized within government and society. And they profoundly resent having to play mind-games or bend over backwards at their workplaces to appease White execs and managers who in some cases are less qualified and competent.

Many can personally attest to racism, but they don't hate *all* White people nor do they consider themselves racists. They smile, act courteous in public, and like all other law-abiding citizens they pose no national security threat. Nobody has to worry about them plotting a bloody revolution to overthrow anything.

Their disgust is mostly expressed in private, in the company of other like-minded Blacks, which is why such matters do not receive the due political attention they deserve. Nevertheless, this Body Politic is dissonant in thought, and if given the opportunity to justly "turn the tables" without inciting violence, or losing their jobs, or jeopardizing the welfare of their families – many would have done so yesterday. More than anything else, concerns for their security and livelihood keep them in check, not their patriotism or love of country.

It is no secret that America has ways to make life difficult for "troublemakers," so the average Black person with a decent career with heath benefits and a pension plan isn't willing to risk it all by supporting anything that could be perceived as "non-mainstream." Excuse the analogy, but their pent-up exasperation parallels the hidden infuriation of our forefathers, who when given the chance, would secretly spit in the slaveholder's food and then standby watching with a decoy smile, waiting to serve seconds.

The above descriptions categorize a living, breathing Body Politic of Black men and women that I believe represents a sovereign-receptive audience "in waiting," whose true unfiltered political voice and vision has not been proportionately recognized. But you know what? This is integration, "American style." This is part of the full-course dish we got by ordering "Civil Rights" from America's political menu.

Therefore, as a means towards actualizing our sovereign potential, this Evolutionary Body Politic could benefit by politically and academically familiarizing itself with the assorted versions of sovereignties and ideologies that are being practiced throughout the world.

Forms and Frameworks of Sovereignties

From a sovereign perspective, "Ideology" concerns doctrines, philosophies, and belief systems that shape the psyche and constitute the centrality and characteristics of a peoples' sociopolitical mindset. Or, to borrow from the earlier quote of Winston Churchill, ideology is the thought-process that makes you "American" or "Un-American." Here however, the emphasis is to specify an ideology of our own that can evolutionize our thought process to espouse sovereignty as a primary ideal for ourselves.

Ideologies however can be good or bad, depending on motives and use. At its best, a sovereign ideology creates peace and justice, and works to unite a people into a collective whole, without infringing upon the sovereign or human rights others. It helps to formulate self-interests and the best sociopolitical means by which to provide and protect the everyday needs of society and government.

At its worst, a sovereign ideology works to unjustly advance one people at the expense and disadvantage of another. Ideological clashes of both politics and religion have escalated to levels today where virtually everyone in the world is a potential target of one thing or another. History points to long ugly uses of ideology where people are enslaved, colonized, occupied or militarily assailed. In the aftermath, a peoples' cultural cohesion and sense of nationhood can further unravel or even be vanquished by the imposition of the *foreign* ideology of the victor.

Modern ideologies in general are not neutral in motives, and certainly not universal in application. Inasmuch as, say, Japanese ideology cannot peacefully be applied universally to appease or remedy all nations, the same holds true with every other political ideology. No ideology should therefore be mashed into the face of a people or subtly imposed through conditioning, especially when millions stand up to proclaim they've had "enough."

The ideology of Euro-Americans sounds good, but it has brought neither peace nor stability to the world. As an Evolutionary Body Politic we not only need a fresh ideology for our own sake of survival, but also to help restore kilter to this world.

The fact that Africans in America are not monolithic also has bearing here, because all of us would never agree on everything about anything, particularly an issue as paramount as reconstituting our ideological makeup. But here's something to consider . . . Despite our vast differences in thoughts and beliefs, none of these differences precluded us from adopting the ideology of Euro-Americans. So on the flipside, none of these same differences should therefore preclude us from pursuit of a sovereign ideology of our own, especially considering the innumerable contrarieties between the principles and practices of Americanization.

It is not impossible or unheard of for a people to have legitimate philosophical differences, yet commonly share the same political ideology. Democrats, Republicans, Independents and Libertarians exemplify this with heated partisan and intra-party spats, covering everything from A to Z, from abortion to Zionism. Yet they all are staunch in loyalty to Americanization. Even a fringe guy like Lyndon LaRouche, who is out on a philosophical limb of his own, is still accepted into the American fold.

In fact, your right to select any political party of your choosing without being harassed is supposed to be fundamental to the "freedoms" offered by this society. Philosophical diversity is supposed to be a cornerstone that's reflective of what "true democracy" is all about. My point is that we as Africans in America can also be philosophically different on a sovereign level.

All of us do not have to agree word-for-word, point-for-point in order to manifest our sovereign ideology and identity. It's already been proven through Americanization that being *different* is not a *disqualifier* for nationhood. Nobody therefore has to be converted into anything. We all can retain every drop of our political, social, and religious diversities and yet still be ideologically unified in sovereign ambition, regardless if a person is affiliated with the NAACP or UNIA; the Boulé or the Black Panthers; SCLC or the Nation of Islam; the Daughters of the Revolution or the Republic of New Africa. The key is to lend ourselves to operational unity.

We could benefit greatly from basic research to academically familiarize ourselves with the operational unity and structural makeup of sovereignties being practiced worldwide. Not all sovereignty encompasses formidable governments with vast territories and massive standing armies. Sovereignty differs in forms and frameworks that range from limited to absolute.

Right here in America, sovereignty is exercised by Euro-Americans in absolute form, while another variety is concurrently exercised by Native American tribes in limited forms. Although the US government should rightfully have no "legitimate authority" over Native Tribes (just as with us), the Supreme Court acknowledged in 1832 that "Tribes have the unique status of nations within a state as well as nations within a nation, with the implication that the relationships between the three 'sovereigns' [tribes, states, and nation] are meant to be conducted on a government-to-government basis."[44]

The reason that Native tribes do not appear to be sovereign like other established governments in the world is because, hypocritically, the US government has historically employed its absoluteness of sovereignty as a restrictive force of political and territorial containment. This further nullifies their belief in the concept that "all men are created equal," which ironically was written on the sovereign soils of the native people whom they've historically subjected to sovereign inequality ... What a paradox. According to the *Maine Policy Review* from the University of Maine:

> Without fences and border crossings to help define reservation boundaries, it is difficult for most Americans to comprehend that legally there are no differences between the 560 federally recognized native nations within the United States and other sovereign nations around the world such as England, China or South Africa. It is also difficult for most to believe that individual

tribes are sovereign nations because the US federal government has rarely treated them as such.[45]

The comparatively limited level of tribal sovereignty in the United States today is due to tribes relinquishing certain rights through treaties or agreements, or because rights were taken from them without their consent through specific acts of Congress. Despite these limitations, the Supreme Court has continuously supported the notion that the sovereign rights of tribes remain fully intact unless those rights are specifically and clearly taken away from or given away by the tribes. As a result, each tribe has retained varying degrees of the sovereignty it possessed prior to European contact. Again, it is the de facto rights (rights in practice) of tribes that enable them to exert their sovereignty, which have been given away. These de facto rights often differ, sometimes dramatically, from one tribe to the next, even within the same state.[46]

In Worcester vs. Georgia 1832, Chief Justice C. J. Marshall wrote: "From the commencement of our government Congress has passed acts to regulate trade and intercourse with the Indians; which treat them as nations. All these acts, and especially that of 1802, which is still in force, manifestly consider the several Indian nations as distinct political communities, having territorial boundaries, within which their authority is exclusive, and having a right to all the lands within those boundaries, which is not only acknowledged, but guaranteed by the United States. The Cherokee Nation, then, is a distinct community, occupying its own territory, with boundaries accurately described, in which the laws of Georgia can have no force, and which the citizens of Georgia have no right to enter but with the assent of the Cherokees themselves or in conformity with treaties and with the acts of Congress."[47]

Based on different cultural and historical experiences, native concepts and applications of sovereignty differed (as with Africans in

Africa) prior to European contact. But the overriding fact is that they all existed without foreign influence or interference. After European contact, Native American sovereignty was diluted and has now taken on expressions that are even "non-native."

Nevertheless, all 560 tribes now have sovereign rights and powers to independently: Define their own form of government; Determine the conditions for membership; Administer justice and enforce laws; Levy taxes; Regulate domestic relations of their members; and Regulate property use.[48] Throughout history however, "Congress has been reluctant to allow tribes too much power, particularly in the area of criminal jurisdiction."[49]

Some people may question the benefits of having limited sovereignty. Well, just remember, there is "No Substitute for Sovereignty." In confirming this, the *Maine Policy Review* determined from research conducted over the last 20 years that "When native nations exert their sovereignty and take matters into their hands to create local solutions to local problems, they not only succeed but prosper."[50]

Also, the *Harvard Project on American Indian Economic Development* and other institutions "have not found a single example of sustained economic development on a Native American reservation where the models for development have been imposed or developed by outside agencies, or where native nations have not exerted their inherent and de facto sovereignty. Sovereignty, above all else, determines successful economic development on reservations."[51]

Limited sovereignty however is no longer suitable to the Lakota, the tribe of legendary chiefs Sitting Bull and Crazy Horse. In December of 2007, based on their *"Declaration of Continuing Independence"* Lakota leaders officially informed the State Department of their intent to unilaterally withdraw from all treaties with the federal government.[52] They now are engaged in a full-fledged struggle to seize back their absolute sovereignty.

Russell Means, a Lakota leader, said the US has broken 33 treaties and that the Lakota are acting "... within the laws on treaties passed at the Vienna Convention and put into effect by the US and the rest of the international community in 1980. We are legally within our rights to be free and independent."[53] He also said that Americans who renounce their US citizenship can live tax-free on Lakota land and receive Lakota-issued passports and driving licenses.[54] Lakota leaders have since dispatched envoys to garner support and assistance from other nations.

There's a presumption that the US government "granted" certain rights and powers to Native Americans via the Constitution and various treaties. But again, since Native sovereignty long predates Euro-American arrival, the US government did not grant, but conversely commandeered Native rights and powers through such documents. So the Lakota have every right to re-declare their full sovereignty. Their just and legal right to do so is further defended by the United Nations "Resolution on the Rights of Indigenous Peoples" that was passed in 2007 by 143 majority votes to 4 nays from Canada, Australia, New Zealand, and the United States, with 11 abstentions.[55] It is not coincidental that all these "nay" governments have usurped the sovereignty and displaced the populations of indigenous peoples.

Research into sovereignties will also inform us that a treaty of different sorts, known as the 1929 Lantern Accords, established the modern sovereign state of the Vatican, headed by the Papacy and the Holy See.[56] "Holy See" is Catholic nomenclature referring to the composite authority, jurisdiction, and sovereignty that is vested in the Pope and his advisers.[57]

Aside from embodying a spiritual/religious form of sovereignty, other extraordinary features of the Vatican is that it measures only 0.17 square miles in territory with a scant population of less than 1,000, which makes it the smallest officially-acknowledged sovereign state in the world, with the smallest military in the world (100 ceremonial Swiss Guards) ...Yet remarkably, its doctrinal influence reaches a massive population exceeding 1 billion.[58]

Economically, its national budget is financed largely through stocks, bonds, real estate and contributions from national Catholic Churches, while it also owns some of the world's greatest art and architectural treasures.[59] Politically, the Holy See issues its own diplomatic passports; operates

106 embassies around the world; and has diplomatic relationships with 174 nations, 68 of which maintain embassies accredited to the Vatican in Rome.[60] By preference, the Vatican is a Permanent Observer at the United Nations (without a vote), and as a neutral state it avoids intervention in wars and political disputes unless its mediation is requested from the governments involved.[61]

Research will also show that sovereign movements are fueled largely by the youth of a society, as were our Civil Rights and Black Power Movements. Both Dr. King and Malcolm X were only 39 when assassinated, yet they both were seasoned leaders who received national media coverage wherever they went. Without the fresh minds and physical vitality of young people, a movement can fizzle and fade over time.

Due to mainstream discrediting of the Black Power Movement combined with the complacency resulting from integration, our youths today have little orientation to political struggle beyond that of hanging chads on voting ballots. Comparing the Hip Hop Generation to the Civil Rights and Black Power Generations, there probably has never been a wider gap in outlooks between any other contemporaneous generations. Consequently, the once invigorated cadres and bastions of Black nationalists from the 1960s have aged into a valiant but dying breed of elders without sufficient heirs, whose notoriety and contributions (like countless of our enslaved ancestors who fought against Americanization) will be omitted from the pages of mainstream history.

To countervail this likelihood and further breakdowns between the generations I call on elders and youths alike to thoughtfully consider and recognize that, "Sovereignty is the 21st-century political and ideological continuation of the Civil Rights, Black Power, and Hip Hop Movements combined . . . Sovereignty is the 21st-century nexus of consciousness that can merge and mutually evolutionize all generations in common purpose."

I'm prompted by hip hop extraordinaire Naz, who I admire, to carry this point a step further. He remarked in *New York* magazine that: "I'm never going to turn my back on the younger generation, no matter how crazy and insane they are, and how many drugs they sell. I'm going to have my opinion, but I'm never going to do how the elders do, like they own the civil rights struggle. Thank God for the people who came before us, but they can't tell me nothing."[62]

Naz is not alone. He speaks what masses of other young people think and feel, which is why he sells millions of units. Here, I interpret his words as a call for unrestrained, intergenerational dialogue on matters that have thus far gone unaddressed. I surmise that as long as we ignore sovereign ideals and solutions we will not only continue to lose our youths to the streets, but we will never reach our fullest human potential as a people.

Somewhere within the range of limited to absolute sovereignty is an applicable form and framework that can be precisely tailored to politically fit our needs and interests far better than the flawed workings of Americanization ever will. But there is no handbook manual, complete with instructions. We must possess the sovereign courage and sovereign imagination to create it and defend it.

Again, as Emerson said, "the fruit is in the seed" and "the end preexists in the means."[63] I extend the interpretation of this to mean that events in both nature and human affairs are "cause-specific" . . . Effects are thereby produced through commensurate means and measures. Sovereignty therefore requires the proper capacity of strategic intellect and *De Facto* processes. As a 21st-century people who have been historically disinherited of our sovereignty, the modern sovereignties and fluidities of today's political world provide encouraging precedents to show that the recovery of our sovereignty is not impossible. It is however incumbent upon us to become cause-specific enough to match the task.

Of course there are many legitimate hurdles and complexities. I wrote in *Pawned Sovereignty*: "Our sovereignty raises many questions to which there are no concrete answers at the moment. But these questions have less to do with feasibility, and more to do with the reality that the fate of Black America has perpetually revolved around an orbit that best benefits White America. So naturally, sovereignty has never been seriously examined."[64]

Let me affirm that there are almost 200 nation-states in this world which stand as political proof that sovereignty is not undoable for us. It is unrealistic however, to think that we can acquire any form of sovereignty in rapid fashion, since Euro-Americans have cleverly integrated us into this society in ways that require great political divesting and mutual cooperation for us to ever be extricated. Everything about us is interwoven centuries-deep and so firmly controlled by them that our sovereignty on the surface may certainly seem unthinkable. But since Euro-Americans do not politically own us, nothing should be unthinkable about any aspect or prospect of what we can or cannot do.

As a so-called "free people" we should be free-enough and have authority-enough to contemplate and pursue sovereignty on our own volition. And as a telltale measure of the genuineness of this government and establishment, we need to know and hear straight from their mouths if they acknowledge or denounce our Sovereign Rights to Exist.

Whether or not we decide to espouse sovereign ideals is one thing, but to have Euro-Americans object or scold us for having such ideals is quite another. So, in many ways our *Sovereign Evolution* is just as much a test of their earnestness to "spread freedom," as it is a test of our willingness to stand up for our freedom.

Considering that all sovereignty is not absolute, it is not unrealistic to think that we can acquire incremental stages of sovereignty with timetables and benchmarks to move towards greater degrees of absoluteness. Because our relationship with Euro-Americans is atypical in so many ways, I presuppose that our sovereignty could likewise be atypical, at least initially. Even in the absence of designated territory, we need to originate our own *Doctrine*, *Documents*, and *Declarations* to legitimize our quest and proclaim our aspirations to the world community.

Although this may defy convention as we know it, remember the aforementioned people of Kiribati and Maldives whose lands are being submerged under sea. They too, along with others, may face the need to defy convention in order to protect or advance their sovereign interests. To place this in an appropriate 21st-century frame, I predict that as the political needs and demands of people accelerate and converge with modernity, it will in turn give rise to sovereign variations that the world has yet to see.

The main reason I highlighted Native Americans and the Vatican is because their unconventional sovereignties demonstrate that sovereignty does not necessarily entail or require sizable territory, exports of great scale, or military prowess. Their structures offer precedents for future signature-brands of unique sovereignty.

Protocols and resolutions passed by the United Nations also substantiate a framework for this. International attorney, Dr. Mustafa Ansari, advocates along these lines in his book, *Defining Change Under UN Laws and Presidential Orders*, which he wrote "pursuant to the designs of international law as reported in the 56th and 59th Sessions of the United Nations."[65] He legally addresses what he calls "Authority Transfers" that would provide us with jurisdiction over territory, schools, civil matters and criminal affairs.[66]

In addition to these "Authority Transfers," I advocate that like the Vatican and the Lakota, we need sovereign jurisdiction to issue our own passports and other national documents. It should be unsettling and unacceptable to us as African people that a European government "owns" our passports, as I outlined in the segment on "Indoctrination."

Passports are a crucial element to distinguish our political self-identity when we travel abroad, especially since America craves war and administers foreign policies that we neither ascribe nor control. In the process we become "accomplices by association" to forms of aggression and hegemony of which we ourselves are casualties. Those of us who denounce the US government's militarism and foreign policies, take no delight in being forced to travel with "it's passport," having to bear such an unwanted onus.

While it exceeds the scope of this work to delve further into applications of sovereignty, suffice it to conclude that we need to petition the United Nations at every level to benefit from all established protocols and resolutions, and begin to engage a course of *De Facto Sovereignty* to: Define our own form of government and declare our own political and ideological self-identity; Originate our own *Doctrine, Documents, and Declarations*; and, Establish foreign relations and allies to recognize and support the legitimacy of our cause.

As outlandish as these *De Facto* acts may appear, it shouldn't escape notice that we have always had cultural tendencies to engage in certain behaviors that are really "sovereign traits" in disguise. For instance, we have our own "national" anthem; the Negro National Anthem. We have our own flag; the red, black, and green liberation flag.

In fact, over the last 3 years I've surveyed my audiences and Black people in general to inquire if they sang the US national anthem when it's played and if they would wave a US flag in public. By conducting your own mini-survey you'll find that, like in boxing, it's a "split decision." A great percentage will neither sing the US national anthem nor wave the US flag. Most of these same people will also express a greater regard for the Black national anthem and our liberation flag. Though this may seem inconsequential; it indicates that the true political self-identity of such Black people is an open question . . . because remember, according to the *US Foreign Policy Encyclopedia*, being "American" is an ideological commitment and a willingness to believe in certain principles and values.[67]

Among our other "sovereign traits," we have our own salute; the clinched-fist Black Power salute that has now incarnated into the "fist bump." We have our own independent approach to worship; the Black church has always been an institution unto itself, formatted with spiritual appeals for us and by us, as affirmed by the aforementioned *ABC News* report, "Two Nations Under God,"[68]

Worshiping for us is deeply steeped in sovereign African traditionalisms, which is why, unlike Euro-Americans who worship in a comparatively bland and motionless manner, we dance and shout and turn church into a celebratory event that reaches heights that White folks

259

don't even reach at New Year's parties. Black preachers moan and groan with the intensity of African mystics in villages who chant to summons powers to bless and heal. Choirs drip sweat as though performing a sacred African rite to bring about spontaneous change. Congregants complete the atmosphere, dressed in their most colorful best, free to emote and participate with impromptu shouts of testimonies and affirmations of praise.

Given that spirituality has always been central to our experience, any form of sovereignty that we embrace will definitely comprise spiritual components. It's not unusual to find a common realm where spirituality of some form is interrelated to the sovereign content of people, as I've clearly shown with American Exceptionalism, the Juche of North Korea, Islam in Arab nations, and quotes from Plato and Aristotle. Permit me therefore to conclude on a spiritual note by drawing two points of "sovereign predestination" from the Biblical story of "David and Goliath" (I Samuel, Chapters 16 and 17).

First, even though Saul was the king at the time, the story reads that David became spiritually mandated and anointed to be king. Saul physically occupied the throne with all appearances of royalty and power, but he in effect represented a fallen authority doomed to failure. It was only a matter of course and time before David would physically take the throne. Meantime, Goliath was teeny-tiny business along the way.

Second, Saul attempted to "equip" David for battle against Goliath with his personal armor (helmet, breastplate, and sword) which was specially made with the best materials available. No other armor was of greater quality or better suited for war. After all, Saul was a warrior king. And so his offer to David was a high and rare honor. But through the course of his "sheepherding," (symbolizing seemingly trivial tasks) David had gained levels of valor and intellect that gave him a different approach to warfare and leadership. So he refused the "king's armor."

Though his approach was underrated, he knew he represented a transitioning of the politics, leadership, and warfare of that time. He therefore had no intentions to adopt any of Saul's old and ill-fated ways.

Instead, David equipped himself only with his "sling, staff, stones, and shepherd's bag," (symbolizing seemingly inconsequential things that ultimately have decisive impact). To the natural eye, all indications were that he was overmatched without the "king's armor." But the reason we marvel at David today is because of his "sling, staff, stones, and shepherd's bag" – Not because of the "king's armor."

And so it is with Americanization, which in our case is analogous to the "king's armor." It too presumably represents the best and most secured ways that life can offer. Like David though, we as Africans in America have always had our own underrated armor that we acquired through our centuries of "sheepherding." We persevered during times of enslavement and segregation, fighting *against* the "king's armor." Millions of our forefathers perished, yet millions more of us now exist.

So, we should never get confused about the spiritual essence of our strength or who we are as a people, because clearly we exist today by virtue of our "sling, staff, stones, and shepherd's bag" – Not because of the "king's armor."

Moreover, we must also understand that our future strengths and triumphs do not hinge on the "king's armor," because like David, we too are predestined for our own sovereign identity. As Marcus Garvey said, we cannot allow others to "interpret our relationship to our Creator. . . . To spiritually regulate one's self is another form of the higher education that fits man for a nobler place in life."[69]

In deliberating our future as a people, we need to factor into account that we have already paid exponentially more in blood than we've commensurately received in sociopolitical returns. We have more than met our fair share of political dues. We owe nothing to any people other than ourselves, and we have nothing to prove to any people other than ourselves. Based on all the uncountable millions who have fought and died to resist Americanization, it's only just and reasonable that a portion of their blood be redeemed in sovereignty.

As we move forward in Political Time and Linear Time, we cannot allow the contributions and sacrifices of men like Nat Turner, Gabriel

261

Prosser, Abdul Rahman, and Joseph Cinque to go unreturned. They along with untold other men and women are in a sense the aspirational "Founding Fathers of our Sovereign Rights." Let me put this in an analogy, using Nat Turner as an example to pose the question: Where was he fleeing to during his opposition? The reality is that his destination was to escape the "existence" of everything that was superimposed upon him. Of course he could not do so. But we have every capability today to establish a "sovereign existence" to honor and fulfill the aspirations of such men and women.

In the final analysis of contemporary world politics, true sovereignty manifests from the full sociopolitical, economic, ideological and spiritual self-expressions of a people, without interferences or unwanted involvement from foreign influences. Because of greed, ideological clashes, and man's outright inhumanities against man, the coexistence of true sovereignties will be one of the greatest 21st-century challenges of governments and societies.

Unfortunately, those who do not possess the vision, courage, and strategic intellect to fulfill and defend their Sovereign Rights to Exist are guaranteed to be perpetual political-sharecroppers and economic-cupbearers of those who do. To avoid such a servile fate, time and history demand our urgent political efforts to cultivate the necessary consciousness for a *Sovereign Evolution* to actualize our *Manifest Destiny from "Civil Right" to "Sovereign Rights."*

<><><><><><><>

Glossary

Americanization – A designation to refer to the ideological/sociopolitical mold and belief system that constitutes the character and conduct of America. It is the trademark fingerprints of the US that make Americans "American." It is an Anglo-European "Process of Thought" that leads to a "Way of Life" which ultimately becomes a "Nature."

Black Liberation Theology – A bona fide Protestant-based Christian theology like any other Protestant theology, differing only in that it emanates from the tribulations and yearnings of Black people to relate and appeal to God to address our particular hardship circumstances. The establishment discredits this theology, because rather than ascribing to blind patriotism (for God to always "bless America"), it does not shy away from deeming America as a transgressor or the object of imprecations when and where appropriate.

Black Nationalist – According to Webster's it is a so-called "member of a group of militant blacks who advocate separatism from whites and the formation of self-governing black communities," as opposed to Black people who are "Nationalist," which Webster's defines with greater dignity, as "advocates of or believers in nationalism, or members of a political party or group advocating national independence or strong national government." The notion is as though there's something wrong or controversial about being "Black" and being "Nationalist."

Civil Rights, Integration, Citizenship – The 3 political components of freedom for Black America, as opposed to "Sovereignty, Independence, and Statehood" which are the 3 higher realms of freedom espoused and exercised by Euro-Americans.

Common History – To have "common history," people must not only experience the same event or conflict, but they must similarly support the same side, positions, and outcome. If their historical paths converged, but they experienced or supported opposing sides, positions, and outcomes, then they have a "related history."

Consent of the Governed – The agreement and will of a people to be governed by a government. According to the US Constitution, "Governments are instituted among Men, deriving their just powers from the consent of the governed."

Controlled Chaos Drill – The deliberate allowing of mass confusion and disorder (to simulate a civil uprising) within society by a government, to gauge what people will and won't do under pressure and dire extremes. The government then brings in emergency medical and security forces to assist and restore order (e.g., the aftermath of Hurricane Katrina).

Converted by Time – "Societies are made for man, not man for societies," but over the course of time and exposure, people can become inclined and accustomed to regard particular thoughts, beliefs, and customs as true and right, even if they are false and immoral.

Created Equal – The politically misconstrued concept, founded in the US Declaration of Independence ("All Men Are Created Equal"). The assumption is that it refers to having "equal rights" (i.e., civil rights and voting rights), when in reality the concept specifies and advocates the rights of Euro-Americans to "assume among the powers of the earth, [their] separate and equal station," or in other words – "Sovereign Equality," not "Integrated Equality."

De Facto – Literally in fact, refers to political acts whereby repressed people politically conduct themselves to "act as if" they legally and officially possess sovereignty.

Déja-Vu Defeats – A term to refer to the repeated electoral defeats of Black people from state to state who have run for Senate and Gubernatorial seats since the 1960s.

Diplomatic Immunity – Legal protection from prosecution for high-level government representatives that was established at the Vienna Convention on Diplomatic Relations in 1961.

Dissent of the Governed – The right of people to take De Facto stands to oppose government abuses and injustices. According to the US Constitution, "Governments are instituted among Men, deriving their just powers from the consent of the governed."

Doctrines, Documents, and Declarations – Instruments that politically define a people, express their ideology, and legitimize their political ideals. These instruments instill pride and patriotism in citizens and garner respect and recognition from other governments and nations.

Doll Test – Psychologists Kenneth Clark and his wife, Mamie Phipps Clark, designed this test in the 1940s using Black and White dolls (identical except in color) to study and determine racial perceptions and preferences of Black children, ages 3 to 7. Recent "Doll Tests" show that Black children still overwhelmingly prefer White dolls, just as in the 1940s.

Double Occupancy and Triple Occupancy – Terms that refer to two or three generations of Black men or women who are incarcerated concurrently, at times in the same penitentiary.

Emancipation Proclamation – The "military document" signed by Lincoln and his Secretary of State, in which he unilaterally authorized himself with the political power to initiate the process to Americanize African people, without consent or a bilateral agreement with the 4 million African people in question.

Ethnonationalism – The notion that members of a nation are part of an extended family, ultimately united by ties of blood, as opposed to "Americans," who are united by beliefs of common ideology.

Euro-American – Refers to the Anglo, Western European people who founded US government and society, who now populate America and comprise the establishment.

Euro-Christianity – Christianity that has its roots in the Protestant Reformation of Europe, which now influences US government and society on all levels, despite the notion of "Separation of Church and State."

Evangelicals – Protestants who, according to Webster's, are "marked by militant or crusading zeal," and who emphasize "salvation by faith in the atoning death of Jesus Christ through personal conversion; authority of scripture; and importance of preaching as contrasted with ritual."

Evolutionary Body Politic – A real but unrecognized segment of Africans in America who share overlapping dislikes and distrusts of government and society, and who are open to sovereign discourse and possibilities.

Exceptionalism – The belief and doctrine that America "is a unique nation, blessed by God to play a special (religious/political/economic/military) role in the world." It fosters the false notion that Euro-Americans can "forgive themselves." It has played a major psychological role to justify ongoing immoralities and hegemony that began with the enslaving of Africans and decimating of Native Americans.

Global War Economy – The annual trillions spent by the US government and billions in profits received by corporations from the Military Industrial Complex.

Government – Webster's speaks of things like the: "Continuous exercise of authority over and the performance of functions for a political unit; and a small group of persons holding the principal political executive offices of a nation, responsible for the direction and supervision of public affairs." But contrary to what is assumed, Webster's does not mention anything about a government being "representative of the people," which is supposed to be prototypical of a "democracy."

Human Quest for Sovereign Powers – The historically contiguous and ongoing pursuit of man for uncompromised freedom to exercise self-government with a political and ideological self-identity.

Indoctrination – A term which signifies that people have adopted the doctrines (traditions, ethos, ideals) of their nation. Hence, they become "Indoctrinated" or *In* the *Doctrine* of their *Nation*.

Kunta Identity – Refers to the historically sovereign cultures and constructs from which many enslaved Africans originated, which gave them an African sense of self-identity and significance. This identity had to be deconstructed in order to transfigure Africans into a European mindset to accept and prefer a "Toby Identity" of Americanization.

Manifest Destiny – As a general concept, it infers "an unstoppable human cause or event." In the case of Euro-Americans, it applies to their westward expansion of territory in the past. At present it encompasses their international reach for wealth and resources, well as their sovereign and ideological dominion to ensure that US government and society remain under the control of Anglo-European principles, practices, and policies. In the case of Africans in America, it implies our need for a *Sovereign Evolution from "Civil Rights"* to *"Sovereign Rights."*

Military Industrial Complex – The elaborate and sometimes covert network of interlocking corporations that have cozy relationships with the

Defense Department, the State Department, and the Pentagon, that receive contracts to support the military and/or supply war-related essentials.

New KKK – "Kids Killing Kids" in Black communities.

Ownership Transferal – With the Emancipation Proclamation, ownership of Africans transferred from private to public. Slavery entailed "private ownership" by individuals via chattel property. Emancipation entailed "political ownership" by federal government via citizenship and taxes. Iron shackles from slaveholders were replaced by birth certificates and forms of identification to secure us under the political jurisdiction of the US.

Pawned Sovereignty – Pawning is a transaction where people exchange an item with a particular value for a cash-sum of lesser value, under the pretext that they may come back to reclaim the item. Most transactions emanate from desperation and/or criminality of some sort, so the item is resold at a profit that benefits the pawn shop. "Pawned Sovereignty" refers to the historical condition and present political reality of Africans in America, being that we have essentially pawned our sovereignty (of great value) in exchange for civil rights (of lesser value). Others now benefit far more from our labor and loyalty than we do. We have paid exponentially more in blood than we have politically received in return. However, we have a historical and ancestral obligation to reclaim our sovereignty with a *Sovereign Evolution: from "Civil Rights" to "Sovereign Rights."*

Placebo Progress and Politics – Changes in government and society that appeal to our political emotions, but otherwise leave our ailments largely uncured. Placebos (Civil Rights, Integration, Citizenship) function as "conditioning agents" to give us perceptions of power, when in reality these agents lack the necessary political properties for us to achieve the status (Sovereignty, Independence, Statehood) of Euro-Americans.

Political Economy – The aggregate capital, massive spending, and revenue streams attached to electoral politics. It relates to the exorbitant price tags that hang on every seat of high elected office, along with all the resulting favoritism and privileges that are all part of a flourishing multibillion dollar "Economy" with its own "Presidential Industry."

Politically Unauthentic – People who lack "Sovereign Consciousness" are bound to find themselves parroting the words, ways, and positions of whichever sovereign power they reside under, thereby making them "Politically Unauthentic."

Political Symmetry – Refers to a state, where authority and influence in government and society are equally managed and controlled between two or more groups. Equality in the case of Africans in America has never meant or involved the "equal sharing" of power or a ratable redistribution of wealth. Being integrated with Euro-Americans has had the sociopolitical effect of making us more "like" them, instead of "equal" to them.

Propaganda – The manipulative use of information by a government to gain and sustain the patriotic loyalty of society.

Related history – If historical paths of people converged, but they experienced and supported opposing sides, positions, and outcomes, then they have a "related history," (like Jews and Germans during WWII and like Euro-Americans and African Americans from 1619 to the 1960s).

Slavemasters – Slaveholders who propagate their ways as standards to be desired and emulated by the enslaved. Euro-Americans have intentionally recorded the history of slavery to always portray them as the "master," not the "enemy" of African people.

Society – The voluntary social grouping and ways of people with a nation that should reflect their unadulterated history, values, and culture, which also should be proportionately represented in government without superimpositions from other governments or nations. "Societies should be made for man; man should not be made for societies."

Sovereign Equality – A political concept that is expressed in the US Declaration of Independence ("All Men Are Created Equal"), which advocates the rights of a people to politically occupy "separate and equal stations" of self-government.

Sovereign Evolution – The natural sociopolitical progression of a peoples' journey to reach sovereignty. In the case of Africans in America, it involves our transitioning from emancipation to segregation to integration at present, with the final phase of sovereignty now upon us to complete.

Sovereign Nucleus – A small but courageous and effective group of men and women whose influence drives the thrust of consciousness for a sovereign movement. *The Uhuru Movement Led by APSP*

Sovereign Wealth Funds – Financial institutions of foreign governments that invest in the economies of other nations.

Sovereignty – Though it is a modern notion of political authority and self-government, sovereignty has been expressed and applied since antiquity. It infers the inherent and actionable rights of a people to self-government without interferences or unwanted involvement from foreign influences.

Sovereignty, Independence, Statehood: The 3 political components of freedom for Euro-Americas which represent the highest levels of political freedom, as opposed to "Civil Rights, Integration, and Citizenship" which are lower subcomponents of the freedom known to Africans in America.

System of Educational Thought – The political/ideological/nationalistic paradigm and purpose for which education is taught, so as to influence and direct the minds of students in a given society. In the US, education is influenced and directed towards Americanization, which is why education is associated with being "White," which in turn is why Black children also "learn" to prefer White dolls.

Three-Fifths Clause – Constitutional clause designating (for census purposes) that every 5 slaves would be counted among the general population as 3 free persons, to ensure that slave states would have appropriate congressional representation.

Toby Identity – The new domesticated identity of enslaved Africans (and descendents) after having their African identities deconstructed and transfigured for Americanization.

Toby vs. Kunta – Represents two diametrically opposed "sovereign constructs" during slavery, vying in a spiritual and ideological struggle of life or death. There could be no peaceful coexisting of sovereign identities, since "Kunta" was anchored to a fixed sovereign nature and fixed sovereign manhood that had to be deconstructed and transfigured entirely, in order to fit the sociopolitical skin of "Toby."

Un-American – Being "American" is an ideological/patriotic/nationalistic commitment and belief. US citizens who therefore promote or live according to principles that run counter to conventional viewpoints, policies, and institutions can be labeled "Un-American."

Un-Birth of a Nation – A term that relates to a nation (people-wise) that is not a nation (nation-state) in the historic sense, because it skipped the process and evolution of democracy where it becomes "born" into a functionally sovereign government and society, as in the case of Africans in America.

Ungovernable – Refers to "De Facto" acts of a repressed people who refuse to consent to be governed.

Un-Sovereign – The political state of a people who lack sovereignty and are therefore forced to pay Un-sovereign Consequences as a result.

"Whites Only" Political Water Fountain – A term referring to the imbalanced racial composition of Congress and Governorships, where qualified Blacks have historically been underrepresented.

White Supremacy – A term mostly used by Blacks, which applies to racially unjust conditions and conduct from Euro-Americans. But I contend that if we used the concept and consciousness of sovereignty as our political lens of interpretation, it will become clear that what we *perceive* as "White Supremacy" are, in actuality, expressions and affirmations of "White Sovereignty." We therefore need our own expressions and affirmations of sovereignty.

Footnotes

Chapter 1

[1]*New Worlds, New Sovereignties Conference*, Melbourne, Australia, June 6 – 9, 2008: http://www.newsovereignties.org.

[2]Webster's Universal Encyclopedic Dictionary, Barnes and Nobles (Merriam-Webster Incorporated, 2002): 1762

[3]Ibid.

[4]Ibid.

[5]Ibid.

[6]Stanford Encyclopedia of Philosophy: Sovereignty18 June 2003, http://plato.stanford.edu/entries/sovereignty.

[7]National Black United Front, www.nbufront.org/html/MastersMuseums/ JHClarke/JHC vmuseum.html.

[8]*Prince Among Slaves*, PBS Documentary, 4 February 2008, Directed by Bill Duke, Narrated by Mos Def, http://www.pbs.org/previews/ princeamongslaves/.

[9]Terry Alford, *Prince Among Slaves*, (Oxford University Press, 1986).

[10]*Prince Among Slaves*, PBS Documentary.

[11]Dr. Bayo Lawal, *From Palace to Plantation to Glory*, (Documentary), "Teachers Guide," 2008.

[12]Ezrah Aharone, Pawned Sovereignty: Sharpened Black Perspectives on Americanization, Africa, War and Reparations, (Bloomington Indiana, AuthorHouse, 2003): 5.

[13]ABC News http://www.abcnews.go.com/WNT/story?id=3002001&pag e=1.

[14]Ibid.

[15]Ibid.

[16] Randeep Ramesh, "Maldives Seek to Buy a New Homeland," *The Guardian*, 10 November 2008, http://www.mathaba.net/rss/?x=611083.

[17]Ibid.

[18]Twenty-Five Treaties Most Central to the Spirit and Goals of the United Nations, http://cyberschoolbus.un.org/treaties/racial.asp.

United Nations International Laws, http://www.un.org/law.

United Nations Treaty Collection, http://untreaty.un.org.

[19]Kim McLaughlin, "Arctic Sovereignty Talks in Greenland (STV. TV Reuters)," *Mathaba News Agency* http://www.mathaba.net/news/ ?x=593500.

[20]John Ward Anderson, "Iran Releases 15 Captive Britons," Washington Post Foreign Service, 5 April 2007: A01, http://www.washingtonpost.com/wp-dyn/content/article/2007/04/04/ AR2007040400334.html.

[21]Oceans and Laws of the Sea, http://www.un.org/Depts/los/convention_agreements/convention_overview_convention.htm.

[22]Ibid.

[23]Ibid.

[24]*The Washington Diplomat,* http://www.washdiplomat.com/02-03/ a5_02_03.html.

[25]Webster's, 1762.

[26]*The Philosophy & Opinions of Marcus Garvey*, Compiled by Amy Jacques Garvey, (Dover, Massachusetts: The Majority Press, 1986): 5.

[27]Kwame Nkrumah Quotes, *Think Exist*, thinkexist.com/quotes/kwame_nkrumah/.

[28]Mike Underwood, "At last, Michelle Obama proud of America," *Boston Herald*, 19 February 2008, http://news.bostonherald.com/news/2008/view.bg?articleid=1074519.

[29]Ralph Waldo Emerson, "Essays of Ralph Waldo Emerson," Book League of America, New York, 1941: 35.

[30]"Kosovo Declares Independence From Serbia," *MSNBC*, 18 February 2008, http://www.msnbc. msn.com/id/23203607/.

[31]J. Victor Marshall, "Bush's Double Standards on Russia-Kosovo," *Mathaba News Agency*, 28 August 2008, http://www.mathaba.net/rss/ ?x=604261.

[32]Answers.Com, http://www.answers.com/topic/list-of-countries-by-date-of-independence.

[33]Jerry Z. Muller, "Us and Them: The Enduring Power of Ethnic Nationalism," *Foreign Affairs*, March/April 2008, http://www.foreignaffairs.org/20080301faessay87203/jerry-z-muller/us-and-them.html.

[34]Ibid.

[35]Webster's: 595.

[36]Harriet Tubman Quote, http://thinkexist.com/quotation.

[37]Ibid.

[38] *The Philosophy & Opinions of Marcus Garvey*, 18.

[39]Ibid, 7.

[40]Africa Within http://www.africawithin.com/nkrumah/big_six.htm.

[41]Kwame Nkrumah Quotes, *Think Exist*, thinkexist.com/quotes/kwame_nkrumah/.

[42]*Castro's Revolution in Cuba 1956-1959* www.onwar.com/aced/data/cite/cuba1956.htm.

[43]Margie Mason, "On Vietnam's Independence Day, Haunting Reminders for America," *Associated Press*, 8 May 2004.

[44]George Will, "War President Should Level With Us," *The Washington Post*, 7 April 2004.

Chapter 2

[1]Webster's 472.

[2]Ibid, 795

[3]Ibid, 1747

[4]Thomas Paine, "Common Sense," http://www.ushistory.org/Paine/commonsense/sense 2.htm: 1

[5]Peter Williams, "England: A Narrative History," *Britannia.com*, Part 7: "The Age of Empire: The American War of Independence," www.britannia.com/history/naremphist4.html.

[6]Reverend Jesse L. Jackson, Sr., "Defending the Constitution," *Tribune Media Services, http://www.blacknews.com/pr/constitution101.html*

[7]Aharone, *Pawned Sovereignty*, 63.

[8]Paine, "Common Sense."

[9]Emerson, 193

[10]American Exceptionalism, FixedReference.org, http://july.fixedreference.org/en/20040724 /wikipedia/American_exceptionalism.

[11]Webster's, 1216

[12] Paul Starobin, "Us and Them: The Fires of Nationalism in a War-Torn World," *The Star Ledger*, 8 Aug. 04: Section 10, 1.

[13]Turkey Arrests Official for Gum Indiscretion, *The Star Ledger*, 25 April 2006: 9.

[14] Ecuador Deports a US Activist, *The Star Ledger*, 5 August 2007: 8.

[15]Terry Eastland, "When Prayer and Politics Converge," *The Star Ledger*, 5 September 2004: 5.

[16]Ben Sargent, *The Star Ledger*, 3 July 2006.

[17]Websters', 536.

[18]"Authorities in China 'Clean' Stones," *The Star Ledger*, 9 April, 2006: 12

[19]Greg Sandoval, "China Bans LeBron James Nike Ad," Washington Post, 7 December 2004: E 2, http://www.washingtonpost.com/wp-dyn/articles/A41825-2004Dec6.html.

[20]Ibid.

[21]Oaths of Enlistments and Oaths of Office, http://www.army.mil/cmh-pg/faq/oaths.htm.

[22]Elizabeth Moore, Slavery Lesson too Advanced, Mom Says, *The Star Ledger*, 5 October 2007: 17.

[23]Ibid.

[24]Ibid.

[25]"Tavis Smiley Launches Tour to Tap Emerging Leaders at Nation's Historically Black Colleges & Universities," *BlackNews.com*, 9 September 2007.

[26]Justin Pope, "New Campus Clash: Conservatives Call for Diversity," *The Star Leger,* 26 December 2004: 33.

[27]Ibid.

[28]Ibid.

[29]Alton H. Maddox Jr., "Recording Black Stories from Black Scribes to Black Journalists," 15 March 2007.

[30]Marcus Garvey: Life and Lessons Sample Documents www.isop.ucla.edu/africa/mgpp/lifesamp.

[31] Paine, "Common Sense,"XXVII/

[32]Women's History, http://womenshistory.about.com/od/quotes/a/margaret_fuller.htm.

[33]www.blackcollegewire.org/news/060327_hampton-hair/.

[34]*Imus in the Morning*, 4 September 2008.

[35]Lisa Irizarry, "Jet, Ebony and Other Mags Presented Blacks with Positive News About Themselves," *The Star Ledger*, 17 August 2006: 25.

[36]Karl R. Popper, "The Open Society and Its Enemies," Vol. 1 (London: Routledge and Kegan Paul, 1980), p. 138.

[37]Ibid.

[38]Michael DeLang, "The Open Society Revisited," 14 March 2005, http://www.swans.com/library/art11/delang01.html

[39]David Barstow, "Behind Analysts, the Pentagon's Hidden Hand," *New York Times,* 20 April 2008, http://www.nytimes.com/2008/04/20/washington/20generals.html.

[40]Ibid.

[41]Jean Cocteau, chass.colostate-pueblo.edu/history/syllabi/mathis02.html.

[42]Mimi Hall, "Mandela is on US Terrorist Watch List, *USA Today*, 1 May 2008: 2A.

[43]CNN.com, http://www.cnn.com/2006/WORLD/meast/08/12/mideast.main/index.html

[44]Donna Abu-Nasr and Ali Akbar Dareini, "Leaders in Iran and Syria Cheer Hezbollah 'Victory,'" *Associated Press*, 8 August 2006.

[45]Ibid.

[46]Ibid.

[47]Peter N. Williams, *England: A Narrative History*, www.Britannia.com/ history/ naremphist4.html.

[48]Ibid.

[49]Ibid.

[50]Brent Staples, Book Review of "Rough Crossings: Britain, the Slaves and the American Revolution," by Simon Schama, *New York Times*, June 4, 2006

[51]Good Morning America "Has America Reached Racial Equality Poll" *ABC*, 12 October 2008.

[52]Constitutional Facts, Http://www.constitutionfacts.com/qbody1.shtml.

[53]"Thought For Today," *The Star Ledger*, 11 June 2006: 45.

[54]*The Philosophy & Opinions of Marcus Garvey*, 19.

[55]Today's Almanac, *The Star Ledger*, 9 November 2007.

[56]The Myth of Unity, *The Star Ledger*, Editorial.

[57]"Today's Almanac" *The Star Ledger*, 11 August 2005: 21

[58]"Early America, Archiving Early America," *EarlyAmerica.com*, http:// www.earlyamerica. com/earlyamerica/milestones/paris/.

[59]Kwame Nkrumah Quotes, *Think Exist*, thinkexist.com/quotes/kwame_ nkrumah/.

[60]"Senator Barack Obama Sees Parallels With Abraham Lincoln," *Chicago (Associated Press)*, 9 July 2005: http://www.BlackNews. com/pr/obama101

[61]Southern Christian Leadership Conference (SCLC), August 1967, www.hartford-hwp.com/archives/45a/628.html

[62]*Peace Work Magazine*, "Race: The Enduring Problem of the 20th Century," December 1999 – January 2000, http://www.peaceworkmagazine.org/ pwork/1299/1210a.htm.

Chapter 3

[1]"Outcry Over Campaign Gives PETA Pause," *Star Ledger*, 14 August, 2005: 35

[2]Today, *NBC*, 20 October 2007.

[3]Diane Brady and Christopher Palmeri, "The Pet Economy," *Business Week*, 6 August 2007: 45.

[4]Headlines and Legends, *MSNBC*, Joe Madison Interview, 3 September 2005

[5]*The Associated Press,* "Black US Lawmakers Angry About Federal Response To Katrina," 6 September, 2005.

[6]Matt Zoller Seitz, "The Whole Picture," *The Star Ledger*, 3 September, 2005: 21.

[7]Ibid.

[8]Ibid.

[9]Ibid.

[10]*The Phrase Finder*, "Let them eat cake," http://www.phrases.org.uk/meanings/227600.html.

[11]Robert Cohen, "FEMA Chief's Qualifications Come Under Fire, *The Star Ledger,* 7 September, 2005: 4

[12]"Feds to Investigate Post-Katrina Bridge Blockade," *The Associated Press,* 10 August 2006

[13]Gary Webb, *Dark Alliance: CIA, the Contras and the Crack Cocaine Explosion.* And let's not forget the Tuskegee Experiment.

[14] *MSNBC News Live*, 30 April 2007.

[15]Lara Jakes Jordan, "FBI Reopens 100 Civil Rights-Era Cases," *USA Today*, 27 February 2007, http://www.usatoday.com/news/washington/2007-02-27-3879412986_x.htm

[16]Jerry Mitchell, "Grand Jury Issues No Indictment in Till Killing," *Clarion Ledger*, 27 February 2007.

[17]"Florida Revisits 1951 Bombing," *Associated Press*, 16 August 2005.

[18]Emily Wagster Pettus, "Man Gets 3 Life Terms in Killing of Black Teens," *Associated Press*, 25 August 2007.

[19]"Survivors of Tuskegee Study Get Apology from Clinton," *New York Times*, 17 May 1997.

[20]Bethanne Kelly Patrick, "Black Soldier's Achievements In World War II Ignored For Over 50 Years," *www.Military.com*.

[21]"Tuskegee Airmen Enjoy Highest Salute," *Associated Press*, 30 March, 2007.

[22]Wayne Wooley, "Full of Tales, Survivors of Unit Reunite Today for Medal," *The Star Ledger*, 29 March 2007: 1.

[23] Patrick.

[24]Wooley.

[25]"Tuskegee Airmen Enjoy Highest Salute," *Associated Press*, 30 March, 2007.

[26]Erin Texeira, "America's Belated Apologies Seek to Heal Slavery's Wounds," *Associated Press*, 9 March 2007.

[27]Jim Abrams, "House Formally Apologizes for Slavery and Jim Crow," *Associated Press*, 30 July 2008.

[28]Texeira.

[29]"Georgia to Pardon Woman Excuted 60 Years Ago," *The Star Ledger*, 16 August 2005.

[30]Ibid.

[31]"Florida Revisits 1951 Bombing."

[32]Lauren Markoe, "Senate Apologizes for Failing to Ban Lynching," *KRT News Service*, 14 June 2005.

[33]"Lawmakers Seek Apology for Senate Inaction on Black Lynchings," *Associated Press*, 1 October 2004.

[34]Ibid.

[35]Ibid.

[36]"Parks Will Lie in Honor Inside Capitol," *Reuters*, 28 October, 2005.

[37]Jennifer Loven, "Bush Authorizes Rosa Parks Statue," *Associated Press*, 2 December, 2005.

[38]"Rosa Parks Act" Aims to Pardon Rights Activists, *The Star Ledger*, 18 March 2006: 7.

[39]Marisol Bello "House Dems Fault Feds for Jena Copycats," *USA Today*.

[40]*The Philosophy & Opinions of Marcus Garvey*, 9

[41]Kelly Heyboer, "What's in a Word? Maybe a Small Piece of History," *The Star Ledger*, 30 Dec. 2004: 1

[42]Ibid.

[43]John Mooney, "Words," *The Star Ledger*, 28 December 2005: 6.

[44]"In Iran, No More Pizzas, Just 'Elastic Loaves,'" *Star Ledger Wire Services*, 30 July 2006.

[45]Ibid.

[46]"Viacom, CBS Formerly Split," *CBS/AP*, 3 January 2006, http://www.cbsnews.com/stories/2006/01/03/business/main1176111.shtml.

[47]DV Republic http://www.dvrepublic.com/story.php?n=121&x=1.

[48]Texeira.

[49]Suzette Hackney, "In Detroit, Good-bye to the N-word," *Detroit Free Press*, 10 July 2007.

[50]Jonathan Tilove, "Where Have All the Black Men Gone," The Star Ledger, 8 May 2005: Section 10, Page 1.

Chapter 4

[1]Jerry Z. Muller, "Us and Them: The Enduring Power of Ethnic Nationalism," *Foreign Affairs*, March/April 2008, http://www.foreignaffairs.org/20080301faessay87203/jerry-z-muller/us-and-them.html.

[2]*US Foreign Policy Encyclopedia*: Exceptionalism, http://www.answers.com/topic/ exceptionalism.

[3]*The Eleanor Roosevelt Papers*, "House Un-American Activities Committee," http://www.nps.gov/archive/elro/glossary/huac.htm.

[4] Jerry Z. Muller, "Us and Them: The Enduring Power of Ethnic Nationalism," *Foreign Affairs*, March/April 2008, http://www.foreignaffairs.org/20080301faessay87203/jerry-z-muller/us-and-them.html.

[5] Seymour Martin Lipset, American Exceptionalism: A Double Edged Sword, (W. W. Norton & Company 1997)

[6] *The Eleanor Roosevelt Papers.*

[7] *US Foreign Policy Encyclopedia*: Exceptionalism, http://www.answers.com/topic/exceptionalism.

[8] Lipset.

[9] Nedra Pickler, "Obama: I'd Send Troops to Pakistan," *Associated Press*, 2 August 2007.

[10] Kim Chipman and Michael Forsythe, "Clinton, Obama Skirmish Over Pakistan, Lobbyists at Labor Forum," http://www.blomberg.com, 8 August 2007.

[11] Imus in the Morning, *MSNBC*, 31 January 2005

[12] Federal Bureau of Investigation, "The History of FBI Headquarters: The J. Edgar Hoover FBI Building," http://www.fbi.gov/libref/historic/hooverbuilding/hqhistory.htm.

[13] MalcolmX.org, www.malcolm-x.org/quotes.htm.

[14] *US Foreign Policy Encyclopedia*: Exceptionalism, http://www.answers.com/topic/ exceptionalism.

[15] Public Law 97-280 96 STAT. 1211 (97th Congress).

[16] *US Foreign Policy Encyclopedia*

[17] Jeff Diamant, "Americans Find an Unwavering Ally in God," *The Star Ledger*, 17 September 2006: 1 Section 10.

[18] Diamant

[19] http://www.quotedb.com/quotes/879.

[20] "Kim Jong Il, Revered and reviled," *The Associated Press,* 5 July 2006.

[21] "Welcome to North Korea" (Television Documentary), *WLIW New Jersey*, October 5, 2006.

[22] Merland Rise Church www.merlandrisechurch.org.uk/northkorea.htm

[23] Robert Cohen, "Court Leaves 'Under God' and Nation's Pledge Intact," *The Star Ledger Washington Bureau*, 15 June 2004.

[24] Ibid.

[25] Robert Paul Reyes, "God Mad At America Claims New Orleans Mayor Ray Nagin," *American Chronicle*, 17 January 2006, http://www.americanchronicle.com/articles/4897.

[26] Will Lester, "More Americans Want Religion, Politics to Mix," *Associated Press*, 7 June 2005.

[27] Diamant.

[28]Ibid.

[29]CNN Transcripts, American Morning, http://transcripts.cnn.com/ TRANSCRIPTS/ 0501/19/ltm.04.html

[30]William J. Federer, "Separation of God and State?" *WorldNetDaily. com*, 11 October 2003. Here are just a few (Boldfaces are my own):

[31]Federer

[32]*Associated Press*, "Scammers Find Bonanza Riding on Angels' Wings," 14 August 2006

[33]Ibid.

[34]Ira J. Hadnot, "Fewer Black Pulpits are Political Stumps," *The Star Ledger*, 15 Aug. 2004: Section 10: 5

[35]Ibid.

[36]Ibid.

[37]ABC News: "Two Nations Under God," abcnews.go.com/politics/5050/ story?id=6015620.

[38]Verena Dobnik, "Scalia Rejects Religious 'Neutrality' in Government," *The Star Ledger*, 23 Nov. 2004: 3

[39]Oaths of Enlistments and Oaths of Office, http://www.army.mil/cmh-pg/ faq/oaths.htm.

[40]David Gibson, "Preparing US for War is Once Again a Faith-Based Initiative," *The Star Ledger*, 24 Sept. 2001: 6.

[41]Ron Jacobs, "American Exceptionalism: A Disease of Conceit," *CounterPunch*, 21 July 04: www.CounterPunch.org/jacobs07212004

[42]*Imus in the Morning*, 20 March 2007.

[43]Webster's, 630.

[44]Laurie Goodstein, "Evangelicals are Growing Force in the Military Chaplain Corps," *New York Times*, 7 December 2005: A18.

[45]Ibid.

[46]Eastland "When Prayer and Politics Converge

[47]Starobin.

[48]Media Matters for America, http://mediamatters.org/ items/200608310005.

[49]"Pat Robertson calls for assassination of Hugo Chavez," *USAToday.com*, http://www.usatoday.com/news/nation/2005-08-22-robertson-_x.htm, 22 August 2005.

[50]Starobin

[51]John Farmer Jr., "Who Are We?" *The Star Ledger*, 27 March 2005: 1 Section 10.

[52]Ibid.

[53]Ibid.

[54]Thomas Paine, *The Rights of Man*, (1792), history.hanover.edu/courses/excerpts /111paine.html.

[55]Interview with Dylan Foley, *The Sunday Star Ledger*, 19 September 2004: 6 Section 10

[56]Ben Ammi, *God the Black Man and Truth*, (Chicago, Communicators Press, 1982, 1985) 93.

[57]Arms Control Association, *United States Geological Survey*.

[58]"US Admits Weakness at Uranium Storage Site," *The Star Ledger*, 16 October 2006: 11

[59] *"A UN without America,"* www.actionforunrenew.ndo.co.uk/pages/usout.

[60]Kim Gamel, "US Proposal 'Insults' Iraq, Leader Claims," *Associated Press*, 11 December 2006.

[61]Carol J. Williams, "An Angry Maliki Has Strong Words for Critics in US," *Los Angeles Times*, 27 August 2007.

[62]*MSNBC News Live*, 19 March 2007

[63]Dafna Linzer, "Search for Banned Arms in Iraq Ended Last Month," *Washington Post.com*, 12 January 2005: A1.

[64]"Powell Says the CIA Erred on Iraq Weapons Lab Data," *Reuters*, 17 May 2004.

[65]Grant McCool and Nguyen Nhat Lam, "US 'Agent Orange' Ruling Disappoints Vietnamese Victims," *Reuters*, 2008, http://www.mathaba.net/rss/?x=583083.

[66]Edith M. Lederer, "Annan: US Troops Should Not Be Exempt From War Crimes, *Associated Press*, 18 June 2004: Star Ledger, 15.

[67]Ibid.

[68]US Punishes Mexico for Joining Global Court," *Associated Press,* 9 March 2006.

[69]Ibid.

[70]Ibid.

[71]Ryan Lenz, "Army Prober Offers Graphic Testimony in Iraq Rape Case," *The Star Ledger*, 8 August 2006: 11.

[72]"What is the real death toll in Iraq?" *Guardian.Co.Uk,* http://www.guardian.co.uk/world/2008/mar/19/iraq.

[73](Statistic from the Iraqi Ministry of Planning and Development Cooperation): AlterNet Staff, "Occupations Toll: 5 Million Iraqi Children Orphaned," AlterNet, 18 December 2007, http://www.alternet.org/waroniraq/70886/?page=entire.

[74]"CBS News with Katie Couric," *CBS*, 8 May 2007.

[75] Dana Priest, "Soldier Suicides at Record Level," *Washington Post*, 31 January 2008: A01.

[76]Ardeshir Ommani "Iraq War and US Soldiers' Suicides," *Mathaba News Agency*, 31 March 2008, http://www.mathaba.net/news/?x=587220.

[77]Ann Scott Tyson, "Army Tries Unique Interactive Video to Stem Flow of Suicides," Washington Post, 9 October 2008.

[78] Wayne Woolley, "War's Hidden Toll: Army Desertions Soar 80 Percent Increase Tied to Combat Stress," *The Star Ledger*, 17, November 2007.

[79] *BBC World News*, 8 December 2006.

[80]T.A. Badger, "Jury Finds GI Guilty of Abuses at Prison," *Associated Press*, 15 Jan. 2005.

[81]"60 Minutes," *CBS*, 10 December 2006.

[82]*MSNBC News Live*, 13 September 2007.

[83][Sources that verify this are: *ABC News*, 18 November 2005; *CounterPunch Magazine*, "The Hard Hand of War: Rape as an Instrument of Total War," 4 April 2008; "The Taguba Report: (Major General Antonio Taguba) Investigation of the 800th Military Brigade" (see *New Yorker Magazine*, 25 June 2007); *Mathaba News Agency*, "Sexual Terrorism: The Sadistic Side of Bush's War on Terror," 14 May 2008, http://www. mathaba.net/rss/?x=592095.]

[84]Anne Gearan, "Powell Ex-Aide: Bush Left Issue of Captives to His Hard-Liners," *Associated Press*, 29 November 2005.

[85]*BBC News*, "POW Footage 'Breaks Convention,'" 24 March 2003, http://news.bbc.co.uk/1/hi/world/middle_east/2881187.stm.

[86]John Koopman, "Real Jessica Lynch Tale Has Yet to be Told," SFGate. com, 17 November 2003.

[87]"The Truth About Jessica," *The Guardian Unlimited*, 15 May 2003 http:// www.guardian.co.uk/Iraq/Story/0,2763,956255,00.html.

[88]Mark Tran, "'Little Girl Rambo Decries' US Propaganda," *Guardian Unlimited*, 24 April 2007.

[89]Anne Plummer Flaherty, "Powell Leads Senate Charge Against Bush on Terror Detainees," *The Associated Press*, 15 September 2006.

[90]*US Foreign Policy Encyclopedia*: Exceptionalism, http://www.answers. com/topic/exceptionalism.

[91]Jacobs, "American Exceptionalism."

[92] Mattias Karen, "World Wide Military Tab Again Hits $1 trillion," *Associated Press*, 8 June 2005.

[93]Ibid.

[94]*Stockholm International Peace Research Institute* (SPIRI) "2008 Year Book on Armaments, Disarmament and International Security," http:// yearbook2008.sipri.org/files/SIPRIYB08 summary.pdf

[95] Scheer, "Cashing In On Terror"

[96]OurDocuments.Gov, www.ourdocuments.gov/doc.php?doc=90

[97]Joshua Freed, "Combat Keeps Arms Factories at Full Capacity," *The Star Ledger*, 27 May 2004: 12

[98]"US Sent Taiwan Nuclear Missile Components by Mistake," AFP, *Mathaba News Agency*, 25 March 2008, http://www.mathaba.net/news/?x=586587

[99]Lolita C. Baldor, "US is Investigating How Fuses for Missile Were Sent to Taiwan," *Associated Press*, 25 March 2008.

[100] Chuck McCutcheon, "Companies Invest in Intelligence," *Newhouse News Service*, 2 July 2006.

[101]Ibid.

[102] *MSNBC News Live*, 15 May 2007.

[103]Matthew Mosk and Michael D. Shear, "Giuliani's Firm Sells Investment Business," *The Washington Post*, 6 March 2007: A 4.

[104]Ibid.

[105]Pete Yost, Ridge Visited Lobbying Firm Exec," Associated Press, 13 Jan. 2005.

[106]Ibid.

[107]Ibid.

[108]Ibid.

[109]Robert Scheer, "Cashing In On Terror," *TruthDig.com*, 30 October 2007, http://www.truthdig.com/report/item/20071030_scheer_column_cashing_in/.

[110] "Negroponte Promised to Sell "War Stock," *Associated Press*, 27 February 2005.

[111]"Making Money Off Iraq," *Parade*, 27 November 2005: 6

[112] Elliott Spagat, "Lawmaker Admits Graft and Resigns," *Associated Press*, 20 November 2005.

[113]Ibid.

[114]Matt Kelley, "Reconstruction Audit Shows $1B in Problems," *Associated Press,* 30 July, 2004.

[115]Ibid.

[116]Matt Kelley, "Companies Hired for Work in Iraq Penalized in Past," *Associated Press,* 27 April 2004: 10.

[117]Ibid

[118] Ibid

[119]Drew Griffin and Kathleen Johnston, "Military Uses Slot Machines to Fund Overseas Recreation," *CNN*, 23 May 2007, http://edition.cnn.com/2007/US/05/22/military.gambling/. [120]Ibid.

Chapter 5

[1]Tamar Nordenberg, "The Healing Power of Placebos," US Food and Drug Administration, *FDA Consumer Magazine*, January – February 2000, http://www.fda.gov/fdac/features/2000/100_heal.html.

[2] Ibid.

[3] Ibid.

[4]http://www.ci.richmond.va.us/citizen/city_gov/mayor/biography.aspx.

[5]Albert Einstein "The Negro Question," 1946, http://www.nsbp.org/einstein_racism.html

[6]Shashank Bengali, "Kenyan Ruler Defies Reconciliation Pleas," *McClatchy-Tribune News Service*, 8 January 2008.

[7]*The Guardian*, Guardian.co.uk, "The Deal," 16 September 2008, http://www.guardian.co.uk/world/2008/sep/16/zimbabwe1?gusrc=rss&feed=worldnews.

[8]Samira Jafari, "Retracing the Path to Equality," *Associated Press*: 7 March, 2005. "

[9]"Stepping Up the Fight for Voting Rights," *Star-Ledger Wire Services*, 7 August 2005: 15.

[10]Jesse Jackson, Jr. Website: http://www.house.gov/jackson/VotingRightsFAQ.htm

[11]Don Schanche Jr., "Jackson: Voting Rights Renewal Vital in South," *The Telegraph*, 27 June 2002: 3A.

[12]Jafari

[13]Ibid.

[14]*Star Ledger Wire Services.*

[15]Ibid.

[16]Ibid.

[17]Jesse Jackson, Jr. Website: http://www.house.gov/jackson/VotingRightsFAQ.htm

[18]Peter Williams, "England: A Narrative History," *Britannia.com*, Part 7: "The Age of Empire: The American War of Independence," www.britannia.com/history/naremphist4.html.

[19]Jennifer Loven, President and NAACP Chief Trade Viewpoints, *Associated Press*, 22 Dec. 2004: 10

[20]*Covenant with Black America*, Introduction by Tavis Smiley, (Chicago: Third World Press, 2006):125.

[21]"Celebrities Remember Ossie," CBS News, www.cbsnews.com/stories, 12 February 2005.

[22]"Obama Gets Secret Service Protection," *International Herald Tribune*, 3 May 2007, www.iht.com/articles/ap/2007/05/03/.

[23]"MSNBC Live News," MSNBC, 26 May 2008.

[24]*Imus in the Morning*, 13 December 2006.

[25]*Imus in the Morning,* 19 September 2008.

[26]Chris Matthews, "Decision 2006: Battleground America," *MSNBC*, 2 November 2006.

[27]"Sharpton's Relatives Were Slaves to Thurmond's," *New York Daily News*, 25 February 2007.

[28]*Politics1.com*, "Presidency 2004," www.politics1.com/sharpton.htm. Despite his civil rights notoriety and connections to the "White world," he's been unable to win any public office,

[29]CNN.com, http://www.cnn.com/2006/POLITICS/06/12/byrd.access/index.

[30]Ibid.

[31]Ibid.

[32]*TheStar.Com*, "Strom Thurmond, 100: Longest Serving US Senator," 27 June 2003, http://www.thestar.com/Obituary/TtoZ/article/107800.

[33]Ibid.

[34]Ibid.

[35]"Eyewitness News Close Up," *ABC*, 13 August 2006. My question is: Who and what exactly are "our kind?"

[36] "What Dean's Saying," *The Star Ledger*, 12 June 2005: 2

[37]Gary Allen with Larry Abraham, *None Dare Call It Conspiracy*, 1971, http://reactor-core.org/none-dare.html. They further state:

[38]Ibid.

[39]Robert N. Taylor, "Republicans Want Blacks To Become More Conservative; They Offer No Change," *National Black News Journal*, 21 May 2001.

[40]"This Week with George Stephanopoulos," *ABC*, 13 May 2007.

[41]Ibid

[42]Loven.

[43]"Open Line," *KISS FM Radio 98.7*, 16 July 2006

[44]Nedra Pickler, "Bush Says Social Security Plan Aids Blacks," Associated Press, 26 Jan. 03

[45]Christi Parsons, "Keyes' Loss Resets Bar On Margins of Victory," Chicago Tribune, 4 November, 2004.

[46]David Mendell and John Chase, "Barak Obama's Landslide Victory Set Stage for National Role," *Chicago Tribune*, 3 Nov. 2004.

[47]Maura Kelly Lannan, "Keys Launches Senate Campaign," *Associated Press*, 10 Aug. 2004.

[48]Tucker Carlson "The Situation with Tucker Carlson," *MSNBC*, 27 June 2007.

[49]Webster's 1216 and 185.

[50]Andrea Elliott, "Muslim Voters Detect a Snub From Obama," *New York Times*, 24 June 2008: http://www.nytimes.com/2008/06/24/us/politics/24muslim.html?pagewanted=1&_r=1&th&emc=th&adxnnlx=1214368499-HZB/4fbFoACU7B%208YcFjmA.

[51]http://uhurusolidarity.blogspot.com/2008/08/what-about-black-community-obama-uhuru.html.

[52]Ibid.

[53]Glen Ford, "Four More Years of Black Irrelevance," *Mathaba News Agency*, 2 April 2008, http://www.mathaba.net/news/?x=587537

[54]"Lynn Cheney: VP, Obama are Eight Cousins," *Associated Press*, 17 October 2007, http://www.msnbc.msn.com/id/21340764/.

[55]2008 State of the Black Union.

[56]*Today*, NBC, 26 May 2008.

[57]"Black Congressman Explains Why He Hasn't Switched Camps," *The Star Ledger*, 2 April 2008.

Chapter 6

[1]Brian Donohue, "Black Leaders Decry a Backslide Toward School Segregation" *The Star Ledger*, 15 July 2004: 5.

[2] Ibid.

[3]Ibid.

[4]Scott Bauer, "Ohmaha Schools to be Split by Race," *The Washington Times*, 14 April 2006, www.washtimes.com/national/20060413-115910-4251r.htm.

[5]Ibid.

[6]Ibid.

[7]Ibid.

[8]Bill Mears, "Divided Court Rejects School Diversity Plans," *CNN.com*, 28 June 2007, http://www.cnn.com/2007/LAW/06/28/scotus.race/index.html.

[9]Ibid.

[10]Donohue.

[11]Edmund S Morgan, The Birth of the Republic 1763-89

[12] Aharone, *Pawned Sovereignty*, 26.

[13]US Census Bureau; Social Security Administration.

[14]John Gibson, "Barack Obama's Fannie Mae/Freddie Mac Connection," *Fox News.com*, 16 September 2008, http://www.foxnews.com/story/0,2933,423701,00.html.

[15]Massie Ritsch, "Bundlers for McCain, Obama Are Among Wall Street's Tumblers," Open Secrets, 18 September 2008, http://www. opensecrets.org/news/2008/09/bundlers-for-mccain-obama-are.html.

[16]Ibid.

[17]Sharon Theimer, "Bush Rewarded 246 Top Fund-Raisers With Posts," *The Star Ledger*, 19 September. 2004: 5

[18]Ibid.

[19]Ibid

[20]"2008 Presidential Race, Presidential Expenditures," *OpenSecrets*, 7 June 2007, http://www.opensecrets.org/pres08/expenditures.asp?cycle=2008.

[21]Lindsay Renick Mayer, "Spending Money to Make Money," Capital Eye, 6 June 2007, http://www.opensecrets.org/inside.php?ID=264.

[22]"Governors' groups put focus on fundraising," *Associated Press*, 6 August 2006, MSNBC.com http://www.msnbc.msn.com/id/14207427/wid/6448213/.

[23] Ibid.

[24] Rolando Garcia, "Kerry Looks to Woo Black Vote With Ads, Little-Known Speaker," 15 July 04: 8

[25]"The Presidents," *the History Channel*: 17 February, 2007.

[26]Sharon Theimer, In Fund-Raising Race, Kerry and Democrats Were Big Winners, *Associated Press*, 13 December 2004.

[27]"Kerry Would Be Among Richest US Presidents," Los Angles Times, 27 June 2004.

[28](Genard footnote)

[29]"Today" show, February 1, 2005.

[30]James E. Mcgreevey, *The Confession*, (William Morrow, 2006), 78-82.

[31]"Who's the RichestIn Congress?" *Parade*, 7 May 2006

[32]Matt Stearns, "Out of Office, They Stick Around D.C. to Cash In, *KRT News Service*, 26 December 2004.

[33]Ibid.

[34]"Medvedev: US supremacy eternally over," Mathaba News Agency, 3 October 2008 http://www.mathaba.net/rss/?x=607756.

[35]John Gray, "A Shattering Moment in America's Fall from Power," 28 September 2008, http://www.guardian.co.uk/commentisfree/2008/sep/28/usforeignpolicy.useconomicgrowth

[36]Martin Kelly, "How many American presidents were assassinated?" *About.com: American History*, http://americanhistory.about.com/od/uspresidents/f/faq_assassinat.htm.

[37]Patrick Martin "Electoral College Votes for Bush, Sealing an Anti-Democratic Election," *World Socialist Web Site*, 19 December 2000

[38]Ibid

[39]Rep. Nancy Pelosi, House Majority Leader, "This Week," *ABC*, 16 March 2008.

[40]Ibid Edmund S Morgan, The Birth of the Republic 1763-89

[41]Delia M. Rios, "Meet the Voters Whose Ballots Really Do Count," *The Star Ledger*, 3 Nov. 04: 18

[42]John Farmer, "Challenger's Hardest Task is Breaking 'Electoral Lock,'" *The Star Ledger*, 31 Oct. 04: 6

[43]Martin, Electoral College__

[44]Farmer

[45]Ibid Farmer

[46]Elisabeth Bumiller and David E. Sanger, "Bush and Putin Exhibit Tension Over Democracy," *New York Times*, 25 February 2005: 1

[47]Delia M. Rios, Protected By History, Scorned By Voters, *The Star Ledger*, 3 Nov. 04:

[48]http://www.house.gov/jackson/VotingRightsFAQ.htm.

[49]Jacobs, CounterPunch

[50]"The Price in Blood: Casualties in the Civil," *Civil War Home*, Warhttp://www.civilwarhome.com/casualties.htm.

[51]Family Forest, FamilyForest.com, http://www.familyforest.com/Kerry_Bush_Cousins.html.

[52]Denise Lavoie, "Obama and Clinton Have Kissing Cousins," *Associated Press*, 25 March 2008.

[53]Family Forest, http://www.familyforest.com/Kerry_Bush_Cousins.html.

[54]Robert Cohen, "Not the First Tie, Likely Not the Last," *The Star Ledger*, 3 Nov. 2004: 18

[55]Ibid.

[56]Ibid.

[57]Ibid.

[58]Ibid.

[59]Walter Mears, "Rutherford B. Hayes Wasn't Such a Bad Guy," *CNN.com AllPolitics.com*, 11 December 2000, http://archives.cnn.com/2000/ALLPOLITICS/stories/12/11/recount. hayes.ap/.

[60]"The American Presidency: Rutherford B. Hayes," *Grolier Multimedia Encyclopedia*, http://ap.grolier.com/article?assetid=0134100-0.

[61]Ibid Patrick Martin, Congressional Democrats Ratify Bush Election Coup in US, *World Socialist Web Site*, 8 January 2001

[62]Ibid. Remember, this was the "Pre-Obama Age," so the Senate was operating with its usual number of Blacks – Zero.

[63]Federal Election Commission, http://www.fec.gov/pubrec/2000presgeresults.htm.

[64]Martin, Electoral College.

[65]Ibid

[66]Ibid

[67]United States Senate, "Vice President of the United States (President of the Senate), Chapter 2: Constitutional Origins and Structural Changes of the Vice Presidency, http://www.senate.gov/artandhistory/history/common/briefing/Vice_President.htm.

[68]Ibid Martin

[69] *Hearing of the Senate Judiciary Committee on the Nomination of Clarence Thomas to the Supreme Court*, Friday, 11 October 1991

[70] Ibid

[71]Lani Guinier, "What We Must Overcome," *The American Prospect*, March 4, 2001

Chapter 7

[1]Students of the World, http://www.studentsoftheworld.info/infopays/rank/PNB2.html.

[2]Doyle McManus, "Kissinger: Iraq is Not Ready for Democracy," Los Angeles Times, 20 November 2006.

[3]Ibid.

[4]Craig S. Smith, "Chirac Says War in Iraq Spreads Terrorism," *The New York Times*, 18 November, 2004: A8.

[5]Garvey 13, 14.

[6]Mark DiIonno, "Trapped in a Matrix of Glorified Violence," *The Star Ledger*, 15 April 2008: 9.

[7]Ibid.

[8] US Justice Department.

[9]2006 Joint Economic Committee Study, chaired by Senator Charles E. Schumer (D-NY)).

[10]David Crary, "Group Paints Bleak Picture for Black Men," *Associated Press*, 17 April 2007.

[11]CBS Evening News with Katie Couric, *CBS*, 2 April 2008.

[12] Sir John Geive, Deputy Governor of the Bank of England, Speech at the Sovereign Wealth Management Conference, London, 14 March 2008. (available at Bank of International Settlements http://www.bis.org/review/r080319d.pdf).

[13]CBS Evening News with Katie Couric, *CBS*, 2 April 2008.

[14]CBS Evening News with Katie Couric, *CBS*, 16 April 2008

[15] *US News and World Report*, 4 October 1999.

[16] Jonathan Tilove, "Where Have All the Black Men Gone," The Star Ledger, 8 May 2005: Section 10, Page 1

[17] Ibid.

[18] The Satcher Health Leadership Institute, *Morehouse School of Medicine*, http://www.msm.edu/x784.xml.

[19] Ben Ammi, 63.

[20] "60 Minutes," *CBS*, 22 April 2007.

[21] Ibid.

[22] "Cam'ron Apologizes for '60 Minutes' Interview," http://www.vibe.com/news/, 26 April 2007.

[23] Ibid.

[24] Albert Einstein Quotes, www.phnet.fi/public/mamaa1/einstein.htm.

[25] Brown v. Board of Education of Topeka, Kansas, see: www.loc.gov/exhibits/brown/brown-brown.html.

[26] Ibid.

[27] Ibid.

[28] Kiri Davis, "A Girl Like Me," www.mediathatmattersfest.org.

[29] Ibid.

[30] 2006 Report from the Schott Foundation for Public Education.

[31] "Hispanic And Black High School Graduation Rates Very Low," 26 February 2004, http://www.parapundit.com/archives/001959.html.

[32] Erik Eckholm, "Plight Deepens for Black Men, Studies Warn," *New York Times*, 20 March 2006

[33] "High School Drop-out Rates Rise," *PBS Online NewsHour*, 28 June 2006, http://www.pbs.org/newshour/bb/education/jan-june06/dropout_06-27.html.

[34] "Black Kids Motivated by Black-Themed Books: Educators Hope it Translates to Better Reading Skills," *EurWeb*, 18 August 2004, http://www.eurweb.com/articles/morenews /08182004/morenews1594408182004.cfm.

[35] Ibid.

[36] John Henrik Clarke, "Notes for an African World Revolution: Africans at the Crossroads," *Africa World Press*, (Trenton, NJ: 1991): 18

[37] Jeff Diamant, "Jews Finish Talmud Study in Style," *The Star Ledger*, 2 March 2005: 15.

[38] Ibid.

[39] Ibid.

[40] Clarke, 18

[41] Roxanne Dunbar-Ortiz, "From Jamestown to Virginia Tech: Colonization and Massacres," *Counter Punch*, 16 April 2008, http://www.mathaba.net/rss/?x=589077.

[42]www.TavisSmiley.com.

[43]Leutisha Stills, "Black Leaders ... or Leading Blacks," *The Black Agenda Report*, 14 February 2007.

[44] Stephen Brimley, "Native American Sovereignty in Maine," *Maine Policy Review*, http://www.umaine.edu/mcsc/MPR/Vol13No2/brimley/brimley.htm#16.

[45]Stephen Brimley, "Five Hundred Sixty Nations Among Us: Understanding the Basics of Native American Sovereignty," *Maine Policy Review*, http://www.umaine.edu/mcsc/MPR/ Vol13No1/Brimley/Brimley.htm

[46]Brimley, "Native American Sovereignty in Maine."

[47]Worcester v. Georgia, Author: US Government, Year Published: 1832, http://www.civics-online.org/library/formatted/texts/worcester.html

[48]Brimley, "Five Hundred Sixty Nations Among Us."

[49]Ibid.

[50]Brimley, "Native American Sovereignty in Maine."

[51]Ibid.

[52]"Lakota Declare Themselves Truly Independent and Sovereign," *Yahoo News*, http://news.yahoo.com/s/afp/20071220/lf_afp/usindigenoustreatywithdraw;_ylt=Al5SEQqQ4j45R2kejRvI28p34 T0D, 20 December 2007.

[53]Ibid.

[54]Ibid.

[55]Declaration on the Rights of Indigenous Peoples, *International Work Group for Indigenous Affairs*, 14 September 2007, http://www.iwgia.org/sw248.asp. (See Declaration): http://www.unhchr.ch/huridocda/huridoca.nsf/(Symbol)/E.CN.4.SUB.2.RES.1994.45.En

[56]US State Department, Bureau of European and Eurasian Affairs, *Background Note: Holy See Profile*, January 2008, http://www.state.gov/r/pa/ei/bgn/3819.htm.

[57]Matt Rosenberg, "The Vatican City is a Country," *About.com*, http://geography.about.com/od/politicalgeography/a/vaticancountry.htm.

[58]US State Department, http://www.state.gov/r/pa/ei/bgn/3819.htm.

[59]Rachel Sanderson, "Vatican Nets a Surplus, But is Wary," *Reuters*, 12 July, 2005.

[60]Rosenberg, http://geography.about.com/od/politicalgeography/a/vaticancountry.htm.

[61]"U.N. Gives the Vatican Rights as an Observer," *The Star Ledger*, 2 July, 2005: 7

[62] Vicki's Dish, *The Star Ledger*, 1 July 2008.

[63]Ralph Waldo Emerson, "Essays of Ralph Waldo Emerson," (New York: Book League of America, 1941): 35.

[64]Aharone, 199.

[65]Dr. Mustafa Ansari, *Defining Change Under UN Laws and Presidential Orders*, www.aareparations.com.

[66]Ibid.

[67]*US Foreign Policy Encyclopedia*, Exceptionalism, http://www.answers.com/topic/ exceptionalism.

[68]ABC News: "Two Nations Under God," abcnews.go.com/politics/5050/story?id=6015620.

[69]*The Philosophy & Opinions of Marcus Garvey*, 17.

Index

D

258

United States 2, 118, 119, 120, 121,
  126, 128, 130, 136, 138, 144,
  147, 149, 154, 172, 186, 209,
  241, 251, 252, 254
University of Georgia 225
University of Lagos 6
University of Maine 251
University of Rochester 132
uranium 142, 150
Urban Institute 240
US Advisory Commission on Public
  Diplomacy 202
US Army Medical Command 144
US Foreign Policy Encyclopedia 118,
  120, 126, 149, 259, 291
US government 21, 26, 37, 41, 42,
  43, 44, 48, 50, 53, 59, 66, 68,
  71, 76, 79, 80, 81, 86, 120, 136,
  139, 141, 143, 148, 149, 150,
  155, 166, 186, 187, 188, 189,
  190, 211, 230, 251, 254

V

Vatican 11, 225, 254, 258
Venezuela 26
Viacom 107
Vienna Convention 12, 253
Vietnam 133, 142, 157
Viet Nam 71
Virginia 60, 99, 163, 164, 215, 244,
  245
Voltaire 224
Vote or Die 207
Voting Rights Act
  VRA 168, 172, 195, 197

W

WABC 63
Wallace, George 161
Wall Street. 199, 200
Washington xiii, 31, 123, 159, 188,
  199, 201, 206, 214
Washington, George 39, 69, 81, 123,

136, 243
Watergate 210
Waters, Maxine 220
West, Cornel 140
West Point 68
White House xvii, 104, 113, 147, 164,
  174, 183, 188, 201, 203, 205,
  210, 215, 218, 237
White Supremacy 13, 38, 80
Wilder, Douglas 163, 164
Will, George 35
Williamsburg 140
World Trade Center 156
World War II 3, 20, 98, 99
Wright, Jeremiah 133, 134

X

X, Malcolm 125, 221, 255

Y

Yale University 215

Z

Zimbabwe 166, 188

Printed in the United States
134570LV00003B/1/P

9 781438 938585